The
British Renaissance

THE BRITISH RENAISSANCE

How to Survive and Thrive despite any Recession

Learn the Secrets of how Six
British Companies are
Conquering the World

JEFFREY FERRY

HEINEMANN : LONDON

First published in Great Britain 1993
by William Heinemann Ltd
an imprint of Reed Consumer Books Ltd
Michelin House, 81 Fulham Road, London SW3 6RB
and Auckland, Melbourne and Singapore

Copyright © 1993 by Jeffrey Ferry
The author has asserted his moral rights

A CIP catalogue record for this book
is available at the British Library
ISBN 0 434 25680 3

Typeset by CentraCet, Cambridge
Printed and bound in Great Britain
by Clays Ltd, St. Ives Plc

For Chrissie

Contents

Introduction

In 1990 a fascinating takeover battle took place in the American state of Massachusetts. The giant British industrial group BTR bid for a troubled abrasives manufacturer, Norton, Inc. In Massachusetts, all hell broke loose. The union leaders at Norton didn't like BTR's proposed rationalisation. They thought that when BTR talked about increasing efficiency and profitability, it meant job losses and new working practices. They whipped up feeling in Massachusetts' State House. Pretty soon tempers among the state senators were as hot as the State House's famous gold dome on a midsummer day. Legislators proposed a law giving them veto power over every foreign takeover of a Massachusetts company. Even the governor, former presidential candidate Michael Dukakis, spoke out against the BTR takeover. Anti-British hysteria reached a level not seen since the Battle of Bunker Hill. In one month, publicity-shy BTR got more publicity in Massachusetts than it received in ten years in the UK. Aghast, BTR walked away from the deal. The publicity caught the eye of other companies and pretty soon a state-owned French chemicals company came forward with an offer, which was quickly accepted. It was just the sort of company the union leaders liked: large, bureaucratic and slow-moving. With any luck, French head-quarters would soon forget they owned the little company in Massachusetts. The little abrasives-maker might carry on for a quarter century or so, their inefficiency subsidised from Paris.

BTR must be doing something right, I thought. (Massachusetts' unions are not the world's most enlightened.) I rang up Chris

Risley, BTR's US press spokesman, to find out what the company was up to. It turned out that BTR had been buying up small American manufacturing companies for several years. Typically, they installed new senior management, refocused their businesses on high-tech products, and increased efficiency on the shopfloor. It usually took them two years to double profits at the acquisition. Sometimes they did it in one.

Risley told me the story of a case from just the previous year. The major American auto manufacturers were going to all their suppliers, demanding they cut their prices by a sizeable percentage *and* improve product quality at the same time. BTR had a subsidiary which made rubber components for Chrysler. The subsidiary refused to give Chrysler its price cut, arguing that their products were already higher than the quality Chrysler required. They said bluntly that they did not see why they should suffer just because Chrysler could not sell enough cars. According to Risley, Chrysler chairman Lee Iacocca got on the phone and told the subsidiary that if they did not accept the price cut, they would lose all Chrysler's business. The little company stood firm. Chrysler duly pulled their business. But six months later, when Iacocca's interest had moved on elsewhere (he was by then busy chastising the Japanese for not buying enough Chryslers), Chrysler came back to the little component-maker. Today, said Risley, the BTR subsidiary did more business with Chrysler than ever before. Why? They simply made the best product of its kind. When Chrysler looked around they found it would cost them even more to get the same quality anywhere else. By investing in its products and its manufacturing, the component-maker had established an unassailable lead over its competitors. It was a textbook case of how technology can be used to build a highly profitable market niche. I asked Risley if he had any documentary evidence for this extraordinary story and he sent me a report on it from the *New York Times*.

Another interesting case was Burger King. In the late 1980s, it was taken over by the British food and drink group Grand Metropolitan. Burger King was then running some very stylish, artistic advertising featuring, among other things, helicopters delivering Whoppers to US marines in nuclear submarines. A turbulent period followed as BK junked its expensive, stylish ads and went back to its roots. Their new marketing was built around two things: the old 'Have It Your Way' customer service pledge and product quality. Their burgers were simply better than the opposition's. They enforced their quality drive by ruthlessly weeding out the franchise-holders who didn't run the shop to standard. Meanwhile, their biggest competitor in fast foods, troubled by slow growth, tried to renew consumer interest by introducing dozens of new products. It spent millions promoting them, hoping to strike lucky. Basically, it was the old 'throw it against the wall and see what sticks' (the strategy, not the burgers). BK was steadily gaining market share. My colleagues on Wall Street liked Burger King's approach much more. The competitor was a pretty universal Sell while, for those Streeters who could get their heads round a company that put a pound sign instead of a dollar sign in front of its profit number, Grand Met was a Buy.

What was going on here? The difference was management. If the British could manage these American businesses better than their American competitors, something pretty special was happening over in Britain. When I moved back to London in 1991, I resolved to find out what it was. This book is the result.

What I found was a renaissance in British management. During the 1980s a new generation of world-beating British companies emerged, in many cases literally out of the shell of the old companies. The new companies are lean, focused, decentralised, motivated and aggressive organisations. They are highly international, doing business in dozens of countries around the world. Sometimes they are great exporters; often, like BTR, they produce and sell locally in many countries.

There are many secrets to their success. But the most important is better people-management. These companies have completely revolutionised their organisations, flattening them, wiping out the hierarchy, and decentralising decision-making as much as possible. They have dispensed with the old baggage of status, prestige and seniority which cluttered up British companies. The new companies are egalitarian, shirtsleeves organisations. They reward most, if not all, of their people with performance-related pay packages, which motivate and involve people in the company's aims and goals. If they are in manufacturing, they have taken people-policies right to the shopfloor and *empowered* their entire workforces. They have given them control over the process, the product and the machines. The result is that these workers no longer 'leave their brain at the door' when they come to work. Look at Unipart, in Oxford: one-time shop stewards today quote productivity figures at you and take such pride in their work that they come in on Saturdays to work on the plant's flower garden or clean the company pond. If you visit Virgin Atlantic's headquarters in Crawley, you are likely to find a secretary leaving work at eight or nine in the evening. When the airline gets a lot of mail, they stay to make sure it all gets answered promptly. They do not get paid to stay late. They just care about the airline and its customers. If you ring computer company ICL, you will *never* hear the telephone ring more than six times. Why? Ask anybody from a senior director to the telephonist to a service engineer, you will get the same answer: It could be a customer on the phone.

The new renaissance companies are incredibly flexible and fluid. Their organisations are constantly changing. People change jobs, the jobs change and the companies reorganise themselves regularly to follow the market and the customer. At Renishaw plc, chairman David McMurtry decided they weren't developing new products fast enough. So he demoted himself to head of Research and Development (R&D) at the Metrology division. When he goes to planning meetings at Metrology, he reports to the division's managing director. When the MD comes to board meetings, he reports to McMurtry. At ICL, every annual strategy meeting for some years now has decided on a major, swingeing reorganisation. ICL chairman Peter Bonfield says if you aren't changing so fast that it's painful, then you're not changing fast enough.

The reason Britain's management renaissance struck with such force in the 1980s is that it was delayed for so long. For years, British industry was in decline. Britain was in a unique position, insulated from the forces of the marketplace: after the First World War, great sections of industry were first cartelised and then protected from outside competition by the huge Empire market. Even after 1945, when formal so-called Imperial Preference was abandoned, many companies sailed, or limped, on, supported by loyal customers in the former Empire. Cosy behind the barriers, they did not modernise, they did not invest and they did not get the best from their people. Instead they grew fat, bloated and bureaucratic.

The upsurge of international competition in the late 1970s, followed by the recession of 1979–81, blasted away the old world. Competition pushed some of the old companies into bankruptcy. Some just shrivelled up and shrunk. But as the deadwood of the old died away, new companies arose to take their place. Thrilled at their liberation, they seized on the newest, freshest, youngest, most exciting new ideas in strategy and management and went to work.

This book contains the story of six renaissance companies. They are in vastly differing industries, but all are world leaders in their businesses. Four are 'turnarounds'. Fifteen years ago, you might not have expected them to survive into the 1990s. Today they are vibrant and growing. They are like young companies again. They have literally changed from companies with their great days behind them to companies with their greatest days yet to come. The other two, Virgin Group and Control Techniques, were small entrepreneurial start-ups a decade ago. In their businesses – airlines and electronic drives – they're world-leading innovators.

I have not tried to cover the companies in their entirety. Instead I have focused on an individual or several individuals, and told the company's story through the individuals' stories. The chapters are written in narrative form, not in the form of staccato slogans or academic treatises. I have kept business school jargon to a minimum. I have tried to let the natural excitement of doing business in today's world pervade the stories. If war is diplomacy carried on by other means, then business is war carried on by other means. Why make it boring?

However, this *is* a management book. There are valuable lessons to be learned from these six companies, lessons in management, strategy and how to cope with today's fast-changing world. The gale of international competition is still blasting its way into fusty corridors of our economy. At each of these companies, I have spoken to the chairman and other senior executives at length, and woven in their valuable, often surprising, insights into business and strategy. Each of the renaissance companies has a unique philosophy.

Turnarounds are especially intriguing. Reversing years of decline, replacing a culture of failure and ossification with a new one of success and opportunity, is perhaps the greatest challenge in business. For the companies in this book, it was a turbulent, controversial and often painful process. Often, hostile takeover, or the threat of hostile takeover, or the threat of imminent bankruptcy was necessary before a company could face up to the radical change it needed. It almost always takes an outsider to lead a really radical, fundamental change. But it was surprising how many veterans of the old culture of failure made a successful transition to the new. Once the lid was ripped off, many of yesterday's yes-men became great contributors to the new, empowered organisation.

The British Renaissance also yields an insight into some of the unique attributes of today's European company. We are moving rapidly to a tripolar world. Europe as a united economic region, and European companies competing with the Far Eastern and North American regions are two of the dominant trends of the 1990s. Yet there are few books on the distinctive traits of the European company. This book is not about that theme, but certain key traits do emerge. One is a great internationalism, a true sensitivity and understanding of other cultures. This is an advantage over many of the companies of the other two regions. The owner of the best-selling, fastest-growing American bourbon in Japan . . . is Guinness! (In Tokyo, they still tell the story of the

American auto chairman – not Mr Iacocca! – who was surprised to discover on his recent lobbying visit that the Japanese drive on the left.) Another difference between North American companies and European is in the approach to people motivation. In the US, motivation focuses on the power of money or corporate recognition or corporate spirit. One must never underestimate the power of money! Yet European companies have shown an innovative ability to appeal to larger issues and dreams, to man's need to leave, as the playwright said, a thumbprint in the sands of time. Management guru Tom Peters admits he looks increasingly to European companies like the Body Shop, the TI Group and Benetton.

I am deeply grateful for the co-operation and assistance I have had from the six companies. In several cases, the companies took some time before agreeing to collaborate with the book; but once they did, they threw open their doors. It is a characteristic of excellent companies that they are open and honest and exercise frequent, comprehensive communication up, down and across the organisation, and with customers and other partners. At each company, I talked several times with the chairman. I spoke with dozens of employees at all levels. I was on several occasions invited to sit in on confidential meetings, including sales and production planning meetings and takeover discussions. I visited companies' facilities in the UK, the Continent and North America. I conducted interviews in cars, trucks, planes and trains.

At various stages executives from the companies read parts of the manuscript, offering comments and suggestions which were highly valuable. I retained full editorial control however and they respected that. Any mistakes are of course my own responsibility.

There is still, of course, much further to go before the British economy takes its place as an equal with the other leading economies of Europe. Britain is still in the second half of EC countries in terms of real living standards. The gap has been closing now for ten years. The recession was a setback for the consumer. But British productivity continued to surge ahead, further closing the gap with its Continental neighbours. There are still many companies that need to undergo a renaissance. There are sectors that have remained sheltered from competition. There are still companies that are too large, too out-of-touch, too monopolistic. But hardly a week passes without some large organisation announcing a radical restructuring or a new international venture. I am optimistic about the second half of the 1990s.

One of the phenomena I came across repeatedly while researching the book was the British executive who left the country years ago but returned in the 1980s, drawn back by the industrial renaissance. Michael Wray was one. Wray left Britain in 1969. He was then an aeronautics engineer of twenty-six with energy and ambition, looking for excitement. He worked at the British Aircraft Corporation, which had two great projects, the Concorde and the TRS2. Wray worked on the TRS2, a hedge-hopping, Mach 1 fighter-bomber. The government killed the TRS2 project because it grew too expensive. To make sure its decision was final and irrevocable, the government ordered the blowtorching of the five TRS2 prototypes. Some of the engineers had worked on the technology inside those planes for thirty years. Young Wray watched them cry at their drawing boards as the planes melted in the torches and resolved to leave. 'It encapsulated everything about England I didn't like, strikes, unions, low investment, low technology and a country that was no longer at the leading edge,' said Wray.

He worked in the US, France, got a business degree, moved to Italy, the Middle East, the US again, and finally Switzerland. It was while in Switzerland that Wray detected a new climate of ambition and achievement in Britain. After seventeen years and seven countries, Wray decided to come back home. He gave up a lakeside apartment in Lausanne, and took a job with the John Crane division of the TI Group.

Six years later, Wray was pleased with his latest, and last, move. John Crane was a venerable old name, but when it came to technology, to going boldly into new markets and new countries, it was at the leading edge. He also noticed that sort of mentality among Crane's customers here in the UK. 'There's a new pride in Britain and in buying British goods,' he said.

Acknowledgements

My greatest debt is to Mike Attwell of Channel Four Television and my publisher Tom Weldon. *The British Renaissance* was conceived in a bar in New York's Hell's Kitchen in the dark days of the 1990 recession. Both Mike and Tom resisted the then fashionable gloom and gave me generous support and encouragement. As I wrote the book, I discovered that my publisher had an uncanny knack for phrasing constructive criticism in the form of praise. His advice was always valuable.

I also owe thanks to the public relations executives at the six renaissance companies. Patrick Fitz-Gibbon of Unipart, Chris Davidson at Guinness, Will Whitehorn at Virgin, John Hutchings at TI Group, Graham Goulden at ICL and Caterina Gianota at Control Techniques. They were helpful and understanding in the face of repeated requests to nose around their territory. This book also would not have been possible without the help of numerous executives, management consultants and analysts. Among them I'd like to thank John Allan, Dan Jones, Tim Simpson, Keith Skeoch, Hamid Anvari and Charles Morris. For invaluable assistance in transcription and statistical work, I'm grateful to Evelyn Denyer, Alison Denyer and Shelley Lacy.

London
May 1993

ONE

Oxford Automotive Components

The Factory of the Future

The factory stood out on its own, in a field, a long, low, white building. Behind were tea plantations, and behind them, in the distance and glinting in the sunshine, lay snow-capped mountain peaks. On the other side of the main road was the town of Kashiwabara, a little forest of single-storey buildings, looking quiet, clean and neat, the typical small Japanese city. Mark Trevelyan loved how well-planned it looked.

Inside the factory it was bright and spotlessly clean, full of uniformed people moving about with a calm purposefulness. Mark stood and studied a flow-line unlike any he had ever seen before. At one end, a man lifted the lower half of a Honda fuel tank on to a waist-high metal dolly. After that, the manual work seemed to end. The Japanese workers spent their time pushing buttons and watching things happen. A man pushed a button and the dolly slid under a welding machine. Small components slid into place against the tank-half, a welding torch descended, and in seconds the weld was complete. The dolly moved the tank-half out, a man lifted it on to a conveyor belt of rollers and gave it a little push towards the next machine. Mark sniffed the air. They must have good ventilation in here. You could hardly smell the burnt metal. He watched the workers having quick little conversations with each other in between watching machines. The fuel tank-half

1

passed through several more processes before it finally met its mate, the upper half of the fuel tank. A machine matched them up, a dolly slid them under another welder and then, in less than ten seconds, a robotic welder created the watertight seam around the entire six-foot circumference of the tank.

A man loaded the complete tank body into another dolly which turned the tank over, plunged it into a vat of water, and held it there while the air pressure inside was cranked up to a level Mark couldn't understand from the Japanese dials and writing on the machine. The worker watched for bubbles. Satisfied, he pushed a button and the fuel tank popped out of the water. He moved it no more than a couple of feet, placed it on to another downward-sloping conveyor line, gave it a gentle push, and off it rolled, a finished fuel tank heading for the paint shop. Oblivious to his fellow visitors, Mark walked up to the top and examined the whole line again, looking this time at the people instead of the machines. It was not like the factory back at Oxford. Instead of being hunched over tank-halves in goggles and helmets, manoeuvring heavy welding torches around, breathing in fumes and trying to see through smoke and soot, these men were calm and cheerful in their crisp white uniforms, relaxed, but always watching with quiet concentration. There was something odd about the way they talked. It took him a few moments to work it out. Finally it dawned on him: they were not shouting. These welding machines were so quiet, you could actually *talk*. A single thought went through Mark's head: 'God, I wish we could work in a nice place like this.'

A night-shift welder on the fuel tank assembly line at Oxford Automotive Components, Trevelyan, thirty-one, was part of a radical experiment, perhaps unprecedented in the entire world. OAC's parent company, Unipart Industries, had selected six shop-floor workers and sent them to spend four weeks at Yachiyo Industries, Kashiwabara, to study Japanese manufacturing equipment and assembly methods. Mostly, though, they were sent to see how the Japanese worked, to drink in and absorb the Japanese system of team-based production. Team-based production, or cell manufacturing, produced the highest quality, lowest-cost motor-cars in the world.

Trevelyan's welding career began in 1972, when, aged sixteen, he quit school to join British Leyland at the sprawling Cowley plant where Austin-Morris cars were assembled. He started at OAC in 1987. Tall, gangly, with short brown hair, Trevelyan was one of the younger employees at OAC. People often noticed the tattoos on his arms below his rolled-up sleeves: on one arm an eagle, and on the other 'Mark' and 'Sue', intertwined in a mix of red and blue. 'Young foolishness' Mark called the tattoos with embarrassment if asked about them, although after twelve years' marriage he was still as devoted to his wife Sue as the day they'd met.

Mark never knew why he had been asked to go to Japan. The only thing he could think of was that one evening in May 1988, he had arrived for work to his usual job of building fuel tanks for the Rover 800 series to find the day shift had altered the layout of the seven-man assembly line. Mark and his mates were moving equipment around, laying the line out as they preferred it when Unipart Industries' managing director David Nicholas happened to walk by. Nicholas introduced himself and asked Mark what was going on. Mark explained that the line was not flowing properly the way the day shift had set it up and their system was more efficient. A small, brusque man who rarely stood still, Nicholas nodded curtly, thanked Mark for his time and was gone. 'I always believed that David Nicholas remembered that day, that he saw, hey, he's organising things, he's getting things running, perhaps he's what we're looking for for the company.

'I don't know, I'm just assuming that, because I always ask myself: why was I chosen? Because I was no different to anyone else.'

In 1988 Oxford Automotive Components was a factory, and a business, in need of radical treatment. Long a part of British Leyland, the factory had been thrust upon Unipart in the early 1980s when Unipart was being restructured in preparation for privatisation. Oxford Exhausts, as it was known in those days, was renowned at Leyland for late deliveries, poor quality and poor service. Poor component manufacture was one of the British car industry's greatest weaknesses. The 1960s was the era of 'big is beautiful'. Companies were integrated, combined, merged and consolidated, in the belief that efficiency would follow. By the 1980s it was clear that massive size only created massive inefficiency, that with no real competition component-makers had little incentive to improve their performance. On the contrary, with uncompetitive manufacturing costs easily hidden in the maze of group accounting, unglamorous component companies, inevitably run by second-rate managers who hadn't made the grade at the main business, staffed with a workforce demoralised by years of being treated as a poor relation, were in what looked like irreversible decline. There was little doubt in Oxford that foisting Oxford Exhausts on to Unipart was the first step in allowing Leyland to look elsewhere for its fuel tanks and exhausts if Oxford could not improve its performance.

In 1986, Unipart's group managing director John Neill started to talk to the City of London about privatisation. The City was united in its views. Five stockbroking firms told Neill the way to get the best price for Unipart shares was to close down or sell Unipart's manufacturing operations. Unipart's main business, delivering spare parts for every car make sold in the UK to garages and shops from Lands End to John O'Groats, was the sort of business that would appeal to investors. With a market including every brand name from Alfa Romeo to Vauxhall, the spares business was not dependent on the British car industry. Unipart was the dominant player in the business, and it was a service. In the 1980s, the City liked services. There was a fashionable theory that manufacturing was something Germans and Japanese were good at. Impressed by the international success of glamour stocks, like Saatchi and Saatchi, British Airways and BET, stockbrokers and politicians began to argue that services – advertising, transportation, cleaning and maintenance – were what the British were good at. The old economists' adage that a people can never prosper by taking in each other's washing was obsolete.

John Neill wasn't interested in these theories. While British Leyland writhed in agonies of poor industrial relations, strategic uncertainty and an inability to design models people wanted to buy, Neill ran Unipart as a kingdom within a kingdom, making it a tightly run, profitable business. Unipart's six-storey, 1960s' Cowley office block was separated from a Leyland factory only by a cyclone fence, but in terms of drive, ambition and philosophy, Neill was light-years ahead of the stolid Leyland management. In the 1970s, he diversified Unipart's business, getting the company into spare parts distribution for all car makes and models. He established Unipart as a valuable, respected brand name in its own right. He opened a retail shop network. 'We have to take control of our own destiny. Otherwise, we'll be doomed,' Neill told his management team. His colleagues at the Leyland auto giant accused him of disloyalty. Why should Unipart distribute parts for other car companies, including Leyland's biggest competitors, they asked. When BL's market share collapsed under the pressure of competition, Neill's foresight was proved right.

In 1986, Neill saw the trend towards global production, transplanted factories and international sourcing of components. 'We're up against the best in the world now,' he said. 'The Japanese are excellent, the Americans are getting their act together, and the Mexicans are terrifying. That's what we have to compete with.'

Neill was tall, gaunt and pale with blond hair greying at the temples, his blue eyes glinting through gold-rimmed glasses as he explained the importance of world-class manufacturing in a soft-spoken voice, traces of a South African accent still discernible. The intensity of Neill's convictions made him sound like a born-again Methodist preacher. His spartan demeanour made a strange contrast with the walls of his sixth-floor office, hung with photographs of nude models. The nudes, from past editions of Unipart's annual calendar, were set in exotic locales: beaches, bridges, mountaintops, one even against a chilly bronze Lenin in Red Square. The annual calendar was one of Neill's more colourful achievements. In the 1970s, he had fought Leyland management for the budgets to shoot these exercises in naked promotion. Most of the auto parts industry employed unimaginative, corner-cutting marketing. The Unipart calendars employed beautiful models, exotic locales, the best paper and printing, and stunning photography. Neill wanted them to be a world-class product to symbolise a company that would also one day be world class. From the moment the calendars appeared, they were a hit with the industry, adorning the walls of thousands of Unipart customers. Photographer Lord Lichfield's journey to Russia to shoot the 1990 calendar took months of negotiation, encountered endless logistical problems, and became perhaps the most costly calendar ever produced. Lichfield's journey was the subject of a one-hour ITV documentary, narrated by Peter Ustinov – several million pounds' worth of free advertising for Unipart.

Behind Neill's leather deskchair and beneath a few naked girls lay a long shelf filled with dozens of books on world-class manufacturing. After 1987, the zeal Neill brought to his calendar was switched to the manufacturing challenge. It took Neill seven years to get Unipart privatised, seven long years of fierce internal battling among British Leyland management and inside the board. In 1980, the Thatcher government extracted a public promise from the Leyland board that they would privatise the company as soon as practicable. Since nobody would buy the loss-maker whole, it had to be sold off in bits. Neill was quick to argue that Unipart would be a viable, profitable company on its own. But Leyland management resisted the break-up of their empire. Austin-Rover boss Harold Musgrove pointed out that no automaker in the world allowed its parts distribution to be carried out by an independent company. Neill countered that he would design an ironclad contract that would give Leyland a service every bit as good as what they could get from a wholly owned subsidiary. Still the Leyland board resisted. Neill finally won his case with a series of presentations to Cabinet ministers Cecil Parkinson and Norman Tebbit. The government owned 99 per cent of Leyland's shares. Quietly, industry ministers twisted some arms in the Leyland boardroom. Finally, in 1984, Unipart got the go-ahead to begin designing a plan for privatisation.

The Leyland board wanted to float Unipart on the stock market, an idea which accorded with the Thatcher government's fervently held vision of Britain as a share-owning democracy. Neill disagreed. He wanted a management buyout (MBO). He wanted Unipart's managers and employees to have a long-term commitment to the company. At first, the Department of Trade and Industry turned a deaf ear to Neill's pleas. British Telecom and Jaguar Cars had been thumping successes as stock market flotations. Why should Unipart be any different? But Neill's merchant banker, Victor Blank of Charterhouse, had good contacts inside Whitehall. Charterhouse pledged they could arrange a buyout, funded by a handful of City investment funds, which would give the government as much cash as a public flotation. If this eccentric industrialist believed his company would be more efficient as a private company, Blank told the mandarins, why not let him have his way? Mandarins, and their ministers, yielded. It would be a buyout.

The next hurdle was the shape of the buyout. The City investors rounded up by Charterhouse wanted to split most of the shares between themselves and Unipart's top three executives. They wanted to gear the company with high debt, structuring it so in three years the investors would more than double their money, while Neill and his two colleagues could walk away multimillionaires. 'This was 1986,' said Neill caustically. 'It was the short-term, get-rich-quick Anglo-Saxon financial system at the peak of its glory.' Neill wanted sixty managers to participate in the buyout, and a tranche of shares to be set aside for employees. 'These people have bet their lives along with me that this company could work,' Neill said. 'There was no way I was going to exclude them.' Once again, he got his way.

At the very last minute, the government dropped a bombshell. It wanted Rover (as Leyland was by now renamed) to sell 100 per cent of Unipart, instead of keeping 20 per cent as previously agreed. It was a repeat of the events preceding the Jaguar privatisation when Rover had wanted to keep 20 per cent of the luxury car-maker but was overruled by Downing Street. This time, Neill sided with Rover. Rover was Unipart's biggest customer and Neill wanted them to have 20 per cent. It was part of his Japanese-style stakeholder philosophy. Shareholdings were part of the glue cementing the relationships between a company and all partners critical to its future.

'We made a promise to Rover in good faith. It would be completely dishonourable to go back on that. You tell the Secretary of State that if Rover doesn't get 20 per cent, then the privatisation is off,' Neill told the ashen-faced bankers seated around a table at Charterhouse. Rover got its 20 per cent.

The final shape of the £55 million buyout allocated 10 per cent of the shares to Unipart management and 12 per cent to the employees, with the remaining shares for the City investors. Neill had just 2.9 per cent (the typical merchant-bank-designed buyout gave senior management 10 per cent or more). Neill battled through resistance from Leyland management, City investors, bankers and the government to secure his unique vision of a customer-oriented, quality-driven automotive components company. In December 1986, he told his Charterhouse bankers that he was going to organise a theatrical stage show using song and dance to explain to Unipart employees the pros and cons, and the hows and whys, of buying a stake in their company. The bankers laughed. A share prospectus set to music? You're mad, they said. The messianic stare in his clear blue eyes made the bankers go quiet. 'I don't want any Unipart employee ever to be able to look me in the eye and say: you knew this was a good deal and you didn't bother going to the trouble to explain it to us.'

Half of Unipart's 4000-strong workforce bought shares in the January 1987 buyout. The minimum purchase was £28, but most who bought spent between £250 and £500. It was an impressive piece of salesmanship and Neill was congratulated by dozens of stockbrokers. In the week after the well-publicised buyout, virtually every broker in the City phoned Neill, seeking to establish a relationship with a company they expected to come to the stock market one day. Neill invited five of them to Cowley to give presentations on their ideas for Unipart's future and how the financial community could contribute to it. All five made the same two suggestions: Unipart should get out of manufacturing, and it should expand its retail business, preferably by acquisition. Every time, Neill challenged them. Aren't the Japanese the best manufacturers in the world, he would ask.

Yes, of course, they would nod.

Well then, what if a British company learned directly from the Japanese how to manufacture as well as they did, and then combined Japanese skill with the natural flair and ingenuity of the British people? Wouldn't such a company be a resounding success? Wouldn't it be more 'glamorous' than a retailer? Wouldn't it be a more enduring glamour than the ephemeral glamour of a retail share, whose glamour would probably evaporate in a year or two?

'Most of them didn't know what I was talking about,' Neill recalled. 'One broker said it's an interesting idea – if it's achievable. He added that he didn't believe it was achievable.'

Neill believed the western auto industry had no choice but to learn from the Japanese. Relations between car-makers and suppliers were a key part of the problem. European and American car companies declined in the 1970s and 1980s partly because of the traditional antagonistic relationships between auto-maker and supplier. It was a short-term, power-based relationship, based on always driving for the lowest price, with little sense of shared destiny. 'Many western companies still believe that is a superior way to secure competitive advantage,' said Neill. 'I think they're absolutely wrong.'

Neill set about building closer, more honest relationships with Unipart's customers, including its biggest, Rover Group. He wanted to emulate the Japanese model: long-term-oriented companies, striving together for continuous improvement and sharing the benefits equally between component-maker and auto-maker. When in 1987, Honda took a 20 per cent stake in Rover, Neill was quick to build a relationship with the Japanese company and its leading supplier of fuel and exhaust systems, Yachiyo Industries. He gave Unipart's manufacturing division, Unipart

9

Industries, a simple objective: become Honda's best supplier in Europe. 'When I play tennis, I like to play with someone who is better than me so I improve my game. I told that to Honda and Yachiyo. I said you play tennis better than we do, we would like to learn from you.'

He believed the secret of Japan's breakthrough in high-quality volume production was in the people. 'It's not investment in capital or information technology, it's investing in people. Empowering individuals, challenging them to work, and creating the space in which they can contribute their intelligence, experience and ideas.' Neill recruited a small team of managers from the British division of American multinational Tenneco who had experience bringing Japanese production methods to Europe. He gave them the task of turning around Unipart's two manufacturing sites, Oxford Exhausts and Coventry Components.

On his first day as general manager of Coventry Components, Frank Burns could not get into his office. The 150 workers were on strike. 'It was their way to say look who's really boss round here,' Burns recalled. The company had a history of dire industrial relations. The regular changes of management, like a skimming stone, left only a momentary impression. On his second day of work, Burns held a 9 a.m. meeting of the company's entire 200-strong workforce. He began by announcing that he intended to turn the company profitable. To do that would require a new sense of co-operation. The company needed to become a single-status factory. 'The first thing I told them was that all the privileged car parking would stop of this very minute, and if you'd like to look through the windows, you can see something going on.' The workers looked out the windows to see a man with a screwdriver removing the plaques identifying the directors' parking spaces. Spontaneously, an enormous cheer went up. 'It was as though you'd given them all a hundred-pounds-a-week pay increase, it really was that important to them.'

The do-it-now action-orientation was a fundamental tenet of Unipart's new management team. When they wanted to do something, they tackled it immediately, telling all and sundry what they were doing and why. 'If you trust people, and they can see that you trust them, and you work closely with them, it's amazing just how well you can do together,' said Burns. 'But you have to put your commitment up front, you have to say to people from day one: I trust you.'

Only a few of the employees of Coventry Components would see the full extent of the new Unipart. Reconditioning old engines was not a part of volume car production. 'Our aim is to back the long-term winners, whom we identified as being primarily the Japanese manufacturing companies. We wanted to give a world-class service to world-class companies,' said Burns. He reached an agreement with a West Midlands company, Beans Engineering, to buy Coventry Components' equipment, and take on most of the men. As a sign of good faith, Unipart paid the costs of the coach to take them from Coventry to Beans' site at Tipton. The 50,000-square-foot factory building became the home of Premier Exhausts, Unipart's greenfield exhaust-building business.

To another ex-Tenneco man, Roger Ball, fell the task of creating Premier Exhausts. 'My brief was to set up a factory that was totally focused on the customer, that was non-union, that had none of the old traditions and obstructions, where the people who worked there would be flexible, mobile, multi-skilled, and would never let the customer down,' said Ball. He recruited half a dozen new young workers in Coventry, selecting men for their positive attitude to teamworking. 'Everybody is psychometrically tested. There's no previous experience necessary. If your attitude is right, we'll train you up,' said Ball. While the Coventry building was being refurbished, Ball took his new recruits down to the Oxford site, now re-named Oxford Automotive Components (OAC), to train them in building exhausts. The exhausts, for the new Rover 200 and 400 series cars, were manufactured on new equipment purchased in Japan, robotic welders, and machines which automatically cut and bent steel pipe. Ball laid out a cellular manufacturing assembly line, producing on just-in-time principles. Developed in Japan, the just-in-time system (or JIT; Ball's favourite joke was telling people it stood for Japanese-Inspired

Terror) meant producing without stock. If it took two hours to produce an exhaust, then the team began building one two hours before it was needed. 'It's like a continuous flow. You put a blob of paint in one end and a finished exhaust comes out the other,' said Ball. The system made enormous savings on working capital; no money was tied up in half-finished pieces of product stacked up against the factory walls. It also meant that if anything went wrong, if say a part was bent wrong and would not fit into a jig, then the entire production process seized up. The entire team would have to turn their attention to sorting out the flaw in the system before work could resume. It therefore shifted the focus of production from quantity to quality, to making sure that every single component was manufactured right the first time.

This concept was the most important single feature of Japanese manufacturing, and yet it was a difficult one for western businesses to grasp. By western standards, JIT would have been a formula for disaster. It should have meant that the production line was constantly stopping, that deliveries were repeatedly late, and costs per unit going through the roof. But at Japanese companies like Toyota, Honda and Nissan, the reverse happened. Productivity and quality were the best in the world, and costs the lowest. The secret was in the people: JIT put the power and responsibility for success in the hands of the five, ten, or fifteen people in each production team. By *empowering* shopfloor workers, JIT inspired them to work, think and produce at levels unmotivated western assembly line workers never even dreamed of. Beginning in the early 1970s and for the next two decades, American companies struggled to understand the Japanese export miracle. An early explanation offered by American academics and businessmen was hidden subsidies from the Japanese Trade Ministry, MITI. Next, it was the low cost of loans. Then it was the Japanese higher level of automation. Then it became 'dumping'. One by one the explanations were produced and discarded when found not to fit the facts. American industry did not find the truth because, in general, they were not looking for it. Proud companies like General Motors or Ford did not want to hear that their problem was assembly-line mass production. That was the heart and soul of their companies.

British companies had an advantage over the American and German companies, the advantage of failure. By 1980, the desperate uncompetitiveness of much of British manufacturing industry was self-evident, especially in the volume car business. Both management and workers were ready for a shopfloor revolution.

In 1988, Unipart's new Rover 200/400 exhaust production went on trial with Rover. Month by month, Ball's team produced a steadily rising number of exhaust systems. The equipment was new, the men were new, and there were teething problems. But every single delivery was on time. 'I drilled it into my people: We never ever miss a delivery date, ever. It's the first rule. Whatever happens, we don't go home, we work all day, we work all night, whatever it takes, we never miss a date. That was absolutely instilled in these guys.' Often, Ball joined the men at the machines. If another pair of hands was needed, a secretary was pulled out of an office. It was a mantra: *We never ever miss a delivery date*. When they stayed late at night, Ball sent out for bottles of pop and snacks. He led them running up and down the factory singing and chanting like US Marines. 'When you create an environment like that, team spirit just accelerates away. You have to struggle to hold it back,' said Ball.

Slim, brown-haired and moustached, born and raised in Birmingham and proud of it, Ball, forty-nine, was a pioneer in bringing Japanese manufacturing methods to the UK. The key formative experience in his career occurred in 1974 when as manufacturing manager for BSA/Triumph, he closed down the once great company's last motorbike factory. In the 1950s and even into the 1960s, BSA/Triumph bikes accounted for 70 per cent of the world market in large (over 750cc) bikes. It was a source of great pride in the Ball family that a family member had worked at BSA every year since Birmingham Small Arms was founded in 1861. After training as an engineer, Roger Ball followed the family tradition into the company in 1959. He fell in love with motorbikes. He arrived at work each morning to see the day's new bikes lined up in rows on their stands, waiting to be tested, engines ticking over, front wheels shivering in the air. The testers, clad in cloth caps and goggles, many of them limping from accidents sustained in earlier racing days, were figures of great respect. 'A new motorcycle has its own smell, of oil, petrol and paint. I would look at those bikes and literally breathe it in. It gets into your blood.' The Japanese entered the market with small bikes, just 250cc. At BSA they laughed, calling them 'tiddlers'. Ten years later, the Japanese owned the industry.

'Some of the mistakes made by the management of the British motorbike industry bordered on the criminal,' Ball declared years later. As a manufacturing manager, Ball lived through the death throes of the industry. In the 1970s, in a belated effort to modernise the factory, Ball won permission to install six automated lathes – and then had to pay eight men to sit in chairs reading newspapers alongside the machines because the union would not agree to new manning arrangements. When the end came, Ball, who considered himself a compassionate manager, a 'people person', had to pay off 600 workers. 'I had grown men with tears in their eyes, asking me how they were going to support their families.' He sold off the equipment, and took a last walk through the empty factory, listening to the echo of his footsteps. A tradition that had begun with his gunsmith great-great-grandfather was ending. 'There was something dreadful about a factory that once was alive and vibrant, full of its own life and culture, and now it was empty.'

A month after that it was Roger Ball's birthday. His wife bought him a Casio watch. He ordered her to take it back to the shop the next morning. 'I swore I'd never have anything to do with the Japanese ever again.' Within a year though, Ball changed his mind. He began to study Japanese industry. 'I wanted to find out what they did that destroyed a market where BSA and Triumph dominated the world and they came along and killed us.' He read every book he could find on Japanese manufacturing. 'I discovered that they do the simple things well. Total dedication to the customer, and letting all the knowledge and enthusiasm of your people, which is your biggest asset, come out.' Ball became a specialist in setting up JIT factories, applying the techniques to auto companies and the historic Birmingham bicycle manufacturer Dawes. For a new challenge, he set up an oil refinery in the Midlands. A large customer was a Shell depot in Trafford Park, Manchester. 'They had their own refinery over the road, but they ordered from us, because we could beat their refinery on delivery.'

In 1989, Ball moved back to Coventry from Oxford and began recruiting staff to the new state-of-the-art factory, Premier Exhausts. The recruitment ad in the Coventry newspaper read: 'Act like a manager. Be treated like a manager'. Premier had contracts to make exhaust systems for Rover and Honda. The Unipart managers never really doubted Premier would win that business. They knew that a greenfield site staffed by young, enthusiastic workers could not fail to produce a quality product. But reforming an old factory was a more daunting prospect. They turned their minds to the challenge of Oxford Automotive Components.

With the brief exception of the war years when it had made parts for Spitfire bombers, Oxford Automotive had been part of the British car industry for seventy years. Sandwiched between a college playing field, a canal and residential north Oxford, the factory sat in a low rectangular brick building built in the 1920s, a mile north of the city centre. Outside the factory doors was one of the world's oldest and most pleasant university towns. The road was busy with local shoppers, tourist coaches en route to historic Woodstock, ten miles up the road. Boys in school uniform walked past, heading to the nearby primary school or cricket fields and undergraduate women flew past on wicker-basketed old boneshakers, late for class, skirts flying in the wind.

Inside the factory in 1988, it was a different world. Like the torture chambers of a medieval dungeon, the factory's glass roof amplified the cold of winter and made a hot summer's day unbearable. Crowded with machinery, some of it dating from before the war, the factory echoed with the clanging of presses and the trundling of trucks. The air was heavy with the soot and sparks of the arc-welders. Ventilation was so poor that at times it was impossible to see more than ten feet ahead. There was scarcely a sign of modern investment anywhere in the factory. So awful was the environment that industrial action often ensued when angry workers claimed the factory was too hot or too cold to work in. On those occasions they would give the management an hour to put in temporary heaters or fans and flee to the pubs over the road. It was a popular joke among the men that they could always count on at least as many strike days a year as holidays. Yet, while every last man belonged to a union, Oxford Automotive was not a militant workforce. Unlike Cowley, the vast Rover site five miles southeast of Oxford, the union had never fallen prey to political trade unionists. At Oxford Automotive, the men, most of them in their forties or fifties, many of them the second generation in their families to work at Woodstock Road, were primarily interested in the quiet life and protecting their livelihoods. But twenty years of decline in the British motor industry, which had led to repeated management efforts to undermine their earnings, tamper with the all-important bonus and piecework systems, and reduce the overtime they all depended on for a decent standard of living, had made them extremely suspicious of a management they regarded as weak, defensive and hierarchical.

The new management team often went off-site to nearby hotels to hold what they called brainstorming sessions. Here they would discuss and plan the company's future, hanging great white sheets of paper on the walls of a hotel bedroom and filling them with diagrams and charts. At these early meetings, it was always an open question whether Oxford Automotive could survive. 'Green-field' was a very attractive and comforting idea to managers trying to introduce the new concepts of production. When Honda built an assembly plant in the States, the first Japanese so-called 'transplant' factory in the west, they went to the little town of Marysville in the Appalachian foothills to recruit a workforce of country boys who knew more about shooting racoon and brewing moonshine than manufacturing. When revolutionary American steelmaker Nucor wanted to build its twenty-first-century electric-arc steel plant, they went to Indiana, plopped their building down in the middle of ten thousand square miles of cornfield, and staffed it with boys straight off the farm. It was not quite so easy to find hillbillies in Britain, but Nissan had pursued the same goal in the UK, going to Washington, Tyne and Wear for people uncontaminated by the bad old habits of manufacturing.

Without the luxury of a billion-pound capital budget, Unipart had been forced to be more daring than the global giants, building Premier in Coventry, despite the city's history of bad manufacturing habits and industrial militancy. Housed in an old interwar building, Premier was a greenfield factory that was brown on the outside and surrounded by blackspots of industrial militancy. Yet the new Unipart management knew it would work because the most important element, the human element, was new. But what about Oxford Automotive? By shifting Oxford's exhaust business to Coventry, Unipart had already lost 150 of Oxford's 500 jobs. Should they go the rest of the way down that road, relocating Oxford's fuel tank business to a greenfield site? Perhaps, thought the new management, the Oxford men *could* adapt to a new way of working. What was needed was something radical, some form of shock tactics.

'Wouldn't it be great if we could pick up the entire workforce and send them to Japan for a month to see what it's like?' said Roger Ball at one of their all-day brainstorming sessions. 'I don't think the finance people would like that much,' replied Frank Burns with a smile. He paused for a moment, and the smile vanished. Then he said: 'But we could afford to send a pilot team to Japan.'

Mark Trevelyan arrived at Narita Airport at 7 p.m. one evening in July 1988. Including an unpleasant three-hour layover in Anchorage, Alaska, it had taken him twenty-one hours to reach Tokyo. It took another four hours to reach the hotel in Kashiwabara. It took an additional two days for his luggage to arrive. He was part of a group of six OAC shopfloor workers, accompanied by one middle-level manager. After a week the manager went back, leaving the shopfloor men on their own with their Japanese hosts. 'Before we left, the managers kept telling us you're ambassadors for the company, don't do this, don't do that. I think they were worried we'd go over there and be your typical English football hooligans.'

The next morning, Mark and his colleagues showed up at Yachiyo's factory promptly at 9 a.m. They joined the Yachiyo Industries staff in the forecourt for five minutes of the traditional morning exercises, before being taken in to meet the managing director. Mark immediately hit it off with Yamira, Yachiyo's MD. 'He was a great practical joker. He used to make me sit next to him, because I was always having a laugh and a joke with the Japanese lads and he loved that.' The work schedule was punishing. They worked every night until seven or eight o'clock, and then went to dinner with the Japanese team they worked with, usually accompanied by some of the Yachiyo managers. On the weekends and once or twice during the week in their four-and-a-half-week stay, they went out for late evenings. These involved a pre-dinner drink in Kashiwabara, dinner in a nice restaurant in Tokyo, and concluded with further celebrations in bars or night-clubs, where they ate more, danced, sang karaoke (Mark discovered he and a Japanese team leader shared an enthusiasm for Frank Sinatra's 'New York, New York'), and drank ample quantities of beer, sake and Scotch.

Mark was impressed with Yachiyo's seven-man production team. They were highly motivated, took pride in producing a quality product and, equally important, they had the resources to do it. At OAC, production workers were not permitted to maintain their own machines, nor check the quality of their work, nor verify the quality of their supplies. The OAC manufacturing system, like that at British Leyland (or General Motors or Mercedes-Benz) was a case of demarcation run riot. At OAC there were six layers above the production workers, from chargehand and foreman up to general manager. In addition, there was an engineering department whose maintenance men were the only ones in the factory permitted to maintain machines, and an inspection department who did all inspection of the factory's inputs and outputs. The overall result was that the production workers were made to feel like brainless automatons. Mark recalled bitterly his first job after school, as an apprentice welder at British Leyland: 'I was pushed from pillar to post. One day it was sweep the floor, the next day it was weld this. If anything went wrong it was always get so-and-so. You were never told why you were doing something or told to do anything yourself.'

The Yachiyo team building fuel tanks for the R8 (Mark always called the car by its production code-name) operated on completely different principles. They had complete control over their own production process: they maintained and repaired the machines; they checked their own quality; under the leadership of the team leader (who actually worked, unlike most British foremen who spent their time with paperwork) they allocated jobs between team members, switching around to avoid boredom and share the load equally as the team decided. 'At OAC I used to make things, but I cut corners, I didn't care whether it fitted the car. I just had a target, a number each day, and I did it. It was job and finish, that's it, go home.

'When I went to Japan I saw that they actually owned every problem belonging to their job. If a machine broke down, the operators, the members of that team *owned* that problem. They knew how to maintain their equipment. They knew how to get all their supplies together before the job started so they had a clear run for a whole shift. It taught me to stand back and think. Rather than put the responsibility on somebody else, I thought, why don't I put the responsibility on *myself* to perform?'

Mark was amazed by how thorough the Yachiyo team were. As preventative maintenance, they checked and rechecked every electrical contact, every air valve and every conveyor belt or track, before they began a major job. 'They were *presumptuous* on a problem. If they saw a problem that could arise they'd say: let's stop it before it does.' And if a major problem did arise during production, the entire team would stop, tackle the problem, and solve it. 'They get straight on to it. At our place, something used to go wrong and, if you're a shopfloor operative, you'd try and convince somebody in maintenance to come over, and it was always "I'll be there in half an hour". I was losing bonus, the company was losing sales, and he was having a cup of tea!'

There is an old joke in Japan about the Honda worker on his way home from work in the evening: as he passes the parked Hondas, he glances at the windscreen wipers. If any are slightly out of place, he stops to adjust them to the foot of the windscreen. Unlike so much western industry, the Japanese believed quality and volume production went together. When they began planning a new factory or a flow-line, they allocated enough investment money for machines to do the job efficiently while reducing the human drudgery. They trained the workforce, often off-site and for months if necessary. Then they turned the team loose on the job, with full responsibility for quality and quantity of their output. The result was men and women who took pride in doing their job well.

Late one night in a smoky bar, while his colleagues danced with the Yachiyo female staff who, as Japanese corporate custom dictated, accompanied the foreign guests on their evening revels, Mark asked Yamira if there would be a job for him at Yachiyo should he decide to move to Japan. Absolutely, said the surprised Japanese. Mark told his colleagues that if he didn't have a family back in Oxford, he'd move to Japan 'tomorrow'. They were, he said, 'smashing people'. He liked the way they worked hard, and played hard, the way they set themselves goals and achieved them. 'The rewards at the end of the day, not only in monetary terms, but to be satisfied that you've achieved something, and that you're achieving something every day because you're *improving* every day, being part of a company that's successful and that's always gonna be successful, and to have a job for life, and to be looked after when you're older . . . it's a fabulous system.'

Returning to the dingy premises of OAC in August 1988 was a disheartening experience. Mark cheered up in November when the equipment arrived from Japan for the new R8 fuel tank assembly line. By January the Japanese team from Yachiyo had set up and proved out the equipment. It was laid out against one wall inside the OAC factory, a forty-foot chain of brightly painted machines connected by conveyors, down which half-carcasses of fuel tanks slid, spun, rose, fell, and finally emerged whole, ready for painting at the other end. OAC men stared with curiosity and wonderment at machines like the automatic solderer, which soldered a bracket on to the carcass with six jets of flame amid a hail of sparks in about eight seconds. A white fence was erected from floor to ceiling around the R8 flow-line to keep the untrained away from the potentially dangerous equipment.

For seven months, Mark and his team continued on old-style manual working. 'The equipment lay there idle, and it was like, what happens next?' The problem was division inside the management. Frank Burns and Roger Ball favoured the full-speed-ahead approach, but other managers feared uproar – possibly an all-out strike – if Mark's team was allowed to begin producing fuel tanks without maintenance, engineering, foremen, and the other demarcations and rules of the traditional system. A compromise solution was reached: Mark and his colleagues began producing, in August 1989, but without control over their whole job. Inspection still checked quality, and maintenance still controlled machines.

While the management debate went on behind closed doors, out on the shopfloor life grew uncomfortable for Mark. Rumours circulated, saying the arrival of the Japanese equipment was the prelude to a Japanese takeover at OAC, or a mass redundancy programme, or both. Another story had it that a handful of men would be trained on the new equipment, and then the plant would be shut down and relocated elsewhere with only a small number invited to take up jobs at the new site. Mark was ostracised by many of his colleagues. 'People would literally ignore you. They'd only speak to you if they had to. You'd hear them talking behind your back, saying "ahh, they're just management puppets" and similar stuff.' Some of the union officials at OAC threatened to block any effort to give new teams different benefits or working conditions.

Mark had a mate at work, Chris Howes. Chris was ten years

older than Mark, but they had become fast friends soon after Mark joined OAC in 1987. Both were welders, and they'd worked the night shift together for months. Both fishermen in their spare time, they had socialised outside work a bit and introduced their wives to each other. But Howes was also a shop steward and in the summer of 1989 he too stopped speaking to Mark. Howes worried that the new machines and Mark's pilot team signalled some new status for the hand-picked workers, or mass redundancies, or worse. 'What's so special about you?' Howes said to Mark.

In August, Mark and his team of four finally transferred from manual working to the automated R8 production line. Mark came in one morning to find a crude hand-lettered sign hung on the white fence, now known universally as 'the cage', surrounding the R8 line. The sign read 'Please Don't Feed the Animals'. The shopfloor hostility had found a new theme. Wherever Mark went in the factory, he was followed by animal noises. Workers threw bits of banana and nuts into the 'cage'. It was childish humour but with a bitter edge.

Mark fought back. When a co-worker accused Mark of putting himself 'above' everybody else, they had a stand-up row in full view of everybody working on tanks. 'I said I *don't* think I'm anything special. But I've had an experience you haven't had, so I've got every right to say this machine is brilliant. I will not be shy about it, I'm gonna tell you how it is.'

But the ever present undercurrent of hostility cut Mark to the core. 'I went home a few times and said to Sue I don't know whether it's the right thing we've done here, because the friends I thought were friends are turning against me.'

Mark often called Sue his 'pillar of strength'. 'I know everybody says nobody's got a wife like mine, but my wife is superb,' Mark said. They grew up on the same Cowley council estate, and met when they were both fourteen. Mark left school at sixteen to go to work at British Leyland, as had his dad before him. Mark lasted only a year before he quit and went on what he called 'all sorts of benders'. It was marriage to Sue that forced him to grow up. They were married at the age of nineteen and had their first child at twenty-one. Growing up with eight brothers and sisters, Mark was a keen supporter of family life. 'I said at the time, let's have 'em early, let's get through the hard work of having children and then we can enjoy our lives later on, if we're still around to enjoy 'em.' Mark got a job in a shoe repair shop and in a short time he was promoted to manager. In 1982 he was offered a job running a larger shop in Tyneside and the Trevelyans moved up north. Things went well until 1985 when the company had to close down many of its shops. Mark was made redundant. For eleven months he was on the dole. They had three children, the youngest only a few months old. Every day Mark looked for work and every day, month after month, he returned home empty-handed. He passed the time reading and eating. 'I must have read thousands of books, so many books I can't remember the names, just to fill the time.' He put on four stone. As the months passed and his savings disappeared, he grew desperate – and angry. If it was not for his wife and family, he said, he probably would have ended up in prison. 'It got to the stage where we had nothing to eat and I had to go begging to the social security, to give me some money to feed my children.' They refused.

'I was almost at my wits' end. I had to ring my mother and I said, look, I've never asked you this before, can you lend me some money?'

Finally, a friend rung from Cowley. The pub where he worked needed another barman. Only a few weeks after they moved back home, the pub manager suggested Mark go for manager. Mark and Sue became trainee manager and manageress, moving around country pubs in Oxfordshire. A year later though, Courage announced it was doing away with managed houses. 'I was given two choices: be sacked or resign. I thought, oh no, here it all starts again.' Luckily, Mark's father-in-law knew of an opening for a welder at OAC.

The ups and downs in Mark's life had given him a determination which not even he fully appreciated he possessed. But it showed whenever he was under pressure. In September of 1990, Frank Burns called him to tell him Unipart wanted to put him on a 'focus career path', a year-long programme involving a short stay at different departments around Unipart and some night courses in business at the Cowley branch of Oxford Polytechnic. 'Never!' said Sue when Mark got home that night. It was like the third chance that neither thought would ever happen. Mark said being chosen as the first one for yet another experiment made him feel 'like a million dollars'.

At work, though, it was the same old story. When he returned to the cage the next morning, he heard the phrase 'management puppet' once again. He turned on a colleague: 'Look, I've been given an objective, I've been given a chance to make something of myself, and if I can do it right, others are gonna have the chance after me. And I'm going for it. Whether you like it or not, I'm going for it.'

At Unipart House in Cowley, Group chief executive John Neill was developing the human resources programmes to back up his empowerment strategy. With 4000 employees, Unipart's main business was the delivery of replacement auto parts to thousands of garages and shops across Britain. Customer service was obviously vitally important. Neill's corporate mission was to make Unipart synonymous with 'Outstanding Personal Customer Service'. He set in motion a comprehensive programme to give Unipart staff the will to deliver outstanding service. Sue Topham, a petite bundle of energy who never seemed to take a breath, was Unipart's head of people development. Starting out as Neill's personal assistant, she had been 'evangelised' by Neill's convictions into an enthusiastic advocate herself. Her enthusiasm more than made up for her lack of formal training in human resources policies. Her current programme had four parts. First was Putting People First (PPF), an all-day seminar in customer service taken by every employee. Publicised by British Airways, PPF was actually developed by consultants Time Manager International. As adapted by Unipart, the PPF course focused on the importance of satisfying the customer, stressing the idea that everybody at the workplace has a customer, even if only the next man down the line. The course also dwelt on personal qualities: positive attitudes, assertiveness, controlling stress and the importance of teamwork. Under the general rubric of customer service, Topham was really running a psychological programme to boost Unipart employees' self-image and self-confidence. 'It made them feel good because most of it wasn't about the company at all. It was about them, their relations with people, and their home lives as well as their work lives.

'Ninety-nine per cent of them walked away different people.'

Topham's second programme, Mark In Action, took the campaign for customer service further. Mark In Action was an award given to Unipart employees or teams who went beyond the call of duty to service the customer. Unipart employees or customers could nominate anybody they thought merited the award. The programme was extremely rigorous. 'We verify the facts and go to an external panel of judges who decide whether each nomination is good enough to merit an award,' said Topham. Award winners received a gold lapel pin and two specially designed, framed Unipart share certificates. They were invited to a buffet lunch with John Neill and all their like management including main board directors. Typically at least seven of the Group's top ten executives attended the lunch. 'It is a high focus event to show our employees the respect we have for them and to inspire others,' Topham explained. Neill never tired of telling the stories of Mark In Action winners. Among his favourites was the case of Ian Bowler, who worked at Unipart's Kidlington (Oxfordshire) oil cooler plant. Bowler was preparing to deliver an oil cooler to the Jaguar plant in Coventry on a Friday afternoon when he discovered the cooler was defective. He took the unit home with him and got up early Saturday morning to repair it. Bowler worked until late afternoon when he stopped to attend a family wedding. Up early again on Sunday morning he finished his work, and delivered the cooler Monday morning at 8 a.m. 'Jaguar never even knew anything was wrong,' Neill would announce as the climax of his tale. To his dismay, journalists rarely printed the story, perhaps because they found it hard to believe such dedication could exist at such a seemingly ordinary Midlands company as Unipart. But a man's desire to belong to, contribute towards, and take pride in, a successful organisation made all manner of achievements possible. Internally, the company publicised the awards with posters, photos of the awards ceremonies and extensive coverage in Unipart's monthly internal communications video 'Grapevine', seen by every employee. By 1992 Mark In Action awards were being dispensed at the rate of four a month. 'When customers hear what we're doing they become very interested. It starts a dialogue where they want to learn more about how we run the awards and they also get more involved in making nominations,' said Topham.

Topham's third people programme, 'My Contribution Counts', was a seminar in how to give presentations. Building on the principles of Putting People First, it was an aggressive effort to break down another of the barriers that separated shopfloor and management by empowering everybody in the company with the ability to give presentations. The seminar began with a quote from Japanese electronics giant Matsushita which was to capture everyone's attention:

> We are going to win and the industrial west is going to lose out. There is nothing you can do about it because the reasons for your failure are within yourselves. With your bosses doing the thinking while the workers wield the screwdriver, you are convinced deep down that this is the right way to run a business. Only by drawing on the combined brainpower of all its employees can a firm face up to the turbulence and constraints of today's environment.

After a day-long workshop, every member of the seminar had to give a lengthy presentation on their job and how it might be improved before a roomful of people. For many, it was their first effort at public speaking since school. Sue Topham waxed lyrical as she described the successes of the programme. Her favourite case was one of the programme's first volunteers, Tracy Towler.

Tracy worked at McDonald's for five years after leaving school and then joined Unipart in the Cowley warehouse. Tracy began her presentation by apologising for her poor spelling and asking the audience to be patient: 'I'm not used to writing on flip charts,' she said. She sat down ninety minutes later, and a roomful of her co-workers stood up and gave her a standing ovation.

Fourth, and perhaps the most radical of Unipart's people programmes, was the Our Contribution Counts or OCC Circles. This was essentially the Japanese idea of the quality circle tailored to Unipart's needs. 'We looked at why quality circles failed in the US, because we knew if we didn't do the research ours would just fail too and we weren't interested in joining that league,' Topham explained. Unipart's own solution was considerably more powerful than the typical American quality circle, and much more flexible than the Japanese model. Any Unipart employee could organise an OCC Circle to solve any problem or improve any aspect of the business where he saw potential for improvement. He could sign up any member of the company he felt necessary to achieving the Circle's objective. Nobody was exempt, not even Neill himself. The man or woman who founded the Circle led it; after consultation with the other members, he set times for its meetings, decided the agenda, led the discussion and decided when the Circle had achieved its goals and was ready to be disbanded. Specially trained 'facilitators' taught Circle leaders the skills necessary to manage an OCC Circle. The investment in terms of staff time would be substantial; but by setting clear goals and including the principle that all Circles would be disbanded when their goals were achieved, normally expected to be within six months, the company was creating a structure that would avoid degenerating into a mere talking shop.

Melvin Thornton worked on the paint line at Oxford Automotive. For months, a recurring moisture leak on the line bothered him. After a fuel tank was assembled, it was hung on an overhead conveyor. The conveyor took it through a hot wash, dried it, spray painted it and dried it again, before the tank was sent off to the next assembly process where secondary components like electronics and fuel pump were fixed to it. Although most of the new model cars used rust-free galvanised steel for the tanks, the two coats of paint were still important to prolong the life of the tank. But the metal stop, or bung, inserted into the intake hole was occasionally letting in minute amounts of water. It remained there through the drying. Droplets leaked out during painting to cause tiny spots of paint flaking. When that happened, the tank failed inspection and had to go through the paint line all over again.

Melvin Thornton had an idea about how to solve the problem. Aged fifty-two, Melvin came from a little village near the picture-postcard town of Bourton-on-the-Water in the Cotswold country-side. He spoke with the rounded country vowels of Gloucester-shire rather than the harsher Midlands accent of most OAC men. In twenty years with the company, he had scarcely missed a single day of work. A model employee, Melvin took little notice of the corporate pronouncements, union campaigns, or waves of rumour that swirled across the shopfloor. Melvin just did his job. In the spring of 1990, Melvin formed an OCC Circle with five shopfloor colleagues. Under his leadership, the Circle designed a new stop. A small round blank of steel with four protruding arms holding it against the tank with tiny springs and ball bearings, Melvin's Stop, as the ingenious little device was quickly christened, was small and robust. A quick twist of a knob on top drew the arms against the tank, forming a watertight seal. 'The beauty of Melvin's stop was that it could be made from scrap metal that otherwise would be waste,' observed Roger Ball.

In June, David Nicholas came back from a trip to Japan. He brought with him a stop Yachiyo had just designed in Japan to solve the same problem Melvin's team was tackling. When Melvin heard that Nicholas had already ordered 500 of the Yachiyo stops, he was furious. 'I hit the roof. I went straight up to David Nicholas and I told him he'd no right to do that because when you set up a task in an OCC Circle, no matter what status you hold in the company, you are the Circle leader and nobody can stop you finishing that project.' Nicholas relented, and Melvin was given a fortnight to prepare a presentation comparing the alternative stops.

John Neill and most of the senior management of Unipart's manufacturing division attended Melvin's presentation. In a quiet meeting room at OAC, Melvin set out the old stop, the Yachiyo model, and his own on a table before launching into his talk. He explained the causes of the moisture problem and each of the proposed solutions. The cost of the Yachiyo model, at £36 per stop, was greater than the £19 for his model. In a full year, his would save the company £35,000. But Melvin stressed quality and durability more than cost. 'I didn't like the Japanese stop. It had too many vulnerable points. I thought it would be damaged with people taking it on and off and chucking it into a box several times a day.'

The Yachiyo order was cancelled. OAC switched over immediately to Melvin's stop. Weeks later, the head of Yachiyo visited Unipart. Melvin was asked to do another presentation on his stop. The Japanese executive and his team listened attentively, taking notes. They were polite but showed little enthusiasm. 'I don't think the Japanese liked seeing somebody doing their job better'n them,' laughed Melvin.

The entire shopfloor watched the affair of Melvin's Stop with intense interest. Melvin had confronted the chief executive of Unipart Industries, David Nicholas, and won. Evidently, management did take the OCC Circles seriously. If Melvin Thornton, a lifelong shopfloor operative, was allowed to design a component, then the old demarcation system was dying. It was a change most on the shopfloor privately welcomed. 'Nobody understands a machine better than the fella who operates it all day long,' Melvin was fond of saying in his Gloucestershire accent. Most of the men had always hankered after control of the machines and the process as potentially a far more rewarding way to work, financially and psychologically.

Soon after Melvin's victory, one of the lads on the fuel tank line came up to the cage and asked to have a word with Mark Trevelyan. Was there any chance, he wanted to know, of his getting on to the R8 line? 'But you're one of the guys who sent me to Coventry a few weeks ago,' replied Mark. 'Well, this job's dying and I'm looking for another string to my bow,' said the lad.

Roger Ball came back from Premier Exhausts to take over as general manager of OAC in late 1990. He was to run the factory, but he also had a secret assignment: to examine the overall position of OAC and decide whether the factory should be relocated elsewhere. OAC operated on twenty-eight acres of some of the most expensive land in Oxfordshire. The Woodstock Road site was highly saleable to a residential developer or one of the nearby colleges. There remained the attraction of creating a greenfield site, staffed entirely with young men and women. Ball examined sites in Cowley, Banbury and Witney. In the end, he recommended to David Nicholas that OAC stay where it was. 'We'd seen Premier and the superb results you can get, and we'd seen Mark and the magnificent results he'd got, but it wasn't all the way yet, because he was in an environment that restricted him. His team were bumping on the ceiling of the old techniques and the old work practices.

'You could see that if you could remove the barriers there would be no problem. There was only one way to go. You had to let the people be empowered.'

In June 1991, the management announced a major day-long conference of the entire OAC workforce, in a large conference hall in nearby Cowley. At the last minute, they postponed the conference to early September. 'Everybody thought, well that's it, we're finished, Unipart's gonna pull the plug on us, we're gonna be closed down,' said Mark Trevelyan. The management did nothing to scotch the rumours, probably thinking a bit of uncertainty would smooth the passage for the impending announcement.

On a warm Friday morning in September, 350 OAC employees gathered for the conference. David Nicholas began with a brief introduction, telling the men that Unipart had decided not to close OAC, but to keep the Oxford site open and expand it. An enormous spontaneous cheer went up. OAC would become, said Nicholas, 'the factory of the future'. He handed over to Roger

Ball. Ball outlined the achievements at OAC. Rover, he said, were so impressed with the results of the R8 production line, they were designing a new fuel tank for the Rover Metro, also to be manufactured at OAC on an automated production line. Honda were talking to OAC about substantial orders supplying fuel tanks to Honda's new Swindon plant slated to open in 1992. 'Working in the old system and on the old equipment, you've put enough effort and enthusiasm in to show us the customer will back you up.'

A comprehensive investment programme would now begin to create the factory of the future, said Ball. 'It won't be a brand-new factory, it will be a brownfield site, but we will change from within.' To make production economic at Oxford, OAC would come down from twenty-eight acres to around eleven, which made little difference to the men, since most of that land was unused anyway. The company would modernise the building, replace the roof and create a new, healthier working environment. It would gradually automate the entire factory, moving to just-in-time production throughout. The workforce organisation would be completely revamped: from now on, it would be a single-status factory. Everyone would wear the same uniform. Everyone would get a monthly salary, paid directly into their bank account. Everyone would get the same sick pay: workers would get full pay for days off sick, just as managers did. The factory would be organised into teams, and each team would be fully responsible for its own production. The age-old system of bonuses, which over the decades had taken various forms including pay by output (piecework) or standardised minimum required daily targets (Taylorism), would be abolished. Teams would set their own weekly production targets, and strive to improve at their own pace, according to the Japanese principle of 'continuous improvement'. Existing bonuses up to £60 per week would be consolidated into the men's standard basic wage. On top of that an annual pay increase of 9 per cent would be awarded, as a symbol of the company's faith that the new system would be more profitable for everyone. After that, pay increases would be awarded individually and would be based on annual individual assessments, carried out by team leaders and management.

'In return, this is what we expect from you: a commitment to the customer, dedication and mobility. We do not see a role for a third party coming between us and you, no matter who they might be. We're not going to be a member of an employers' organisation that tells us: you can't change your holidays or reduce your working week because all the firms in our organisation have their holidays at this date or work this many hours. And we cannot have a trade union in the works. We are not going to be influenced by anyone who could stop us giving the customer the service that he *must* have if we're going to have a future.'

The men listened quietly, rapt in attentiveness, as Ball outlined how union de-recognition would work. On Monday morning, all employees would be given a copy of a new employment contract to take away and study. They would have until Christmas to decide whether or not they wanted to sign. If they wanted legal advice on the contract, they could consult a solicitor *at Unipart's expense*. Generous redundancy was offered to anyone who didn't want to stay. 'If you don't want to stop with us, we're sorry about that but we'll treat you well, give you a good start to your new life and, if you need any help in starting your new life, we'll help you with that as well.

'If you do want to stop with us, and we hope you will, there'll be no more compulsory redundancies. Even if we haven't got work for you, we'll put you on to training, because we're always looking to improve the way we do things. There will be no more insecurity, you'll be treated properly.'

Under the new non-union system, if an employee had a grievance against the company, Ball went on, Unipart would pay his expenses for taking outside legal advice. This pledge, effectively the company offering to pay the expenses of someone suing it, captured local headlines. It was the most striking demonstration of the company's conviction that the men would prefer the new system. In planning the Cowley conference over the summer months, management's greatest worry had been the reaction to union de-recognition. Most workers saw unions as a natural part of the workplace furniture; even those who detested the windy politics of union leaders found union back-up helpful on particular issues. Ball later admitted that even as he mounted the podium that Friday morning, he worried union de-recognition could be the spark that might set the entire edifice ablaze. 'We thought long and hard about de-recognition. But at the end of the day, it's the right decision and you have to say: is it right or isn't it? And you have to do what's right, and you have to deal with it.'

Ted Saxton, forty-seven, had worked at OAC for twenty-six years. He was one of the most senior shop stewards at the plant, and looked the part. Big, burly, with a sly grin and a sharp sense of humour, Ted was easily imagined standing outside a factory gate on a freezing winter's morning, warming his hands at a makeshift brazier, turning lorries away from the entrance, and putting a TV reporter in his place when asked a stupid question. Indeed, Ted had spent many mornings on picket lines back in the turbulent 1970s when scarcely a week went by without industrial action somewhere at British Leyland. A natural leader and widely respected at OAC, Ted was not a militant. He was a sensible union man, whose first priority was fighting not for ideology but for the livelihoods of the men and their families. With a wife and three teenage children to support, Ted shared those concerns. Ted's father and grandfather before him had both worked all their careers at OAC. His grandfather had been there almost from the day the factory opened its doors in 1919. It was called Osberton Radiators in those days and Ted still called the factory 'the Rads'.

Ted listened with fascination as Roger Ball outlined the 'factory of the future'. 'I thought, if they really do the things they say they're gonna do, well then this will be brilliant. People were expecting the worst and now we were being offered something better. A lot better.'

The men's mood rose as Ball detailed the plans for new investment. When he began to explain the policy of union de-recognition, Ted looked round. The men were clapping. Cheering the abolition of the union! He thought: 'I'm Ted Saxton, I'm the shop steward here, I can't be seen to clap him.' But Ted saw the point of Ball's argument.

The current management structure, Roger Ball went on, was too bureaucratic for the factory to have the flexibility it needed. Six layers of management between him and the men on the shopfloor were too many. That would be collapsed down to just two. The position of foreman would be immediately abolished. From now on, the foreman's job would be fulfilled by the team leader, with the big difference that team leaders would work on the line with their team. (Foremen rarely touched a piece of metal from one year to the next.) Anybody in the factory could apply to be a team leader, and Ball urged the shopfloor workers to consider applying for the posts. In an astounding day, this was perhaps the most stupefying piece of news yet. The foremen, the little Hitlers of the factory floor, were not only to be abolished, but would have to re-apply for what sounded like their own jobs without the status – and they would have to compete against the men to win those positions!

Then Ball delivered the *coup de grâce*: a new position, group team leader, would be created, to act as head of the team leaders, working with the manufacturing manager. The new group team leader would be Mark Trevelyan.

Mark was sitting in the back of the auditorium. Everybody swivelled around to look for him. Too stunned to congragulate him, they just stared. Many of the men in the room had known Mark and his family for years. They had grown up on the same Cowley estate, the Blackbird Leys. They had watched him, a teenage tearaway like all the rest, who had grown up and settled down, like all the rest, under the twin pressures of family and financial responsibilities. He was one of the lads, shy, proud, a hard worker, never one to stand idle when somebody needed a hand. Like most, he liked a pint of beer and a game of football. Group team leader! He was thirty-three, ten years younger than many of the ex-foremen who would now be working for him.

Mark studied his shoes, embarrassed by the stares. At the podium, Ball drove home the point. 'You know Mark,' he said.

'He didn't go to a posh school, he didn't go to a university, he doesn't wear the old school tie and yet he is being given a chance.

'We want to be in a position where we hardly ever have to go outside to recruit. We want our talent to be homegrown. I expect there to be many more like Mark.'

At the conference's end, Ted Saxton went up to the podium to ask David Nicholas why he wanted to abolish the unions. Nicholas took the shop steward aside and pleaded with him to take a lead in convincing the men to back the new strategy. 'Trust me,' he said. 'And we'll make you a company to be proud of.' He repeated it several times: 'Trust me.'

Ted Saxton arrived at work Monday morning at the stroke of 8 a.m. The factory looked different. As you walked into the main press shop where Ted worked, an overhead sign hung down from the ceiling. The sign was some ten feet across and flashed its message in lights: 'Welcome to the factory of the future'. The entire factory floor was painted. The factory looked and smelled cleaner than Ted could ever remember it. The cleaners and painters had worked from Thursday night straight through the weekend. It was only a cosmetic overhaul, but it was an inspiring indication of management's good faith.

Ted picked up a copy of the new employment contract to study. He knew that many of the men would be seeking him out for advice on the new regime. At home that evening Ted studied the contract carefully. He saw nothing he objected to. On Tuesday morning, he handed it in signed. By the end of the month, 280 out of the factory's 320-strong workforce had followed Ted's example. Only a handful declined, most of them older men preferring to take the severance payoff and early retirement. For three years, the workforce had watched Roger Ball and his management colleagues in action; they had seen the results of their improvements on delivery times and quality levels to their customers: orders from Rover, Peugeot and Jaguar were increasing all the time. On top of that, the immediate benefits of the package offered were a powerful persuader. 'Now we can *afford* to be sick,' commented Melvin Thornton, who also signed his contract on that first Tuesday. The promise of full sick pay was only partly about pounds and pence: it was also hard evidence of management's trust in the men.

In November 1991, the regional office of the Transport and General Workers' Union asked Ted to come to a special meeting in Oxford. The T&G officials wanted to find a way to prevent OAC going non-union. As the new spirit of shared purpose, single-status companies and striving for world-class competitiveness blossomed in British industry, trade union leaders found themselves the only remaining defenders of the class system. Like the editors of *Debrett's Peerage*, their livelihood depended upon maintaining the old divisions. It was an irony not lost upon Ted Saxton, as he faced the angry union officials across a bare wooden table in a sparsely decorated room in Oxford. The old system was dying, and it was time to give the new one a chance, thought Ted, and the dinosaurs of the trade union movement would have no more success standing in the way of progress than the first dinosaurs did in rolling back the Ice Age. The sharp-edged sardonic wit that in the past humiliated anxious middle managers into shopfloor concessions or left haughty strike-covering television reporters at a loss for words in front of their own cameras was now turned against the union officials.

Ted must do everything he could to stop the men signing the new contracts of employment, the union leaders said. 'But I've already signed mine,' he replied, with an innocent smile.

Well then, he must ensure that none of the men applied for the new position of team leader. Why not, Ted wanted to know. They grew agitated as they explained that the team system, like multi-skilling, was a mere front for giving management the capability to further reduce the workforce. The men would become pawns in their own exploitation.

'Well, it might be difficult for *me* to tell the men not to apply,' Ted replied.

Why, they demanded.

'Because, you see, a fortnight ago, I applied to become a team leader.'

In October, Ted had been told confidentially that if he applied for a team leader post in the press shop, he would get preference over other applicants, even former foremen. Roger Ball wanted team leaders to be drawn from the men with the experience of doing the job. '"If you don't take over that team leader role," they said, "we would have to put in somebody who doesn't know what they're talking about as a tool setter, and you'd be passing all your experience on to him."' Ted left the union meeting at a complete stalemate. It was the last anyone at OAC heard from the T&G.

Within six months, Ted's ten-man press shop team reduced the time required for a tool change on the big press from ninety minutes to just eighteen minutes. Tool changes on the great hydraulic presses were a key indicator of manufacturing skill in the auto industry. In Japan, they took minutes; in American factories, hours. It had taken some of the advanced US plants a decade to bring tool changes down to Japanese levels. At OAC, Ted accomplished it in months. 'It was just better layout and organisation really,' he explained. 'But if you'd told me a year ago we'd *ever* do it in eighteen minutes, I'd have said rubbish!'

Mark's old friend Chris Howes also applied to be a team leader. He was asked if he would be willing to go to Japan during the Christmas 1991 shutdown to study Yachiyo's tank assembly for the new Honda Synchro car. He asked who would be leading the group. 'You will,' said Roger Ball. 'I was gobsmacked,' said Howes. 'They must trust me an awful lot to send me to Japan for three weeks in charge of four other guys.'

The structure of the new OAC rapidly took shape. Many of the new team leaders were former shop stewards. These were the men who had the ability and the desire to achieve something. In the past only the union had offered them that opportunity. The new system gave them opportunities to be leaders in a positive, exciting cause, the challenge of making OAC a world-class manufacturing company. That meant increasing productivity, pay and profits. As profits would grow, money would be ploughed back in new investment, giving a new boost to production levels and pay. It was a virtuous circle. Said Ted Saxton: 'When I took over as team leader, I said to my chaps: the job isn't going to change just because I'm team leader. What I want is ideas from you to make us more efficient and keep us in a job. My chaps have responded really well.'

Elsewhere in the factory, quality and productivity improved by leaps and bounds. On the line producing fuel tanks for the R8 (the Rover 200/400 series), output per man-hour finished 1991 at levels 17 per cent above the previous year. Equally important, quality surged ahead as the production teams took responsibility for their own quality. For 1992, the fuel tank line set itself a target of 95 per cent right first time, meaning only 5 per cent of fuel tank assemblies would need reworking before going on to the paint line. As 1992 neared its end, that target was regularly achieved, and the team was considering the more daunting objective of 2.5 per cent for 1993. 'In the old days, probably about 50 per cent of the fuel tanks we built were right first time,' commented Mark Trevelyan.

The process of converting to just-in-time production had begun well before the Cowley conference. Since the conference, Roger Ball had sped it up substantially. By reorganising production in the main 80,000-square-foot factory, reducing the level of stocks of inputs and work-in-progress, he was able to close the 50,000-square-foot building behind the main factory formerly used for stores. 'Stock turn', the number of times the stock in the factory was completely renewed each year, a crucial indicator of how efficiently a manufacturer uses his inputs, shot up from six in 1990 to thirty by end-1992. In other words, while in 1990 the factory needed eight weeks' worth of inputs on hand to ensure smooth production, by 1992 it was producing (more and better) with less than two weeks' worth of stock. Frank Burns said thirty was the best figure he'd seen for the UK auto industry. 'But we know that in Japan Toyota have reached figures in the forties. That's our target.'

As team production and the enthusiasm for employee involvement spread across Unipart, OCC Circles became widespread. In the 1991–92 year, 145 OCC Circles were created, three quarters of them initiated by staff, not management. They saved the company over £2 million, Sue Topham estimated. It was just the beginning, she said, but showed the potential waiting to be unleashed by empowering people. The largest single saving was achieved at Premier in Coventry, where management had earmarked £250,000 in the capital expenditure budget to replace a defective coiling machine which rolled stainless steel for a silencer. The operators of the machine set up an OCC Circle, tracked down the fault in the machine, and corrected it, saving the company £250,000. *Nobody understands a machine better than the man who operates it all day.*

Melvin Thornton did not apply for a team leader position. 'That's a post for a younger man,' he said. Melvin looked forward to retirement and spending time at his Gloucestershire home with its rose garden. Until then, he preferred to be involved in specific problems. In the company, he was famous as the man who taught Yachiyo how to paint fuel tanks more efficiently. He was rung up by employees from other divisions seeking advice for their OCC Circles or requesting his participation, which he usually politely declined. He did however participate in the Circle which devised the new uniform for OAC workers, a bold but simple blue suit with a red baseball cap with the letters OAC in white. Melvin praised the new team-based production system for encouraging all employees to use their brain as well as their hands on the job. 'We're not working harder,' said Melvin. 'We're working smarter.'

Customers, the key to OAC's future, also acclaimed OAC's new production system. After seeing the initial results of Mark's R8 production line, Rover decided to design a fuel tank for their small hatchback, the Metro, which could be manufactured on an automated production line. Rover awarded OAC its 'Sterling' award as a top-quality supplier. The Rover-Unipart-Honda-Yachiyo relationship grew continually closer, with more joint design projects under discussion. In 1992, as Honda completed construction of its giant Swindon assembly plant, the Japanese giant told OAC it wanted them as one of its prime suppliers. OAC would build the fuel tank for the car code-named the Synchro, the family car model which seemed well positioned to reach success comparable to its American counterpart, the Honda Accord, the best-selling car in the American market. Although the British car industry spent the 1991–92 year mired in recession, OAC's sales grew throughout the year, as Rover expanded its 200/400 range, and Peugeot gave the Oxford factory a growing share of its business. The men worked substantial overtime and, not infrequently, Saturdays, which translated into more take-home pay than ever before. 'If this is a recession, then all I can say is I hope it never ends,' commented Melvin.

In the autumn of 1992, OAC won new business from Rover on the old Montego/Maestro models, and clinched its first-ever contract with Swedish car-maker Saab. It supplied the new Honda factory in Swindon. OAC's engineering team redesigned a catalytic converter for a new Rover model, making it lighter, cheaper and more environmentally-friendly than the original, designed-in-Japan model. Neill's claim that one day they would combine Japanese manufacturing skills with British creativity was coming true, sooner than anybody could have expected. 'We are putting it all together, and turning it into saleable, quality consumer products,' Neill said.

Investment in the factory was creating a working environment which a visitor from ten years earlier would scarcely recognise. New lighting was installed in much of the factory. Section by section, the leaky, old glass roof was replaced with a modern, insulated roof. A computerised heating system was installed. Local artists painted a giant 100-foot-long mural across the entire length of one wall. Most striking perhaps were the improvements outside the factory, where a small lake had always been an ugly dumping ground. The debris was removed, the banks of the lake landscaped and carp were introduced. To aerate the water for the factory's new residents, two fountains were installed in the lake. Streams of water shot twenty feet into the air at the lake's centre, lending a refreshing country scent to the air. Some of the men planted a vegetable garden inside a small greenhouse on one side. 'Our next project is to build a canteen with a conservatory overlooking the lake,' said Roger Ball.

'When you walk around OAC, you sense the spirit. You see it in people's eyes, in the way they look at you and the way they talk to you,' said Unipart chief executive John Neill. Neill now presided over two of the most advanced auto component facilities in Britain. In Coventry, Premier Exhausts was completely automated. Catalytic converters were installed into exhaust systems without ever being touched by a human hand. At OAC there would always be old-fashioned manual welding for after-market parts for the older Rover cars, the MGs, Austins, or Minis (most of them exported to Japan now), but automated equipment was gradually taking over each of the production lines for the current models. Both factories were set to be overflowing with business as Honda at Swindon raised production levels towards its target of 100,000 vehicles per annum. The team production system pioneered at Unipart's two manufacturing plants was now being spread throughout Unipart's core business, auto parts distribution. Productivity gains were already evident. In 1992, Unipart reported profits up 29 per cent to £19.1 million on turnover of £661 million. In a generally disastrous year for the auto industry, it was an impressive performance. The performance of Unipart's share price was still more dazzling. In 1987, the Unipart employees were offered a 'share package' which included mostly low-risk preference shares with a guaranteed dividend and only a small portion in riskier so-called ordinary shares. In 1987, the ordinary shares were priced at 5 pence each. In 1993, those shares traded on Unipart's private market at £9-80 each. The typical employee who bought £560 of shares in 1987 had purchased £30 of ordinaries. By 1993, that £30 investment was worth £5880. But Neill stressed that the high share price paid was not a goal in itself but the side-effect or reflection of the company's bright future. 'The way we got where we are today was by saying, how do you build a high quality enduring relationship with *all* your stakeholders, your customers, shareholders, employees, suppliers and communities. How do we all work together to ensure that all stakeholders benefit?'

The most striking transformation of all at OAC was in the men's morale. 'We're aiming not just to be the best in Europe, but the best in the world,' declared Melvin Thornton. Ted Saxton described how, a few years ago, none of the workers liked to be seen in OAC clothing outside of the factory. Today, OAC uniforms are badges of pride, and the distinctive red OAC baseball cap is not an unusual sight on the streets of north Oxford. Every Thursday evening, Ted Saxton goes straight from work to pick up his wife and do the weekly shopping at Tesco's. He always wears his uniform. 'Getting given a nice uniform, having a nice clean work area and rest area, or having a gaffer who knows everybody by their Christian name and you call him David, some people say they're silly little things, but they mean a lot to the lad on the shopfloor,' said Ted.

At OAC, a thoughtful Roger Ball considered the lessons behind the transformation at OAC from a strike-ridden factory facing closure to one of the most successful components companies in Britain: 'Dan Jones says in his book [*The Machine That Changed The World*, an in-depth description of Japanese auto manufacturing philosophy] that you need to have stood on the precipice, and be close to a Japanese partner, to stand a chance of succeeding.

'That's true here at Oxford, but it wasn't true at Premier, where all the news we gave them right from their recruitment was always good news. At Premier, the catalyst was this is a new product, a new factory, a new future. That was enough to set them away.'

Today, Group team leader Mark Trevelyan works in a cramped, crowded room sectioned off from the main factory. Its large windows look out on to the fuel tank lines and the clanging of the hydraulic presses reverberates through the partition walls. OAC is still a brownfield site: in the office, which Mark shares with a couple of other managers, the desk chairs are missing their backs, and the ancient IBM desktop computers are scuffed and battered. On the walls are a couple of glossy Unipart calendars. Nearly every other bit of wall space is covered by hand-written charts showing production outturns, quality targets and other critical production ratios. Mark rushes around from meeting to meeting, stopping everywhere for hurried consultations. One meeting concerns a proposal from one team to reorganise the shift schedule to reduce the night working while maintaining output; another meeting involves new equipment just installed on a line; still another concerns the details of an impending trip to Swindon to meet with their opposite numbers at Honda. Mark says he learns something on every visit to Swindon: 'If you watch the way they inspect every item, every detail of a component, you see they want it to be perfect. They don't want the customer to have a problem, ever.

'That's perfection and that's where we're heading.'

TWO

Guinness

It's Not Easy Being a Dolphin

It was a bitter war. The prize was bourbon and the battlefield was the thousands of ginza and rappongi bars in Japan. It began in 1988 when Guinness took back from Suntory, Japan's largest beverage company, distribution rights to Japan's favourite American bourbon, IW Harper. Nobody did that to Suntory on its home turf! Vowing to give Guinness a black eye, Suntory quickly signed up another American bourbon, Old Forester. Wielding immense clout in the drinking places and supermarkets of Japan, Suntory set out to prise Guinness's IW Harper brand off the bars and shelves and replace it with Old Forester. In its first year, Old Forester notched up impressive sales of 100,000 cases, coming in at number three in the fast-growing bourbon market. Guinness fought back, with aggressive marketing, a jazzy advertising campaign emphasising the American glamour of bourbon whisky, and a determined sales effort asking the bar and supermarket owners to let the customers, not the suppliers, choose their drink.

When the dust settled two years later, Guinness and the customers had won. IW Harper sales grew by more than 10 per cent, holding its number one spot. Old Forester sales fell by 20 per cent, taking it down to number six in the Japanese league. Guinness was pulling down £10 million a year in *profit* on IW

Harper. It was doubtful if Suntory was making much profit at all on Old Forester.

Guinness decided to thank its Japanese supporters, and Guinness chairman Anthony Tennant did it with his usual style. He asked the Scottish Ballet if they'd like to do a tour to Japan, at Guinness's expense. Scottish Ballet chairperson Lady Elizabeth Dalkeith immediately accepted the offer. Guinness was a loyal sponsor, spending more than £100,000 a year sending the Ballet all over the world, to play to audiences usually far bigger than those they drew in their native Glasgow. Tennant knew that Lady Dalkeith and her vice-chairman Oona Ivory knew members of the Japanese Imperial Family. Would they mind inviting them to attend? Lady Dalkeith had met the Emperor's younger son Prince Akeshino when he studied at Oxford and Mrs Ivory had been at Cambridge with Princess Takamodo. Both princes and their wives were delighted to come. The next day's newspapers showed the happy members of the Imperial Family drinking the health of the Scottish Ballet and ballet worldwide with glasses of IW Harper and Old Parr, Guinness's top-selling Scotch whisky in Japan.

The next evening, Brian and Oona Ivory were guests for dinner at Prince Takamodo's private residence. The bustle of Tokyo quickly faded as their car wound through the neat, ornate gardens of the Imperial Compound. The prince and his family inhabited a simple but elegant, modern, low-slung, arch-roofed house. The prince and princess waited at the door to greet their guests. Mrs Ivory presented the prince and her old friend with a gift from Guinness, courtesy of Anthony Tennant. It was a bottle of Old Parr Elizabethan. At $1000 a bottle, it was the most expensive Scotch in the world. As the servants scurried off to fetch whisky tumblers, walking on their knees in the Imperial presence as etiquette required, Prince Takamodo held the Scotch up to the light to admire the bottle. It was beautifully crafted, with delicate white threads twisting through the hand-blown glass. The prince seized the pewter stopper, and looked up at Brian Ivory with a smile.

'Let's crack open a bottle.'

The transformation of Guinness is one of the great turnarounds of modern business history. Fifteen years ago, the two companies that make up present-day Guinness PLC, beer-brewer Guinness and spirits-maker Distillers Company Ltd, suffered from defeatism and decline in equal measures. Under the leadership of Ernest Saunders (1981–87), Anthony Tennant (1987–92) and Tony Greener (1992–), the company remade itself and began clawing its way up the league tables of the world's fiercely competitive drinks industries. Today, Guinness is a lean and decentralised, innovative and superbly internationalist organisation. It is aggressive and expansionist, constantly seeking out new markets, launching or relaunching new products from within its broad portfolio of brands. In place of yesterday's gentlemen-businessmen polishing excuses for lacklustre sales, they are professional marketers, expert in the science of turning age-old brand names into newly vibrant symbols of luxury and quality.

Superlatives stick to Guinness like beer mats to a dirty bar. It is the largest alcoholic beverage company in the world (among all beverage companies, it ranks second to Coca-Cola). It is the largest Scotch whisky company, selling the world's most popular brand of Scotch (Johnnie Walker) and the most popular gin (Gordon's). Measured by profits per barrel sold, it is the world's third most profitable beer company. With pre-tax profit of £795 million on sales of £4.3 billion in 1992, the company boasts higher profit margins and greater cash generation than most of the world's billion-dollar companies. In 1992, one London stockbroker estimated Guinness earns more profit on exports than any other British company. It's not a bad record for a company which in 1981 was facing bankruptcy and was a ripe target for a hostile takeover.

The old Guinness was a sleepy company, family owned and family dominated, its loyalties divided between Ireland where it made most of its profit and where the senior family members lived, and Britain, home of the management who ran the company. It was a slowly sinking ship, although in 1981 the sinking was gathering speed. Beer consumption in its two biggest markets,

Ireland and the UK, was falling. Its diversifications into pharmaceuticals, plastics and a dozen other industries were suffering from recession. Profit margins were down by half to 5 per cent and heading south. Board member and merchant banker Peter Guinness decided that what the company needed was an injection of new thinking, skilled in the modern business of marketing. A headhunter found him a British businessman working in Switzerland for food giant Nestlé named Ernest Saunders. He seemed to have some good ideas, and Peter Guinness arranged for him to meet the company chairman, the Earl of Iveagh, at the earl's stately home just outside Dublin. After a relaxed lunch during which the earl talked about his farms, his pets and his ailing health, Saunders got the job. The Guinness company did not suspect the blitzkrieg that was about to hit them.

In 1981 Saunders was forty-six. Tall, grey-haired and soft-spoken, he was deceptively self-effacing. Born in Austria, he'd come to England as a child of three when his family fled the Nazis. His formative business training was at Beechams, a successful drinks and over-the-counter pharmaceuticals marketer, responsible for brands including Silvikrin, Eno, and Lucozade, and at international food giant Nestlé. Saunders worked for five years at Nestlé's corporate headquarters in Vevey, on Lac Leman in Switzerland. By 1981, he was bumping up against the limits of promotion for a Briton inside the internationalist – but decidedly Swiss at the top – Nestlé. His wife and two children also wanted to return to England.

Saunders was a break with Guinness tradition in several ways: he was a marketing man, in a company which had always seen itself as production oriented. He was not deferential; rather he was an aggressive, perhaps hyperactive businessman, bulldozerlike in his determination. He was powerfully attracted by the historic Guinness brand. It was the opportunity he had been waiting for. At Nestlé he compiled a list of a half-dozen world-class brands which were in decline and susceptible to turnaround. Guinness was on the list. He did not drink the thick black beer but, as a marketing man, he saw enormous possibilities for turnaround and expansion in the world-famous brand's image and sales. 'They may have known the name for different reasons – some from the well-known family, some, the *Book of Records*, or the famous advertising, and sure enough, some for the beer – but it was a name everybody knew, and it was a situation where I believed that if I was any good, as I believed I was in the marketing field, then there was something there and if I got that right, I could rebuild the business around it.'

For Saunders, the switch from Nestlé to Guinness was like a journey back into the business dark ages. Guinness was an old-fashioned colonial company of gentlemen-businessmen. Top of the pyramid was the Guinness board, dominated by the earl, his titled relations, and retainers to the Guinness family. The family went back to Arthur Guinness, an entrepreneurial Irishman who in 1759 brought 'porter', the dark ale originally drunk by Covent Garden market porters, to Dublin. Within a decade Arthur Guinness and Sons was bottling and shipping his brew back to England. In the Napoleonic Wars, British officers drank Guinness stout to revive them from injury or exhaustion. During the nineteenth century the beer followed the flag, winning a loyal following in virtually every corner of the Empire. In the late nineteenth and early twentieth centuries, the Guinness family became famous, especially in Ireland where virtually every famous Dublin church, monument or building was either on land given to the nation by the Guinnesses, built by them or contained orna-ments donated by them. In Britain, Southend became known as the Parliamentary 'Guinness family seat', held by three gener-ations of Guinnesses, including Henry 'Chips' Channon, (MP 1935–59), a social-climbing American who married into the family and whose major contribution to posterity was to coin the phrase 'rivers of champagne', describing the parties he attended in the interwar years.

Benjamin Guinness, the third earl, took over as chairman in 1963. He was just twenty-five, cared little for business and knew less. Under his chairmanship, the company was run like a feudal domain (managing director Tony Purssell referred to the beer operations as his 'private fief'). The mindset at the company was not on the creation of wealth but on its distribution to the deserving lower orders including management, shopfloor employees, and the Irish government pleading for employment-creating measures from the Guinness board. They all shared the assumption that the Guinness wealth was a bottomless well. The company's culture was production oriented: they took great pride in the quality of the beer. Implicitly, they subscribed to the old Victorian maxim of building a better mousetrap and waiting for the world to beat a path to your door. Yet by 1981, the rest of the world had woken up to the fact that drinks were a marketing-led, not a production-led, industry.

In the same year that Saunders joined Guinness, somebody humorously suggested the new Social Democratic Party campaign on the slogan 'A Better Yesterday'. With their near-monopoly eroding in Ireland, foreign competition invading their once sacred Empire markets, and Britain turning away from dark beers, Guinness too saw the world through 'better yesterday' spectacles. The company could not understand change, only preservation. It could not understand growth, only moderating the decline. Inside the breweries, highly trained chemists still bore job titles with the word 'Brewer', as if PhD chemists were meant to be flattered by the Victorian-style craftsman title. The anachronism extended to many areas of management, with titles like 'Brewer in charge of Sales' or 'Brewer in charge of Finance'. Ian Cheshire, a young management consultant brought in by Saunders, saw the old management as symptomatic of Britain's paternalistic management culture of the 1970s. 'They were gents, well bred, chummy, all with nice houses. They saw themselves as neo-aristocrats, behaving decently and selling beer to a grateful public.' There was no sense of direct divisional responsibility or a need to meet profit targets, Saunders recalled. 'They were called "special interest" directors, like government ministers: here's a portfolio and you look after leisure.' Consultant David Hoare felt he had travelled back through time when he joined Guinness in 1981. 'You had to come from Oxford or Cambridge, you had to have a degree in

engineering, and you had to be at least a Blue. Tony Purssell was
very close to the family.'

Guinness's corporate headquarters was a narrow four-storey
office building in Albemarle Street in London's Mayfair district.
Today occupied by mid-eastern carrier GulfAir, the building, with
one office on each floor, was woefully inadequate to the needs of
a multinational with a turnover of £900 million operating in more
than fifty countries. Saunders quickly discovered that the headquarters was tiny because real power lay elsewhere – with the
powerful 'barons' who ran the major divisions such as Guinness
Ireland, the Park Royal (London) brewery, or far-flung Guinness
breweries in countries like Malaysia or Nigeria. Said Saunders: 'I
was forcibly struck by the fact that the only regular reporting from
the hundreds of operating companies scattered around the world
was done by the main subsidiaries' managing directors' secretaries,
who used to ring up the managing director's secretary at Albemarle Street, have a little chat, and by the way report that the
monthly target was unlikely to be met, and she might produce an
estimated lower figure for the year.

'There was never any suggestion of remedial action.'

Before Saunders, Guinness management's fundamental strategy, if such a slack-jointed organisation could be said to have a
single strategy, was that Guinness's famous black stout was in the
long run a declining market and the company therefore needed to
diversify into other business areas. Under the rubric of diversification, Guinness had by 1981 acquired some 200 subsidiaries
around the world in a bewildering variety of industries. To get a
grip on this octopus-like empire and a hard, numerical sense of
where it was going, Saunders turned to management consultants
Bain. The 'Bainies', as they were known, were a mostly young,
business-school-educated, highly motivated international group
who prided themselves on their analytical skills and their ability to
write and implement radical solutions for ailing companies. They
had little time for sentimentality, history or tradition. If the realities
of the marketplace were faced in the cold light of day, almost any
large company, they believed, could quickly improve its bottom

line. 'Fact-based' was one of the greatest compliments in the Bainie lexicon, and their favourite slogan was 'we sell results, not reports'. Saunders walked into Bain's London office without an appointment. He requested a meeting with some Bain consultants and introduced himself: 'I'm Ernest Saunders and I'm managing director of Guinness and I need some help.' Bain consultant Richard Grogan recalled they did not quite believe him: 'We sent a guy out to check.'

In the financial year ending in October 1981, Guinness made pre-tax profits of £41.8 million. When a team of Bain consultants set up shop at Albemarle Street early in 1982, with the task of assessing the state of the entire group, Saunders could find nobody with any idea of how much profit the group would make in 1982 or even how much they had made so far that year. The news was likely to be bad. Recession was hitting both the British and Irish markets hard. Like many a colonial-era company, Guinness depended heavily on markets of the old Commonwealth. Nigeria often accounted for more than a quarter of the group's profits, but in 1981 Nigeria was in the midst of one of its regular politico-tribal-economic crises which looked like eliminating real (ie sterling) profits entirely.

Within a month, the Bain team contacted 250 subsidiaries around the world and produced a provisional total for 1982 of £20 million. The Guinness share price had fallen through most of 1981. The Bainies told Saunders that if Guinness profits did not come in at £40 million or more the share price would collapse and the company would be taken over.

Faced with the prospect of hostile takeover, probably followed by being thrown out on his ear, Saunders swung into action. He created a Bain team charged with examining the loss-making subsidiaries in order to eliminate the problems, closing them down if necessary, and to write them off in the 1982 accounts so the company would be free to focus on growth areas thereafter. One target of this exercise was Tony Purssell, Guinness's chief executive. In theory, Saunders was running only the beer business. Purssell remained Saunders's boss, responsible for group strategy.

The determined Saunders wanted the top job. He believed, probably rightly, that as long as the meek Purssell was above him, he would not be able to carry out the radical surgery the company desperately needed.

One morning in a hotel room, Saunders switched on the television to see Francis Ford Coppola promoting his next major feature film. It would all be made possible, said Coppola, by a very generous investor: the great beer company Guinness. Furious, Saunders commissioned an investigation which swiftly revealed that Guinness's foray into Hollywood film finance had a very real potential to bankrupt the entire company. Following a Guinness board decision to commit $25,000 to film development, Guinness's so-called leisure division had taken a nominal 1 per cent stake in a film partnership. However, as senior or 'managing' partner, Guinness was obliged to indemnify all other partners against losses above a pre-set limit. Bain consultant Olivier Roux served as Guinness's financial controller from May 1983. He produced a balance-sheet write-off of £85 million of unrecoverable losses for 1982. Purssell and Michael Ogle, Guinness director with 'special responsibility' for leisure investments, resigned. Roux, who went on to become Guinness's finance director in 1985, was astonished by the carefree way Guinness directors squandered millions of pounds on businesses they had only the most general knowledge about. Amateurs, gentlemen playing at being businessmen, he called them.

In Saunders's first eighteen months at Guinness, an astonishing 149 subsidiaries were sold off – a rate of roughly two companies a week. The Bain team carrying out the evaluation of these non-beer subsidiaries organised their work to a weekly schedule: every Monday morning they tackled the subsidiaries for the week, with the aim of giving Saunders a presentation on Friday morning, evaluating the subsidiaries' prospects and recommending a course of action: sell, restructure to sell or hold. The Bainies were amazed at the range of interests a beer company based in London and Dublin could amass. 'The phone would go and we'd learn we had a Caribbean island,' said Hoare. The list included pharmaceutical companies, a company producing drugs from snake venom, plastics companies, and one selling build-it-yourself injection-moulded plastic one-man sailboats. Most of the diversifications had a certain tenuous logic. For instance, at one point in the 1970s it looked as if metal beer kegs would be replaced with plastic, so Guinness invested in a plastic-maker. Beer-making was essentially a chemical process, so Guinness leveraged its chemical expertise into pharmaceuticals. Most executives would have bought a book about these subjects. At Guinness, they bought companies.

The worst excesses were in the area of boats and boating, a favoured pastime of several Guinness directors from the Purssell era. By 1981 Guinness owned the largest fleet of yachts in western Europe. Most of them were used in tourism-related ventures, carrying people around canals in Ireland and France. The Bainies flew out to visit these subsidiaries (often the only way to get reliable numbers), started work on the cash flow projections on the airline home, and stayed up through the night to compile the Friday presentation. A biotechnology subsidiary used mirror-stem techniques to replicate the jojoba plant. It had invested £1 million in research and was not yet ready to bring anything to market. At a Friday morning meeting, a Bainie pulled an eight-inch-high jojoba plant from under his chair and placed it on the table before Saunders. 'Here you are, Ernest. One million pounds and it's yours.' The company was sold. The divestitures netted a total of £40 million cash for the group. More important, they allowed the management to focus once again on its core business.

Saunders and his team shared the conviction that Guinness's future lay in beer. The previous regime's strategy was flawed in its defeatist assumption that beer consumption was in long-term irreversible decline. Said Bainie Richard Grogan: 'Even if beer consumption would decline one day, it was still potentially highly profitable. Guinness profits were declining because the company stopped building their brand and because their costs were out of control. And because their diversification programme was catastrophically ill-conceived.

'And into this nightmare stepped Ernest.'

After two centuries of international success, Guinness's famous black beer looked unlikely to finish out a third. Between 1973 and 1981 stout consumption in the UK fell from a 10.5 per cent market share to just 6.2 per cent. The overall beer market in these years was generally buoyant, rising in the 1970s from 37 million barrels annually to 42 million. The 1979–81 recession hit beer hard but, even at the bottom in 1982, consumption was 38 million barrels, ahead of the level a decade earlier. The problem for Guinness was that stout seemed to be a dying taste. In the 1970s, lagers blasted their way into the British market, doubling market share from 15 per cent in 1973 to 31 per cent by 1981. Whether brewed by a British brewer (Heineken, Fosters, Carling Black Label, Skol), by a foreign company brewing in Britain (Carlsberg), or imported from abroad (Holsten Pils, Beck's), many of these lagers had the clout and marketing spend of multinational giants behind them. They arrived chasing the younger drinker, whose tastes were moving away from traditional bitter, ale or stout, in favour of lager. The younger drinker was not only the largest consumer of beer, but he was 'promiscuous' in his taste, trying different beers both in the pub and at home, and taking much longer than his father did before settling on a habitual brew. Guinness did worst among these younger drinkers; it did best among older, traditionalist drinkers. Hence the fear in the company, which had grown to near-paranoia by 1981, that Guinness's consumer base was literally dying off.

With some of the best-known advertising in the world, Guinness ought to have been well-placed to win a marketing war. But Guinness's so-called great advertising was something of an illusion. Although it cost the company £10 million a year and won award after award, it did little to sell the product. It was as if, Saunders grumbled, the company had a division called Famous Advertising, completely divorced from every other division. The pre-1981 management were more interested in prestige than in building the business, and the old advertising reflected those priorities: 'It put the beer on a pedestal,' observed Ian Cheshire. 'People respected it, but they didn't drink it.'

In 1982, Saunders launched a multi-pronged assault aimed at reversing the decline of Guinness stout in the UK market. His first step was to issue an instruction to every department of the company to stop as much as possible the appearance of pictures of little old ladies, men in cloth caps or horses drinking Guinness: these images had become favourites of the press, which liked the idea of Guinness having some mystical revivifying power. To Saunders this was just the reverse of the young, sophisticated, stylish, cult image he aimed to cultivate for the beer. The first reaction of Guinness executives was to deny that these pictures appeared. Saunders had little time for the pre-existing management – 'not a single marketing man among them'. His reaction was brusque but effective: 'I had a montage made up of pictures, taken from the world's press, of little old ladies, cloth-capped men, and horses drinking Guinness. I shoved it around all the marketing departments with a note saying I do not want to see any more of this.'

In the media, advertising is described as inspiration and imagination. For Saunders, the key ingredient was intensive research of the consumer and his preferences. Saunders was relentless in investigating consumers' views and feelings about Guinness stout. Polls of Guinness drinkers were carried out to find out who they were with regard to age, sex, social class, income and every conceivable category. Psychological research was done on a sample of Guinness drinkers to determine why they drank the stuff. A sample of Guinness non-drinkers was interrogated to find out why they did not drink it. Target Guinness drinkers (ie young, male 'session drinkers', the heaviest consuming category) were quizzed to find out what might make them start drinking it. Before it was launched on an unsuspecting public, Saunders's strategy for the resurrection of the black beer was the most exhaustively researched in the history of the beer industry.

The first thing research discovered was that there was some truth in the cliché of the lonely old lady sitting in the dark corner of a pub pouring her bottle of Guinness into a glass. The average draught Guinness drinker was significantly younger than the drinker of the bottled beer. 'That gave us an indication that the way to rebuild this brand was to start on the basis of the draught Guinness, which was a slightly lighter, less bitter product anyway and because it was served chilled, tended to appear even lighter,' Saunders said.

In 1983, Saunders launched a new advertising campaign, built around the slogan 'Guinnless Isn't Good for You'. Posters which displayed the slogan alongside an empty glass seemed almost to mock the long-running traditional advertising, the revered 'Guinness Is Good For You' (usually accompanied by a picture of a glass of the black beer topped with the distinctive creamy head). It poked fun at all beer advertising. It got lots of publicity, much of it unfavourable. 'It was a sort of short-term shock therapy campaign designed to attract young people and make them willing to open their eyes and reconsider Guinness as a drink,' Saunders recalled. The Guinness family hated the new advertising. 'I didn't like it myself but the pre-research showed that this campaign had a real chance of achieving an image shift,' said Saunders.

As the Guinnless campaign began, Saunders recruited Gary Luddington to the key role of marketing director. An earnest, boyish character who looked younger than his thirty-seven years in 1983, Luddington joined Guinness for the challenge of trying to rescue a brand which most of the world believed was dying a slow but certain death. His track record, particularly at Carlsberg where he was involved in the 'Probably the Best Lager in the World' campaign, was first-class. Luddington was immediately impressed by the depth of Saunders's commitment to the marketing effort. 'Ernest was the only CEO I ever worked for who phoned me up and said, have you got enough money because if not we'll get it from somewhere else in the company.'

While the most visible part of the campaign was the Guinnless advertising, behind the scenes Guinness fought the war on many fronts. Research showed that Guinness tended to be consumed by a large spread of occasional drinkers (as opposed to what the industry called 'session drinkers', ie five- or ten-pint-an-evening men). The typical Guinness drinker ordered one when something in a pub reminded him or her of Guinness. Typically it was the sight of another drinker with a glass of the black beer. Luddington came up with the idea of a new plastic bar fount in the shape of a glass of Guinness, complete with the distinctive head. 'What could be better than to put that reminder right there on the counter?' The new fount, replacing the traditional red square emblazoned with the Guinness harp, was installed in a handful of pubs as an experiment. Sales increased dramatically. Saunders ordered the new fount to be put in every UK pub where Guinness was sold. Luddington followed through on the reminder theory by sponsoring pop concerts, putting up Guinness posters at social centres like universities, and running constantly changing Guinness ads in newspapers. 'If something happened in the news, we would run an ad which picked up on it, with an ironic comment or something, so people would get that little reminder saying "oh yes, I quite fancy a Guinness".'

No stone was left unturned. There was a complete overhaul of the beer's 'livery', its logo-bearing pub accessories, to make the image younger and more stylish. The old colours, buff and black, evoked its Irish tradition. The new colours, gold, glossy black and bright red, suggested a young, stylish, modern drink. Guinness had an unusual ready-made brand extension, in the form of Black Velvet. Black Velvet is a mixture of champagne and Guinness occasionally drunk at bars and parties. Saunders mounted a major promotional effort for Black Velvet, charging the sales force with getting it on to cocktail lists at up-market bars like the Savoy. Black Velvet's glamorous aura rubbed off on the beer.

Another problem was the beer's image as fattening or 'heavy'. In reality it had no more calories than most other beers. Luddington's research showed that the warm temperature at which Guinness was served made the beer seem heavy. In recent years, consumer taste had moved steadily to cooler temperatures for beer. British drinkers regarded Irish draught Guinness as better-tasting than the British. But in blind taste tests, drinkers couldn't tell the difference. Luddington's conclusion was that the beer's temperature, lower in Ireland because Guinness is drawn from the keg much more frequently, was the real difference. The result: a massive multi-million-pound programme was undertaken to install coolers on every Guinness bar dispense system in the UK. Under Saunders's insistence to do it all by yesterday, nothing was done in half-measures. 'It was a huge, almost military-style operation,' Luddington recalled.

A year after the Guinnless campaign was introduced, sales of the black beer began to rise slightly for the first time in a decade. But the campaign's effectiveness began to decline. Being in need of a Guinness became a bit of a joke, almost a sign of lack of macho (macho or manliness was very much the key attribute in the relationship between a man and his pint). 'It was quite a shock having to go and tell Ernest that the campaign he had developed wasn't working,' Luddington recalled. Saunders was quick to accept the evidence and seek a new, more positive campaign. When the agency that developed 'Guinnless' could not offer an acceptable replacement, the campaign was thrown open to bids from the rest of the advertising community. Before that could happen though, Luddington had to decide exactly what the brief for the new ad campaign would be. In the go-go 1980s too many marketing managers abdicated this responsibility, expecting the ad agency to do all the work. Luddington believed he and his team had to develop the new brand image, building on the philosophy, history and character of the beer. 'It was *our* duty to think of a new direction, and hopefully the agency would think of a way to carry it out on the ground creatively.'

Working with Cooper Research, a specialist firm of market research psychologists, Luddington developed what may have been the most intellectually challenging advertising brief up to that time. They key concepts were forged during a weekend Luddington and sales director Peter Mitchell spent with psychologist Peter Cooper at his Devon farmhouse. Listing all the attributes of Guinness the new ad campaign would have to communicate, they covered the walls of Cooper's living room with paper. They came to the conclusion that Guinness's attributes, or 'brand values', could be grouped into two distinct, and conflicting, sets: a hard or manly set and a soft, womanly side. They christened these shell and yolk. The shell referred to the beer's macho image, deriving from its hard-living, rugged Irishman, rough-diamond heritage, while the yolk represented the beer's opposing tradition as a uniquely healthy, nurturing, warming drink, which Luddington called its 'wombish' character. This second image also derived from Ireland where Guinness was once commonly recommended by doctors to pregnant women. Back in the nineteenth century, the beer was healthy by comparison with earlier alcoholic drinks like poteen. Luddington decided the new ad campaign would have to tell both stories, shell and yolk. 'On the one hand, you had to underpin the whole thing by saying this brand really is good for you, but on the other, you would use the shell values to attract the hard men and the clever guys.'

Amidst the heightened media interest that admen can always stir up about themselves, several agencies competed for what, at £7 million a year, would be one of Britain's largest pieces of advertising business in 1985 and probably for years thereafter. Ogilvy and Mather won the commission, on the strength of one word. 'Genius' seemed to Saunders and Luddington to encapsulate everything they were trying to communicate with the brand: the cleverness and competitiveness of the shell values and the caring/providing values of the yolk. Saunders watched Ogilvy's presentation, excused himself to go to the men's room to confer with Luddington, and came back to tell the agency they'd won the business.

The first series of TV ads broke the equation back down to its two halves, with a set of 'yolk' ads, depicting changing seasons and other aspects of nature, while a set of 'shell' ads showed various clever lads drinking Guinness in the pub. It was when Ogilvy decided to marry the two concepts into one ad campaign that something incredible happened. Their idea was to find a man who was the epitome of Guinness's shell values and place him in scenes which expressed the yolk values. 'This couldn't be just an ordinary human being. He had to be really enigmatic.' Luddington saw hundreds of actors, before finally settling upon a tall, blond German actor who had played a major role in the hit movie *Blade Runner*. His name was Rutger Hauer. In 1986, Ogilvy unleashed a series of strangely cryptic ads on the television-watching public.

Guinness sales skyrocketed. The sales graph looked like a hockey stick. 'It was the most phenomenal thing I have ever known,' said Luddington. One of the most effective ads was one where Hauer stood in front of an aquarium tank holding a pint of Guinness. The dolphin swam silently towards the window of the tank, looked at Hauer, and swam off again towards the back. Hauer turned to the camera and said, 'It's not easy being a dolphin.' 'It created a dialogue with the consumer,' said Luddington. 'It was almost an interactive campaign.'

Between 1983 and 1989 Guinness sales rose by 50 per cent. Sales of stout beers (Guinness was 90 per cent of the category) rose to nearly 20 per cent of the total UK beer market by 1991. Luddington attributed it to Hauer's 'duality': he was both reassuring and challenging, gentle yet threatening. 'Hauer created this tremendous rapport with the audience. People thought: what does he mean?' The young came back to Guinness in droves. It became a standard at university bars.

Hauer was the most visible part of the turnaround campaign, but behind the scenes every element in Saunders's marketing onslaught played a role. Marketing professors wrote books about the so-called product life cycle, in which brands are born, live and die, to be replaced by new, more timely brands. Guinness stout came back from the dead. For marketing man Luddington, the most gratifying aspect of the revival of Guinness was the virtual disappearance of Guinness's former image. 'If you talk to kids of twenty-two to twenty-five years old about the old cloth cap image of Guinness nowadays, they wouldn't know what you were talking about. They think it's a trendy drink.'

The keystone in the Georgian arch at the front gate to Guinness's Dublin brewery, St James's Gate, is decorated with the impassive sculpted head of a woman, her face and forehead garlanded with hops. Inside the gates was the heart of the Guinness company. Even after the headlong growth of the 1980s, Guinness Ireland accounted for £75 million in annual operating profit, more than a quarter of Guinness's worldwide beer profits. Yet when Saunders first passed through the arch at St James's Gate in 1981, he felt he was entering an industrial museum. The vast sixty-four-acre site, spread along the River Liffey in an industrial part of the Irish capital, encompassed buildings from every period of industrial history. Old railway tracks still ran between the brewery buildings, left over from the brewery's own private railway. In the eastern corner a windmill, now defunct, towered over the long, low, brick brewhouse and warehouses, most of them also disused. In a small turn-of-the-century era building near the front gate is the main reception area, an elegantly simple light, airy, mahogany-columned, high-ceilinged room with a marble bust of Arthur Guinness, the son of an estate manager to the Archbishop of Cashel, who started it all in 1759.

The company rose to worldwide prominence in the Victorian era, under the leadership of the founder's grandson Benjamin Guinness and then under his sons, Arthur and Edward Cecil Guinness, who ran the company from 1868 until 1927. For many years, St James's Gate was the largest brewery in the world. While Edward Cecil retained ironfisted control on the ever expanding brewery business, both brothers took an active interest in Irish civic affairs, British politics and worthy causes. Their endowments to the Irish colony included such Dublin landmarks as St Stephen's Green, St Patrick's Park, the wholesale renovation of St Patrick's Cathedral, the Iveagh Market and acres of Iveagh Trust housing for the underprivileged, providing homes even today to more than 10,000 families. Benjamin's Dublin townhouse was made a gift to the Irish state and today houses the Republic's Department of Foreign Affairs. The British Crown recognised the brothers' endeavours and loyalty to London during this turbulent period for Anglo-Irish relations by creating Arthur Lord Ardilaun, and Edward Cecil, the more ambitious, younger brother who led the company, the Earl of Iveagh. Irish author James Joyce paid homage to the brothers in his famous *Ulysses* (in a passage which he may well have written after downing a few pints of the stuff):

> ... the foaming black ebon ale which the noble twin brothers Bungiveah and Bungardilaun brew ever in their divine alevats, cunning as the sons of the deathless Leda. For they garner the succulent berries of the hop and mass and sift and bruise and brew them and they mix therewith sour juices and bring the must to the sacred fire and cease not night or day from the toil, those cunning brothers, lords of the vat.

From the top floors of some of the buildings in the brewery, a visitor in 1981 could make out through the mists the green hills of Phoenix Park. Bordering Dublin on the northwest, the 2000-acre park contained the home of perhaps the four people who matter most in this nation, whose three and a half million people have never been completely the masters of their own fate: the Irish president, the papal nuncio, the US Ambassador and the third Lord Iveagh. By some law of fate which perhaps James Joyce could have explained, God rarely rolled sevens on the genetic dice for more than two successive generations. While the Victorian Guinnesses were businessmen, builders and leaders of men, the next three generations were of the sort described by obsequious family historians as great achievers in agriculture, landscaping or entertaining.

The third Lord Iveagh, aged forty-four in 1981, was a colourless figure. He had been plucked out of Oxford, where he was studying poetry, and put into the company to take over upon his grandfather's death. Devoted to the country life he lived at his Phoenix Park estate, Farmleigh, he freely admitted his lack of interest in business. His main interests were horses and breeding the rare Charolais cattle he kept at Farmleigh. As for drinks, he enjoyed their consumption more than their production.

Guinness Ireland was the most fiercely independent of the company's many baronies. Since the flotation of the company on the London stock exchange in 1886 (the Irish financial community was barred from participating in the share offering), the family's main aspirations had been in Britain. It was left to Guinness Ireland to work at maintaining the family's reputation in their native land. The paternalistic company supported many efforts by the Republic's government to boost employment. Such largesse became increasingly untenable as lager's popularity grew and Guinness's market share fell from 90 per cent to the 80s and then the high 70s. When profits tumbled, the Irish management slashed investment. St James's Gate became outdated, costly to run and overmanned.

The old brewhouse Saunders saw on his first whistle-stop tour of the business in 1981 resembled one of those turn-of-the-century Heath Robinson cartoons: a vast, dirty, decaying building, the semi-gloom rent by occasional rays of light streaming through cracks in the dirty windows and holes in the roof. Giant copper tanks shrouded in mists of steam emitted a rumbling symphony of hisses, whistles and belches. From the copper tanks, iron and lead pipes protruded in every direction, up towards the rafters, down into the pitch-dark basement, and across the factory floor at shoulder height, obliging workers to bend to get under them. Valves on these pipes, shaped like the steering wheel of an old-fashioned boat, were positioned in the unlikeliest of places requiring men to kneel, climb slippery spiral iron staircases, stand on chairs, or descend into the dankness below to open or close them. In a previous burst of modernisation, 1930s-era thermometers had been attached to the Victorian copper tanks, but a glance was sufficient to confirm they provided nothing like the accuracy needed for modern brewing.

Saunders was horrified by the state of the brewery, terrified Guinness was in danger of violating Irish health laws. 'People used to come from all over the world to see this Mecca of brewing and the condition of the thing was appalling,' he recalled. Only months after Saunders's arrival, Guinness Ireland managing director Mark Hely-Hutchinson quit rather than implement the cost reductions Saunders wanted. His replacement was Brian Slowey, a charmingly pugnacious Irishman whose easy manner cloaked a tough interior. Slowey's task was challenging: delivering Saunders the cost reductions and revamped marketing strategy he demanded without demoralising the St James's Gate workforce or management and without triggering too much interest from Guinness family members, whose intervention could only be a further hindrance. He also had to be careful not to alienate the Irish government, whose goodwill was essential to the business for many reasons, not least their penchant for raising beer taxes whenever the government budget deficit ballooned. 'Rationalisation by its very nature is always tough, but a rationalisation programme at Guinness was tougher because people had been there for generations and suddenly you were saying to them sorry there are no jobs here,' said Slowey.

The Irish cost-reduction operation was all the more difficult because, unlike their British counterparts, the Irish trade unions had not been jolted into realism and reasonableness by a Margaret Thatcher. To win them over, Slowey employed a combination of stick and carrot. The carrot was a £100 million investment programme promised by Saunders. This would pay for a brand-new high-tech, low-cost brewery at St James's Gate with greater capacity than ever. Saunders did not shrink from backing his strategy with big money. With its great beer-making tradition, skilled workforce and easy access to the sea, he believed St James's Gate was the ideal site to produce and export growing quantities of the black beer. Slowey's stick was the threat that, if St James's Gate did not reach the targeted levels of efficiency, beer production would be transferred to the London Park Royal brewery, itself undergoing a cost-reduction exercise under Saunders's direct control. Under Slowey, generations of management secrecy and internal politics were discarded for the straightforward approach of spelling out the full truth to the workforce and letting them see that the best option was a major rationalisation. Shrink to grow was the message. 'We literally sat down with them and said: "Fellows, we can let things go on as they are and I guarantee you within so many years, particularly with Saunders there, we will be a small regional brewer maybe producing for the Republic of Ireland but certainly not for Northern Ireland or the UK and probably not for the world. Or on the other hand there can be a major rationalisation and we will make sure that if you leave you will leave with dignity, which is very important, and you will still think that Guinness is the greatest thing since brown bread.'

As MD of Guinness Ireland, Slowey exercised a lot of clout in the Republic. The company bought some £200 million worth of barley and hops from 6000 Irish farmers every year. It paid hundreds of millions of pounds in excise taxes to the Irish exchequer, making it Ireland's biggest single taxpayer. Vic Steel, recruited from Beechams in 1985 to run Guinness Brewing Worldwide, was amazed to find on his first visit to the Republic Irish prime minister Garrett Fitzgerald making an appointment to come see him at *his* office at St James's Gate. The Republic's government was not pleased to hear in 1982, in the midst of recession and steadily rising unemployment, that Guinness was about to embark on rationalisation. The company had always been a dependable source of jobs, skilled and unskilled, in Dublin. Slowey applied his formidable powers of persuasion. 'I convinced the government that they had to help me convince Saunders [to maintain Guinness Ireland as a major production site], and I said the best way to do that is not only psychological but financial, so we would like a grant.' The government agreed to a subsidy of £10 million towards Guinness's investment programme, the first time the Republic's government had ever agreed to subsidise a programme that involved job reductions instead of gains.

While carrying out the work that earned Saunders nicknames in Ireland like 'axeman' and 'Deadly Ernest', Slowey kept morale up by assuring the Guinness Ireland management that he was protecting them from even more painful measures from London. 'I'd say to my team, fellas, get down on your knees every day and say thanks be to God for the Irish Sea! Let him work over there as long as he likes!' Some of Saunders's emissaries from London were rejected by the Guinness Ireland barony, which, while a vassal to London, remained far from supine. One such envoy was Saunders's first appointment for group finance director, who fell out with key Guinness family members based in Ireland. In that case, Saunders yielded to the family and let him go. Others sent by Saunders were seduced by the wily Slowey. 'I seduced 'em. I make no bones about it. When we heard about someone coming over, I always said: fellas, our objective is, we'll make that bastard smile, and we'll make him Irish.' It was a great achievement by Slowey and St James's Gate managing director Paddy Galvin to cut the workforce while maintaining employee morale and avoiding any strikes or industrial action. Throughout the early 1980s, Guinness's London management dreaded and half-expected a backlash from the workforce, but it never came. In 1989 Galvin was headhunted to Waterford Crystal to help another world-famous Irish brand name sort out its cost problems.

Guinness Ireland's marketing problems, if less visible to the untutored eye than the decrepitude of the old brewery facilities, were no less severe. Guinness's famous black beer had 90 per cent of the Irish stout market while its Smithwick's Ale held 95 per cent of the ale market. But both these sectors were in decline, losing out to lager which was surging in popularity among young people. Ireland was a young nation and Irish youth were at least as fashion-conscious as their British counterparts. 'Our problem was that the people who were drinking Guinness were falling off the edge,' said Slowey. Guinness's 'flagship' lager, Harp, suffering from an unfashionable cut-price image, was steadily losing market share to overseas invaders like Heineken. In 1982 foreign take-overs of some long-established traditional Irish brewers shook Guinness out of its torpor. First, Murphy was bought by Heineken. A year later, the Australian Fosters acquired Beamish and Crawford. Slowey's predecessor was studying these small brewers too but lost out to the fast-moving lager giants. It was the shock

Uncle Arthur, as Guinness was fondly known inside the Irish industry, needed.

Working closely with new marketing director Brian O'Neill, and with plenty of input from Saunders, Slowey revolutionised Guinness Ireland's marketing strategy. Borrowing from the UK strategy, they gave the black beer a younger image. They developed new advertising and invested in dispense systems to serve the beer at cooler temperatures. Once again, the marketing input worked its magic. After years of declining sales, draught Guinness turned around and began growing at 2–3 per cent per annum. More important in the longer run, the beer became trendy amongst Irish youth. 'Nowadays, if you go into the younger generation's pubs and watch the kids, particularly the girls, you'll see that over the last couple years they have switched from only drinking lager to beginning to drink stout as well,' said Slowey.

The lager market required a more radical approach. The old Guinness would have been too proud to brew or sell other people's beers on its home turf. But with the Irish public's growing fondness for foreign products and cultures, the best way to attack the premium lager market was with an established foreign name. Guinness had the distribution clout with Ireland's publicans to lift the right premium lager to significant market share virtually overnight. Slowey began negotiations with a number of foreign beer-makers, signing deals with Furstenburg, a venerable German lager with thirteenth-century origins, and the famous Danish lager Carlsberg. In 1984, Slowey approached Budweiser with an offer to brew and distribute the famous American beer in Ireland.

Budweiser held an astonishing 40 per cent of the US market, the world's largest beer market. But the beer had terrible difficulty winning a toehold in Europe. It was barred from much of central Europe because of a name dispute with its Czech namesake (Budweiser Budvar). It spent millions on advertising in western Europe and still European consumers stuck to the view that the USA was not a proper beer pedigree. Slowey told Anheuser-Busch, the owners of Budweiser, that if Guinness took over marketing control of Budweiser they would make the beer a success. But he wanted control over everything, even the beer's recipe. Anheuser-Busch chairman August Busch III came to St James's Gate and the Kilkenny brewery where Guinness proposed to brew Bud, crawled around under the kettles and kieves with his thermometers and ultimately concluded that, yes, Guinness quality did measure up to the exacting standards set a century ago by his great-grandfather in St Louis, USA. 'After a lot of palaver and discussion with all the top men, we convinced them to go in a particular direction,' said Slowey. It was the first time anybody other than Anheuser was allowed to brew Bud.

Guinness's marketing team went to work. They used rice in the brewing, a unique Budweiser practice which August Busch regarded as indispensable, they changed the flavour, making it less sweet. They made it less strong, cutting the alcohol content from 5 to 4 per cent. They placed the beer in thousands of Irish pubs and supported it with a big ad campaign. The strategy was a resounding success. By 1992, Budweiser held 14 per cent of the Irish lager market, treble its market share in any other European nation. In their enthusiasm for the Irish market, the Anheuser executives (many of them Irish-Americans) signed on as lead sponsor of the Irish Derby – the Budweiser Irish Derby as it became. That turned into an annual bill for £1 million. So, or at least some Anheuser-Busch sources claimed, the American company *still* was not making any money on the beer. Guinness Ireland's managing director in 1993, Colin Storm, disputed the claim, pointing out that each year when Bud and Guinness renegotiated the terms of the marketing spend on the brand, each side tried to play down their profits. Guinness was definitely making a profit on Bud though. 'We wouldn't be selling the brand otherwise,' said Storm.

Back in 1981, Guinness had looked threatened in its fortress, Ireland. The management pursued what Slowey scornfully labelled a 'King Canute' strategy, trying to hold back the irresistible trend towards lager. Invading foreign giant Heineken might have crushed tired old Uncle Arthur. In 1992, it was Heineken who was under siege. With a Cheshire cat grin, Slowey explained:

'We have developed a lager portfolio which surrounds them at different points. Furstenburg is a top-of-the-market lager, Budweiser is the 'scene' lager, which is at present taking market share from Heineken, and Carlsberg is the more mature lager.'

Meanwhile, Saunders's ambitious investment programme was bearing fruit. The new brewery began to come onstream from 1986. The walls and the famous arch remained. But inside, St James's Gate had a brand new heart and lungs. The major components were a new brewhouse (cost: £40 million), a new fermentation area (cost: £50 million), new labs and new, fully automated keg-filling lines. In 1992 the new roasthouse, which roasted barley golden brown, giving Guinness its distinctive ruby-black colour, opened. In the vast kettleroom on the first floor of the new brewhouse, eight shiny stainless steel kettles, each some twenty feet across, boiled the crushed, flaked and roasted barley together with hops, to create a mushy, porridge-like mixture ready for fermentation. With a forty-foot high ceiling and bright wraparound windows, the room was clean, bright and quiet enough to have a normal conversation in. Tradition was respected with a twenty-foot high tapestry of the Guinness harp hanging on the far wall, overlooking the gleaming kettles.

Through a door was the control room, a quietly humming, low-lit room where three operators and a shift manager sat at a bank of computer terminals watching the wall in front of them. On the wall was an intricate flow-chart diagram depicting the hundreds of kettles, kieves, vats, hoppers, tuns and other receptacles connected by a lattice of pipes and tubes. A green light indicated a closed valve, an orange light an open one. The brewery represented by the wall of pulsating lights produced two and a half million pints of beer a day. The computerised process control system (mostly German made, by Siemens and brew engineers Huppman), changed the formula according to the beer, and often according to the country of destination. Guinness stout for the German market contained only crushed barley, since flaked barley was forbidden by Germany's ancient beer purity law. Furstenburg lager was produced for Britain and Ireland at 4 per cent alcohol strength, but at 8 per cent for Belgium. In the old days the valves were opened by hand. At the new brewery, it was done electronically, as was the monitoring of temperatures. 'The quality of the beer has never been better,' commented biochemist Andrew Savage, twenty-five, shift manager on the brewhouse day shift. Savage, three operators, two fitters and an electrician ran the shift, taking the place of some one hundred men twenty years ago. Heavy manual lifting has completely disappeared, as has most of the dirty work. In today's Guinness brewery, most of the work was brain work, performed by highly skilled professionals.

The relative youth of the staff was another big change from the old days. Promotion was faster than ever before, based on ability and performance rather than time served. 'Guinness is one of the best, if not the best, employer in Ireland,' opined Savage who joined the company straight from university. A member of the company's Sharesave scheme which allows employees to invest in Guinness shares at special below-market prices up to certain annual limits, Savage was fully abreast of the company's share price and annual profit results. Guinness's Sharesave was probably the world's first corporate share incentive scheme offered to employees worldwide. Guinness employees in more than fifty countries were given incentives to invest in the company's sterling-denominated shares. For employees who participated, it acquainted them with the role currencies play in an international company, spread awareness of the company's overall goals of growth and profitability – and made them a bit of money too. Andrew Savage pointed out that another form of compensation also contributed to making Guinness a uniquely rewarding place to work: 'We still get an employee allowance of two bottles of Guinness a day.'

The change in Guinness Ireland's financial position was as stunning as the gleaming stainless steel in the new kettlehouse. Said Slowey: 'If you look at where we were in 1982, we more than doubled our profits in five years, in a situation where the GNP in Ireland was falling every year, and after that we doubled them again in the next five or six years.' Could Guinness Ireland raise its profits even higher than the £75 million sterling it earned in

1992? New Guinness Ireland managing director Colin Storm smiled confidently. 'If we don't, I'll be on the next ferry home.'

One morning in November 1984 Dr Alan Forage was sitting in his bath playing with the soapsuds. He was thinking about bubbles. Forage had been thinking about bubbles for several months. He was Guinness's head of research and development, based at the St James's Gate brewery in Dublin. Trained as a botanist, with a PhD in radiation biology, Forage had done research into cancer, genetic engineering of pharmaceuticals, and food safety. But now it was bubbles.

Forage's brief from Guinness head of product development, Kim Slater, was to develop a canned beer that would taste exactly like draught Guinness. The project had been around for some time. When Forage joined Guinness in 1980, the company had just introduced an experimental product, a take-home bottle which came with a syringe. The consumer poured the beer into a glass, and then 'injected' a gas and beer mixture from the syringe into the beer to produce a foamy head just like that on a glass of draught Guinness. The product did reasonably well in Japan, but met resistance from consumers in Ireland. They found it too fiddly and not worth the additional price. The syringe product was never launched in the UK.

With Saunders's arrival, the take-home draught Guinness project took on a new urgency. Saunders was keen on the new marketing trend for beer brand extensions. In the old days, Coke or Heineken or Bacardi was a unique, single product. But in the 1980s, marketers discovered that 'extending' a brand by launching different versions could not only tap new markets but improve the consumer's image of the original product: Coke gave birth to Diet Coke, Carlsberg spawned Special Brew, and in the States, Miller beer found a gold mine with Miller Light. Luddington renamed bottled Guinness 'Guinness Extra', positioning it as the traditional product for the older drinker. Draught Guinness was younger, trendier and more upmarket. As the Pure Genius advertising began to lift sales of the draught, a take-home product that appealed to the same young market became a top priority. Canned beer had a younger image than bottled beer, so Saunders wanted take-home draught to come in a can. Another reason Saunders was keen to inject some new fizz into Guinness's take-home market was that profit margins were much fatter in the take-home business. In the on-trade, Guinness's margins were always under pressure from the large British brewers who controlled two thirds of the pubs. In the more freely competitive take-home market, Guinness didn't have to sacrifice profit to win shelf space.

'The brief was to develop a new product that came in a can, that would open in as conventional a way as possible, and that the consumer would recognise as a draught,' said Forage. His Latin temperament showed in his regular bursts into passionate discourses on the ingredients of beer, the onerousness of health and safety legislation, or the role of DNA in beer fermentation. The challenge of take-home draught beer was not only to make it consumer-friendly, but also inexpensive. The consumer would pay a few pennies more for a can of real draught beer, but not a lot more, Guinness's marketers told Forage.

Market research showed that what made draught Guinness's taste different from the bottled stuff was the famous creamy head. The head was produced by nitrogen gas, packed with the beer to maintain pressure inside the kegs. Lagers were pressurised by carbon dioxide dissolved in the beer. When carbon dioxide rose to the top of a glass of lager, it formed large, round bubbles, which quickly escaped into the atmosphere. Nitrogen formed smaller, lens-shaped bubbles which clung to the surface of the beer. Their oblong shape reflected light, making the head appear white. Sliding silkily over the tongue, the bubbles gave the beer a creamy texture unlike that of any other beer. In the pub, this miracle of physical chemistry was easily accomplished every time the barmaid pulled a pint of Guinness, the pressurised nitrogen rising through the dispense system with the beer. The problem facing Alan Forage was how to turn every can into a pub dispense system in miniature.

Forage watched the trail of bubbles his fingers made in the bath as he moved them through the water. For months, Forage and his team of a dozen researchers experimented with buttons, plungers and other devices to create pressure. He was leaning back, staring at the tiles on the bathroom wall when the idea struck him.

'I went back to first principles. A sudden change in pressure creates bubbles. If you create a bubble, as it goes from the bottom to the top, it creates more bubbles in its path. So all I have to do is put some bubbles in at the bottom.' The act of opening the can would trigger the change in pressure (as the can fell to the pressure of the outside atmosphere). All Forage needed was to find a way to hold pressurised nitrogen at the bottom of the can.

On Monday morning, Forage explained his idea to his colleagues. The initial plan was to put something like a ping-pong ball with a tiny hole in it at the bottom of a can. The ping-pong ball would be full of liquid nitrogen, inserted at $-73°$ C. Beer is drunk at around $5°$ C. When a can was opened, the nitrogen, evaporating into gas, would surge out through the hole. Bubbles of nitrogen rushing upwards would dislodge more nitrogen from the beer, and the army of rising bubbles would create a full creamy head of beer. It took two months of experiments with inserts in different shapes and sizes before they achieved consistent results. Once the success rate reached 5 per cent, Forage knew they were on the right track. Getting it from 5 per cent to nearly foolproof was the easy part.

But many challenges remained. The next problem was how to produce the new system cheaply, reliably and efficiently. This was as big a challenge as discovering the basic concept. They needed to be able to produce the insert, put it in the can, get the air out of it, put the nitrogen in, and ensure it stayed at the bottom of the can throughout the travels and disturbances a can of beer sustains between brewery and consumer's mouth. At every step, Forage was breaking new ground for the drinks industry. 'If Murphy's Law applies, it applies three times over on this project. It was only the tenacity of the team that made it finally work,' he said.

The solution was a plastic doughnut-shaped insert, about three quarters of an inch high, held to the bottom inside of the can only by friction. Guinness installed a new machine on its canning line at Runcorn, Cheshire, to stuff the inserts into the cans. The cost of the development of Canned Draught Guinness came to some £5 million, making it the largest single R&D project in the company's history. The most expensive element was the design and manufacture of the machine to stuff the insert, sucking the air out as it pushed it to the bottom of the can. Using only a friction fit to hold the insert in place was an especially safe, reliable and cost-effective solution.

As soon as Guinness Brewing's marketing unit got their hands on Canned Draught Guinness, CDG as it was quickly dubbed, they rushed it into research. The results were better than they could have dreamed. Consumers simply could not tell the difference between real draught and the CDG product. Of course, once they saw it being poured from the can, they claimed the canned product tasted worse. That gave birth to the first advertising slogan: 'Hard to Believe. Easy to Swallow.' In 1988 the marketers conducted a small test in a single region. Among customers who tried CDG, the repurchase rate was 70 per cent. 'A really good product normally gets around 35 per cent,' said Forage. 'This was the most successful thing we'd ever seen.'

When in 1989 the product was launched nationally, the results exceeded all expectations. Within two years, Canned Draught Guinness was the seventh best-selling beer in the British take-home market. Indeed, when its 1991 sales of £43 million were added to canned Guinness Original's sales of £56 million, total take-home sales of the black beer were well ahead of market leader Heineken's sales of £73 million. 'Cannibalisation' – the substitution by consumers of CDG for Guinness Original – was undoubtedly a side-effect of the CDG launch, but since the price and profits on the high-tech product were some 25 per cent above the Original, that was not all bad news for Guinness.

Forage singled out not a scientific breakthrough but a management change as the single biggest factor behind the success of CDG. The key, he said, was the existence of a product champion, in the form of Kim Slater, head of product development at

Guinness Brewing Worldwide (GBW, the division encompassing all beer activities). Without a senior product champion, Forage would never have had the support to turn his Sunday bathtime vision into a working product. 'There were so many plausible arguments somebody could have used to put us behind the eight ball,' said Forage. 'One colleague in production said it would never work, another said it would be impossible to package the widget (the insert). It would have been so easy to say no.'

Before Saunders, research and development reported to the production department. Saunders gave Slater's development team the authority to drive an R&D project. In 1988, reorganisation at GBW formalised that relationship, putting research and development under GBW's central strategic unit, known as the business development unit. Forage reported, via the head of business development, to the marketing director. Forage's team, which by 1992 included fourteen people in Dublin, eight at Park Royal and eight at Guinness's Spanish beer subsidiary Cruzcampo, worked in an internal supplier-customer relationship with any division of GBW that needed its assistance. In addition to production and marketing projects, Forage even participated in the M&A (merger and acquisition) team which assessed Cruzcampo prior to the 1990 acquisition. Said Forage: 'R&D is a strategic asset for the whole company. It looks into the future, from six months to ten years out.'

At his quiet ground-floor office, in an interwar building separated from the main Park Royal brewery by a grass field where Guinness cows still graze and a sports ground where workers compete in summer in the Guinness Bowls League, Forage finds the solitude necessary to contemplate his next industry-shattering breakthrough. On the white wall are two small prints: a 1920s-era 'Guinness is Good for You' poster and beside it, an ad from Her Majesty's Patent Office featuring a photo of the clear plastic insert with a message urging inventors to register their inventions. Forage claimed he did not mind when, in 1991, GBW chairman Brian Baldock and a representative of the Park Royal workforce collected the Queen's Award for Technological Achievement, for invention of canned draught beer. 'It wasn't only me. Lots of guys worked nights and weekends to make it work.' He added he took greatest pleasure from seeing other brewers copying his invention – taking care of course not to violate Guinness's patents. 'I seem to have created a whole new sector of beverages. Almost like the cat's eye in the road, it's becoming a commonplace of everyday life. That's very satisfying.'

Clearly visible in the Patent Office advert on his wall was the number 42 pressed into the plastic on the widget. 'In the book *The Hitchhiker's Guide to the Galaxy*, you'll find that the number forty-two was the meaning of life,' Forage said. He paused. 'But in our widget, it's just the mould number.'

Although Canned Draught Guinness went national only three years after Saunders left the company, in some respects it represented the culmination of the revolution Ernest Saunders wrought at Guinness. CDG was a revolutionary product in an industry that usually records changes over centuries rather than years. It was a breakthrough made possible by the establishment of a marketing-led, customer-focused culture throughout the company. Guinness refused to break down profits by individual beer products, but one independent London stockbroker estimated that in 1992 Canned Draught Guinness brought in £14 million of profit in the UK alone.

Company revolutions are always achieved by many people. But there is usually one man at the head of each revolution. At Guinness, Saunders was that man. It was his all-embracing vision of where the company had to go and his dogged, determined drive to overcome all barriers in getting it there that made it possible to overthrow what had become by 1981 a defensive, negative culture. Most managing directors take their job with a brief, precise list of objectives scribbled on an imaginary piece of paper. Those objectives are typically realistic, achievable and often limited. With a company in deep trouble, it is often enough simply to raise a depressed share price. When Saunders joined Guinness its share price hovered around 50 pence, valuing the entire company at just

£100 million. In those days, Saunders received visits almost weekly from investment bankers seeking to buy Guinness. Had he aimed, say, to double the share price, he could doubtless have achieved that in a couple of years, and moved on to a less risky MD job at a larger company.

Saunders dismissed those investment bankers contemptuously as 'asset-strippers'. He was by nature unable to envisage halfway solutions, unable to see himself as one of those managing directors hopping from company to company like from stone to stone in a muddy pond, never looking back. He wanted to make Guinness world class. Saunders's vision of what Guinness ought to look like was conditioned by his previous experience. His model was Beecham's, where he'd worked from 1963 to 1973. His admiration of Henry Lazell, then Beecham's managing director, bordered on hero-worship. He admired the way Lazell ran an international company on strict and demanding financial targets yet still took a personal interest in the brands – visiting local supermarkets to check the shelves for Beecham product Lucozade or interrogating ad agency executives on whether they were using Brylcreem. Saunders always spoke about the 'privilege' of working for Lazell. 'Henry Lazell was one of the founders of marketing in this country,' he said.

At Guinness, Saunders tried, and succeeded, in applying Lazell's approach: he combined the managing director's strategic role with a close interest in marketing. His grasp of detail constantly impressed his colleagues. 'He was an extraordinary combination I've never seen before or since, creative and intuitive, and simultaneously rigorous, logical and detail-oriented,' recalled Bain consultant Grogan. 'He was a two-or-three-briefcases-a-night guy. He made decisions on everything. Nothing was left to chance. We used to think he would kill himself from overwork. Nobody else at the company gave of himself the way Ernest did.'

If Saunders appeared to colleagues as often cold and occasionally ruthless it was because he was by nature shy (he didn't possess the natural bonhomie which characterised many beer industry veterans), but also because he *was* ruthless: he was horrified by how poorly the Guinness of 1981 was performing and how little the management – overpaid and lazy in his view – did about it. 'They were just the wrong people. They came from a generation that had no accountability, who knew the results were appalling, but just didn't seem to care. The people who joined me knew I cared about the company, knew I was working day and night to turn it around, and they were people who wanted the challenge and *enjoyed* the challenge of turning a company like that around.'

The effect, of course, was that holdovers from the old regime were often treated brutally. 'You couldn't imagine two cultures clashing more profoundly,' recalled Ian Cheshire, Saunders's personal assistant at Guinness. 'It was like the American Indians and the Europeans. It was mass wipe-out. The two cultures couldn't co-exist.'

Guinness went on to become one of Britain's top ten companies and one of the most respected drinks companies in the world. Saunders accomplished the most difficult part of the job, the initial turnaround. Marketing veteran Gary Luddington was the point man on the campaign to restore the black beer's success in the UK, perhaps the most daunting of the tasks Saunders faced. Cheerily voluble as marketing men tend to be, Luddington grew quiet and thoughtful when describing Saunders's responsibility for what happened at Guinness. 'If you'd have said in 1982 that Guinness would be where it is today, nobody would have believed you. Nobody.'

Luddington gave the largest share of the credit to Saunders. 'Those years were the first and probably the only time in my life where I applied everything I knew and watched it really work. It was many people's ideas, advice and efforts. And yet at the end of the day, it was one man's real vision and energy and determination to get it where it was.'

He recalled a decisive moment in 1985, when they went to the Guinness board for approval to spend £1 million on just two TV ads, the first in the Pure Genius campaign. It was a big risk for everybody, including Guinness UK managing director Peter Lipscombe, who had just joined the company from Beecham's. 'Peter had spent all his life making Diocalm commercials where £10,000 was a lot of money and here he was having to ask Ernest to sign off on a million pounds,' Luddington recalled. Saunders backed it immediately and pushed it through the board. Guinness beer went on to prove wrong marketing professors' fondly held theories about the inescapable 'product life cycle', a lesson Luddington believed more companies ought to learn. 'A lot of brands have died in the UK because of management safety, refusing to back them or pulling out too early, too much short-termism,' he said.

Finance director Olivier Roux broke with Saunders over the DTI investigation and went on to testify in court against his former boss. Nevertheless, he was categorical in his praise for Saunders's contribution to the Guinness revolution: 'Ernest was the smartest CEO I ever worked with,' Roux said.

'When he decided to spend £100 million in Ireland or £20 million on Park Royal, these were very risky decisions. They could have bankrupted the company. He took the risk. And he made it work.'

Saunders had his faults. His greatest fault was his inability to delegate. In his determination to change Guinness at maximum speed, he tried to take direct control over as much of the company as he could. Phil Rhodes, who succeeded Olivier Roux as group controller in 1985, said the management chart looked like a comb. 'It was ridiculous. Every single important profit centre reported direct to Ernest.' Because he did not trust the Guinness executives to implement the necessary changes (sometimes he was right) he relied on the Bain consultants, who became known inside Guinness as Ernest's secret police. 'It used to be said that every time a Guinness executive got on a plane, there was a guy from Bain sitting two rows behind him,' recalled Luddington. During the Distillers takeover battle of 1986, Guinness public relations director Chris Davidson was shocked to find he was working with eighteen different outside public relations consultants, all hired by Saunders.

Bain's work was often highly valuable. Luddington found their ability to cut to the core of issues and evaluate strategic issues quickly and thoroughly from a fresh, outsiders' vantage point a valuable asset for line executives immersed in the day-to-day issues of running the business. But Saunders relied too much on Bain, using them to keep control on the business. Guinness Ireland MD Brian Slowey described them as a 'second arm of management'. Slowey described a pattern of meetings with Saunders. 'He might disappear or be called away somewhere for half an hour and as he walked out he would say continue, but who do you continue with, the people from Bain? So I had to wonder: who was I really working to? Was it Bain or was it Saunders?'

Because of Saunders's suspicion of St James's Gate, Slowey saw the worst side of Saunders's management style. In the UK marketing operation, Gary Luddington saw the best side: Saunders was keen to bring in middle managers, delegate, share decision-making, and listen to argument. But it is striking how few senior divisional chiefs Saunders brought in to the group over his five years. It was not until 1985 that he appointed Vic Steel as managing director of Guinness Brewing Worldwide, and in his memoirs (*Nightmare*, written by his son James) Saunders revealingly describes Steel as 'dependable'. Saunders's PA, Ian Cheshire, who worked as closely with Saunders as anyone, believed he was not power-mad, happily delegating all financial issues to Olivier Roux. But, perhaps because of a lack of self-confidence, he found it hard to trust people. Said Cheshire: 'Ernest was naturally quite shy and he took a long time to open up. If you got on the inside he was extremely loyal, perhaps over-loyal to certain people like Tom Ward.' Ward was the American lawyer who played a key role as Saunders's adviser and confidant in the Distillers takeover.

Saunders defended his excessive centralisation of power as necessary, given the dire state in which he found the company in 1981. 'I'd been put in to turn it around, and I calculated there were certain things I could do regardless of the non-management and all the other problems, because I refused to let excuses get in the way.' He also defended his reliance on Bain. 'One of the things I could do was to hire in a resource which I reckoned I could plug in like a Hoover to get me the analysis I needed, work on the projects I needed, give me the information to take decisions across all these hundreds of companies, and that I could gradually tone down as I hired permanent people. What I didn't want to do was to have a permanent overhead of people that in the longer term I might not want.'

But the moment of toning down never came. One senior Bain consultant argued that, by the end of seven years' continuous work, Bain had been active in the beer business for at least three years too long. Nor were Bain's services cheap. Their annual bill peaked at some £15 million in 1986 when they worked at both Guinness Brewing and Distillers. 'Bain's programme was extremely powerful, but it was a two- to four-year programme. By years five, six or seven you should have your own management doing it, with occasional consulting support,' commented a former Bainie.

Excessive centralisation played a critical role in Saunders's downfall, over the scandal surrounding the Distillers takeover. Guinness was poised to win a £2.6 billion takeover battle for the world's largest whisky company. It would have elevated him to the big league as one of Britain's foremost businessmen. It was precisely the moment when he should have been building bridges to important friends, colleagues and allies. Instead he was burning them. In March 1986, supermarket chain Argyll launched its third bid for Distillers, upping its offer to £2.5 billion. Saunders wanted to outbid Argyll with a third Guinness offer. His three key advisers, finance director Roux, merchant banker Roger Seelig and stockbroker David Mayhew, opposed the idea. At that late stage, the cash value of the bid had become irrelevant, they said. The decision was going to be made on the relative merits of the two management teams, and Guinness was clearly ahead. Saunders's own reputation and record was their trump card – his opposite number at Argyll, James Gulliver, was increasingly viewed as a wheeler-dealer, not a marketing expert.

Some men cannot live with failure. Saunders could not live with success. He could not accept the advice of moderation, that victory was already in the bag. Although Guinness did not make a third bid, Saunders broke with his formal advisers, relying instead on an informal group including his old friend from Nestlé days, American lawyer and Guinness director Tom Ward, Tony Parnes, a 'freelance' but well-connected stockbroker, and millionaire investor Gerald Ronson. The informal group organised 'fan clubs' of secret investors in Guinness shares, to push the share price up, raising the value of Guinness's bid. Roux saw the 'fan clubs' as possibly illegal and completely unnecessary. His relationship with Saunders became openly antagonistic. In June 1986, after the bid was won, Saunders, again advised by Ward, decided to retract a promise to the City to make Scottish banker Sir Thomas Risk chairman of the merged Guinness-Distillers. It was a stupid decision, made by a man perhaps losing his grip on reality. It antagonised the whole of the financial, business and political Establishment. A month later, industry minister Michael Howard warned Saunders he was 'minded' to commission a formal inquiry.

If, earlier, Saunders had put in place a comprehensive set of senior managers at Guinness and trusted their advice, he might have avoided the disastrous decisions of early 1986. Guinness Ireland MD Brian Slowey possessed finely tuned political antennae, yet he was never in Saunders's inner circle. He believed Saunders's ultimate failing was his political *naïveté*: 'If you're a very big company it is very important that you work well with people like the Establishment and the civil service. You pull them in with you, you make them share in the success and the benefits, and if you do break with them, if you are going to have a battle royal, you make sure you pick the pitch and you know what the end result is going to be.'

As his success and power increased, instead of becoming a team player, Saunders became even more of a loner. He had cut himself off from Guinness's line management by using Bain to reform and revolutionise the company. In 1986, he cut himself off from his Bain advisers. The 1986 transfer of £6 million of Guinness money and property to himself and Tom Ward may have been criminal, or a temporary lapse, or perhaps as Saunders claimed, a misunderstanding. By then, Saunders had made too many enemies, inside Guinness management, on its board and outside.

A sophisticated criminal would have ensured his board was full of yes-men or fools. Saunders' *naïveté* showed again in that his finance director Olivier Roux was fiercely independent. Bizarrely, he was not even employed by Guinness. A Bain employee, Roux had told Saunders, a year before the Distillers takeover, that he wanted to leave Guinness and set up his own consulting business. After the Distillers takeover, Saunders ordered a company Rolls-Royce fitted with two telephones – one of the prizes for the chairman of a top ten company. Roux continued to drive his Volkswagen Golf. When the government inspectors came calling, the man with a Volkswagen did not hesitate to give it up and tell the truth, implicating the man with the Rolls. The man who should have been known for one of the greatest corporate turnarounds in British history became more famous for his role in a squalid criminal scandal.

'People used to say he was the "axeman" or the "iceman". But that wasn't Ernest. What Ernest loved most of all was the Guinness brand,' said former Bain consultant David Hoare.

'If Ernest died and you cut him open, you'd see brands.'

THREE

United Distillers

'Everything About It Has To Shout Quality'

The thing Nigel Shattuck always remembered about the old Distillers Company Ltd was that the company secretary rode a bicycle to work every morning. DCL was one of Scotland's largest companies selling its most glamorous export yet its executives lived a mean, austere existence. Its awesome stable of renowned brand names included Johnnie Walker, Gordon's Gin, Pimm's and White Horse. Yet for two decades, the brands fell further behind more aggressive international competitors, losing steadily in market share, profitability and, their most precious asset, reputation. By 1986 DCL was a modest company, with a lot to be modest about.

Before 1981 Guinness management sat impotently watching their beer lose market share; Distillers management actively contributed to their own decline. In the 1970s they made a disastrous decision to flood the market with whisky, in a vain attempt to boost sales in the face of weak demand. The result was a downward trend in the price of Scotch and erosion of its image as a luxury, prestige drink. In the United States, Scotch and cognac sold at similar prices in the 1950s and 1960s. On the big screen Spencer Tracy and Cary Grant drank Scotch and soda. By the 1980s, cognac sold for double the price of Scotch. Michael Douglas drank cognac or fine wines. Scotch was increasingly seen as something one's father bought. In Europe, meanwhile, Distillers was badly wrongfooted by the European Community, which ruled in the 1970s that spirits brands had to be similarly priced across the Community. Johnnie Walker sold at lower prices in the UK than on the Continent. Lacking the marketing skills to deal with this challenge, Walker simply withdrew its Scotch from Britain, the world's second-largest Scotch market.

The Distillers Company was formed by a series of mergers in the 1920s. They were negative, defensive mergers, made for all the wrong reasons. They achieved their short-term aim of suppressing competition and maintaining employment in the Scotch whisky industry. But the company's initiative was smothered under layers of stubborn, conservative management bureaucracy. The great brand-name companies, including Dewar's, Johnnie Walker, Haig, Buchanan and White Horse, sacrificed their entrepreneur-driven aggressiveness under the new corporate structure. But large size gained them little as the company refused to integrate the brand companies. Thirteen major brand companies retained their autonomy, inside an unwieldy, tortuously complex 'federal' structure. Inevitably, internal politics and family connections took precedence over corporate performance.

The brand companies continued to be dominated by descendants of the founders. In 1986, the chairman of Distillers was John Connell. His father had been managing director of Gordon's Gin, and his brother David was MD of Johnnie Walker Scotch. Ian Ross, the man slated to take over Johnnie Walker before Guinness intervened, included among his qualifications the fact that his father had been Distillers chairman and his uncle had been MD of VAT 69. Johnnie Walker executive Nigel Shattuck recalled interviewing for a personal assistant in the early 1980s. He saw a nice young chap whose main interest was the jazz band he played in. At his previous job, the man had a poor record of getting to work on time. Shattuck rejected him. The next day a colleague rang to suggest Shattuck reconsider. The young man was the grandson of a former Distillers director. Shattuck refused to change his mind. Days later, the young man was hired by Buchanans, another Scotch subsidiary.

Like a family business fallen on hard times, the culture was dour, grudging and provincial. Rona Cameron, now with Guinness's public relations department, was a trade journalist covering Distillers in the early 1980s. 'The thing I always remembered about Distillers was that the secretaries had bigger offices than the directors,' she said. Company cars only became generally available to management in the mid-1980s. 'You were badly paid, you got no share options. All you got was a few bottles of whisky at Christmas,' said Shattuck. Management was old and inward-looking. 'Dead men's shoes' was the governing rule for promotion. The higher one rose, the greater the importance of family and factions. There was no uniformity of culture: some of the companies were aggressive, while other were more lackadaisical.

The group was bedevilled by rivalries between the brand companies, between top men at each company fighting for seats on the group board, between families and even inside families. Corporate headquarters in London, Distillers House, was nick-named the 'Kremlin' for the intrigue that went on. Years after the takeover, a reporter was stunned when he asked David Connell about one particularly bad strategic decision. Connell's reply: 'If you look into it, you'll find that decision was taken by my brother.' David Connell spent his early career with White Horse and felt Johnnie Walker people were too conceited and successful. When he took over at Johnnie Walker, he determined to bring them down a few notches. (David Connell was one of the best of the Distillers executives, pushing the Walker brand forward, especially in Continental Europe. He was one of the few to stay on and rise to a senior position under the new regime.)

Drinks distributors around the world marvelled at how Distillers men always seemed to smile more when they took market share from one of their sister companies than from a genuine competitor. In the late 1970s, Brian Slowey was MD of Cantrell and Cochrane, a large spirits distributor in Ireland. He recalled how he made millions from the rivalries between Distillers companies.

'Every year it gave me no end of joy to negotiate with each of the individual barons. I would say to Haig, "fellas, the marketing manager of Johnnie Walker is giving us more money" and he'd say to me "we can't have that", he'd give me more money, and then I'd be back on the phone to Johnnie Walker.'

For aggressive drinks distributors from Dublin to Sydney to Kinshasa, a contract to distribute a Distillers brand was usually a gold mine. Distillers made millionaires out of dozens of them. Usually they were foreigners, sometimes drinks industry veterans, sometimes just entrepreneurs with an eye for a deal. The Spanish Ferrer family, whose Afersons company distributed Johnnie Walker, became far richer than any Distillers shareholders. Distillers executives spoke enviously of the wedding of the Ferrers' Porsche-driving son Carlos. The caviar, it was whispered inside the 'Kremlin', was handed out like baked beans – all paid for by the awesome profits from the Red and Black – Johnnie Walker Red and Black Label.

'It is wrong to say that Distillers couldn't spell the word marketing, but the problem with Distillers' marketing was that it was all conducted by the distribution companies, and all our own brands competed with each other,' admitted Distillers director David Connell. Distillers' problems had much in common with the problems of Guinness before Saunders's arrival. Both companies were production-oriented, and needed to make the big jump to a marketing-led organisation. Both companies had too many family members and their sycophants in senior management positions. Both companies suffered from a schizophrenia over their national identities which got in the way of focusing on building the business. The old Guinness did not know whether it was Irish or English; the old Distillers did not know whether it was Scottish or English. Distillers executives talked a lot about Scotland, its distillery communities on Speyside, and the shareholders in Edinburgh. But the top men lived in Surrey, worked in the 'Kremlin' in London's snooty St James's Square, and possessed neither the resources nor the will to make Scottish employment their overriding concern. Hardening of the corporate arteries had all but immobilised the company. By 1986, a shake-up from the outside was essential, someone to knock heads together among these thirteen autonomous companies comprising more than one hundred brands and to set about realising the true potential of Scotland's most famous export. The Guinness take-over was that outside force.

On Friday 16 April 1986, Guinness controller Phil Rhodes enjoyed a glass of champagne in the Portman Square boardroom with the rest of the head office staff, celebrating the success of the takeover at the invitation of the ill-fated Ernest Saunders. 'There we were, this small group of people who'd made one of the biggest bids in British corporate history and won. Suddenly our share price was on the back page of the *Evening Standard*. We were one of the Top 30 companies in Britain. It was kind of hard to believe.' To recover from the intense pressure of the bid, they took Saturday off. Sunday morning, Rhodes was back at his desk. As head of the control team, he was in charge of the daunting task of restructuring Distillers.

A soft-spoken accountant, before Guinness Rhodes had worked in Glaxo's finance department where he had built the pricing model for Zantac, Glaxo's anti-ulcer compound which became the most profitable drug in history. At Distillers, Rhodes's two objectives were to restructure Distillers and at the same time cut costs out of the organisation. He worked closely with a team of Bain consultants. The theme for the Distillers revolution which went on in various forms until 1992 was carved out in June 1986, and portrayed in a slide which formed part of all the internal presentations on the company. The slide read: 'Distillers today is a loose federation of individual brand companies. In the future it should be a single multinational brand marketing company.'

Rhodes and his team were dumbfounded by what they found at Distillers House. The old Guinness had had its corporate indulgences, but they paled by comparison. Distillers headquarters, in historic St James's Square, were housed in the building where the Queen Mother was born. Enlarged by combining two of the elegant Georgian town houses, the offices were stuffed with expensive antiques and the corridors were long, dark and heavily carpeted. The furniture was kept spotless by a full-time French polisher. The company also employed a part-time art historian to oversee their valuable collection of paintings. Pride of place was given to 'The Monarch of the Glen' which hung in the boardroom. 'The size of the head office budget made my eyes water,' said one member of the control team. In short order the furnishings, together with the contents of the well-stocked wine cellar, were sold at auction. What bothered the Guinness men most was the excessive drinking that went on in Distillers House. Distillers executives seemed to believe that selling spirits required sampling them as often as possible. Every office had a well-stocked drinks cabinet. Instead of a tea lady, Distillers had an ice lady, who went along the corridors every day at 4.30. One week after the takeover, Guinness corporate finance director Simon Duffy went to lunch at Distillers House. 'I was offered a G and T and I said no thanks. I gave great offence.' Rhodes's team had an informal competiton to see who could come up with the most euphemisms for 'let's have a drink'. Some Distillers executives fought back, complaining to the press about the beastly behaviour of alleged 'storm troopers' from Bain. After the eruption of the scandal in December, some newspapers carried their gripes sympathetically. Thanks to the time-honoured device of the nonattributable quote, the inroads made into the liquid lifestyles of executives chauffeured in from Surrey each morning was portrayed as a threat to the honour of Scotland.

In March 1987, the scale of the revolution became clearer to Distillers when, now restructured into a single company and renamed United Distillers, they moved into Landmark House, a modern, thirteen-storey office block in Hammersmith, west London. Some of London's finest West End real estate went on the block: in addition to Distillers House, the London head-quarters of Buchanan's, Dewar's, Haig and Johnnie Walker, all of them within a half mile of St James's Square, were sold. While an important objective in siting the new United Distillers (UD) was to be convenient for Heathrow Airport, Guinness did not mind at all that Landmark House was an austere, concrete-and-glass tower alongside a motorway flyover, overlooking one of London's largest and ugliest roundabouts. It was a powerful way to put across the message that United Distillers' purpose was not executive indulgence but growing sales, profits and brand image. Group headquarters Portman Square, a squat, 1960s-era office block, brewing headquarters at the Park Royal brewery, and Landmark House made a triumvirate of not uncomfortable but highly utilitarian head offices.

On 9 March 1987 Anthony Tennant joined Guinness as group managing director, ending two months of crisis management by the non-executive directors. Tennant's availability for the job was a stroke of luck for Guinness. Aged fifty-six in 1987, Tennant had been in the drinks industry for twenty years. He had taken over Grand Met's drinks division International Distillers and Vintners (IDV) in 1976 and in the succeeding eleven years moulded a disjointed federation of baronies into an aggressively managed, tightly run machine, boasting brands like the world's number one vodka Smirnoff, and the world's best-selling French wine, Le Piat d'Or. By the time he quit IDV, its profits had risen tenfold to more than £200 million.

For Tennant too, the availability of the top job at Guinness was lucky. Only weeks before, Grand Met chairman Stanley Grinstead had fingered Tennant's rival Allen Shepherd as his successor at the food-drinks-hotels-and-pubs conglomerate, angering the ambitious Tennant. When Grinstead beseeched Tennant to stay with Grand Met, Tennant replied: 'First, I shall case the joint.' When a headhunter rang offering 'something suitable' which turned out to be the chief executive job at Guinness, Tennant was gone.

If Ernest Saunders was Guinness's Robespierre, then Tennant was its Napoleon. The changes Tennant wrought, in his discreet, gentlemanly way, were at least as radical as those of the Saunders era. And, by giving the company a well-defined management structure, Tennant's changes were more stable and enduring. Guinness executives soon realised that the company's shareholders had got the best of both worlds. Saunders's manic intensity and propensity for bet-the-company risk was ideal for Guinness when it was a medium-sized beer company in deep trouble, while Tennant's strategic overview, deal-making prowess, ability to delegate and lifetime of relationships in the beverage industry were perfect for maximising the value of the rich inheritance of underexploited brands from Distillers in 1987. Guinness had another concern in 1987: maintaining management morale and rebuilding its reputation, in the face of the unfolding Distillers takeover scandal. Eton- and Cambridge-educated, Tennant was descended from a family of nineteenth-century Scottish business-men, related to playboy and Royal friend Lord Glenconner, and son of a onetime Member of the Queen's Bodyguard. His wife Rosemary was one of the Hendersons of Henderson Adminis-tration, one of the bluest of blue-chip City investment institutions. His pedigree contrasted sharply with that of the self-willed 'outsider', Saunders. A not-so-subtle message went out through the corridors of power and the columns of newspapers that Guinness was now in safe hands.

Tall, broad-shouldered, with jutting jaw and large black-framed spectacles, Tennant's bulk always made him seem a size too large for his impeccable suits. He began his new job literally with a blank sheet of paper: 'All the files had been taken away and there was no briefing from my predecessor available either. I had nothing to go by except my own views about how the operation should be conducted.' He quickly decided to focus Guinness on its two core businesses, beer and spirits. Non-core businesses were sold, including the Underwood's chain of retail chemist shops, Champney's health farm and other health-related projects Saunders had acquired. Tennant's alacrity paid off. The cheque for the Martin's chain of newsagents, sold in the summer of 1987 for £202 million, reached Portman Square on Black Monday, the day of the October stock market crash. Delay would probably have led to a price renegotiation. The Martin's deal showed that in strategic matters Tennant was as tough and singleminded as his predecessor. He decided to sell Martin's without even consulting the newsagent's senior management. 'There were some nice people running that business, and they were a bit sad that I didn't even meet them before taking the decision, but had I done all that, it would have been too late,' he admitted. Brian Baldock, whom Tennant made managing director of Guinness Brewing Worldwide, organised a party to mark Tennant's first anniversary at Guinness. Tennant's surprise gift was a bulldozer full of fertiliser. 'We're giving you this,' Baldock explained, to general laughter, while Tennant looked on in bemused astonishment, 'so you can do to your garden what you do to us: cover us in it and say grow faster!'

Tennant was scathing about Saunders's management style and his reliance on management consultants Bain. 'The degree of centralisation and the appalling inefficiencies that resulted from it, I'd never seen anything like it,' he said. He criticised Bain in public. But, although he sacked other Guinness advisers, he did not sack Bain. They continued to work for both Guinness Brewing and United Distillers. Bain's contribution was especially valuable in setting up new overseas distribution companies. But Tennant also created permanent management structures, systems and areas of responsibility appropriate to a large company. For the key job of managing director of United Distillers, Tennant turned to a Guinness non-executive director, Tony Greener. Tennant and Greener had done business in the early 1980s, when IDV signed a deal to bottle a Scotch for Dunhill (Dunhill Old Master). Tennant felt Greener had the intuitive understanding of luxury brands and the marketing skills United Distillers needed. The appointment demonstrated the difference between Tennant and his predecessor: Greener was tough and independent-minded. He had run a large company for a decade. Saunders had never been willing to accept such a strong figure below him.

At IDV, Tennant achieved great success with the group's flagship Scotch, J&B, but he always felt one hand was tied behind his back – by his biggest competitor, Distillers. With 40 per cent of world sales of Scotch whisky, Distillers' policy of competing on price held all whisky prices down. Worse, it eroded the prestige image of Scotch. American consumers were always seeking symbols of status and prestige. In the 1980s, the ultimate decade for glitz and glamour, Distillers had actually succeeded in reducing the prestige of Scotch through repeated price-cutting. 'They turned it into a non-aspirational drink,' Tennant grumbled, his great head shaking in disbelief. At last, as boss of all the Distillers brands, he was able to take the lead in resurrecting and rebuilding the image of Scotch. Tennant believed Scotch had to be marketed as a luxury product. Like perfume or an expensive car, a bottle of Scotch said something about the person who owned it. The most important single indicator to the consumer of high quality was price. The price of Scotch was way too low. But it could be raised only in the context of a broad-ranging marketing programme educating the consumer that a man's brand of Scotch (three quarters of all Scotch is drunk by men) said a lot about him in terms of taste: the ability to recognise it and the ability to afford it. 'You're talking about image, you're talking about occasional purchase, and the values of Scotch in the consumer's mind, and the aura that surrounds it.'

Distribution was the key. Each national distributor made all the crucial marketing decisions determining the success or failure of the product. He set the price, he chose where to sell it and he created the advertising to back up the sales effort. As an old-fashioned exporting company, the old Distillers was not involved in those decisions. Its interest in a case of Scotch disappeared the moment it was hoisted on to a boat in a Scottish dock. At IDV Tennant had seized control of distributorships around the world from virtually the day he had taken over as managing director there. When he joined Guinness, United Distillers (UD) owned distributors accounting for only 20 per cent of its sales. Working at breakneck pace, Tennant travelled the world, sometimes buying up an existing local distributor, sometimes setting up a new one, sometimes creating a joint venture in partnership with an existing distributor. Buying companies at the rate of one a month, in six years at Guinness Tennant spent more than £2 billion on acquisitions. Ironically, while Tennant pursued his great takeover spree, worthy Members of Parliament proclaimed that the age of the takeover was dead, buried by the 'Guinness affair'! Ernest Saunders was a clumsy amateur in the takeover game. Tennant was a seasoned pro.

An important move into distribution was in the American market, where Tennant sought to buy Schenley Industries from American financier Meshulam Riklis. America was the world's largest Scotch market and UD brand Dewar's America's number one Scotch. Schenley had distribution rights to Dewar's, as well as a motley assortment of locally produced spirits brands. Israeli-born Riklis was a colourful figure who claimed the phrase 'junk bond' was invented in a 1970 telephone conversation he had with financier Michael Milken. In 1986 Schenley gained ownership of the Dewar's brand name in America from Saunders in what looked suspiciously like part of the machinations before the Distillers takeover. (Riklis took a significant stake in Guinness at the height of the takeover battle.) By the late 1980s, Riklis had lost his enthusiasm for the takeover game and was devoting more time to nurturing the career of his young-actress wife, Pia Zadora.

In a scene Alfred Hitchcock would have appreciated, Tennant and his banking advisers from Morgan Stanley pursued Riklis across the American Midwest as he watched his wife's performances. Japanese drinks company Suntory also wanted to buy Schenley. Their representatives joined the odd cavalcade. In snatched meetings in hotels and theatre lobbies, Tennant and Riklis agreed a deal, Selling Schenley to Guinness for $480 million. The unspoken threat that if Riklis sold to anybody else Guinness might whip up renewed publicity over the murky circumstances that surrounded Riklis's acquisition of the Dewar's rights probably helped Tennant win the deal. Tennant and Riklis got on well. 'I rather liked him,' said Tennant. He had good reason to. By 1992, the Schenley acquisition, which included a rough diamond in the shape of American bourbon IW Harper, had paid for itself many times over.

The most daring, innovative and profitable of Tennant's deals was the complex set of arrangements he reached with Moët

Hennessy Louis Vuitton LVMH, the French luxury goods giant. In one giant leap, the deals hoisted UD's distribution presence in more than a dozen countries. To do it, Tennant had to risk hundreds of millions of pounds of Guinness cash in an unstable, dissension-racked French company. By playing his cards shrewdly and patiently, and never losing sight of his ultimate goal, he emerged two years later with a new, innovative joint venture structure for drinks distribution which was the envy of competitors.

In March 1987, Moët Hennessy chairman Alain Chevalier approached Tennant with a proposition. Would he like to establish a series of joint venture distribution companies around the world with the venerable champagne and cognac producer? The ventures would market Moët's champagnes, Hennessy's cognacs, and UD's products too. For Tennant, Chevalier was like the genie emerged from the (cognac) bottle to grant him his greatest wish. Hennessy cognac had powerful distribution companies in many parts of the world, including the Far East. The Far East was the greatest omission of the old Distillers Company. Japan and the fast-growing Asian tiger economies were some of the world's most profitable markets. If UD and Moët Hennessy pooled forces, overnight and at minimal cost to Guinness, UD would have a sales presence in these vital markets. In addition, Moët Hennessy's leading American wine and spirit distributor, Schieffelin and Somerset, would work for UD too.

Chevalier made the generous offer because he was seeking a poison pill. Moët Hennessy's share price was leaping in early 1987 as secret buyers accumulated stakes. Chevalier didn't want to be taken over by a stranger who might take apart the cognac and champagne empire he'd diligently constructed over more than a decade. The Guinness joint ventures would help repel a predator because Guinness would have the right to break them in the event of a takeover of Moët Hennessy. The threat of such disruption might scare away potential predators. In time, the two companies established fourteen joint ventures around the world.

Tennant saw that the joint ventures would soon be as vital to

UD as they were to its French partner. 'I suggested to Alain Chevalier that it was very important to avoid anybody disturbing the partnership, and that it might be a good idea if we had a long-term shareholding and we discussed whether it should be five per cent, or ten per cent, or more.' But in June 1987 a new player entered the game. Still frightened of a hostile bid, Chevalier agreed to merge his company with Louis Vuitton. The new company, Moët Hennessy Louis Vuitton LVMH, was the world's largest luxury goods company, and one of France's largest quoted companies. Vuitton's interests, including Louis Vuitton luggage, Givenchy perfumes, and Veuve Clicquot champagne, combined with Moët Hennessy to produce a company with a turnover of £1.3 billion, roughly half the size of Guinness. The merger delayed, but still did not kill the takeover threat.

In July 1988, Bernard Arnault finally broke cover, with a 15 per cent stake in LVMH. Although he owned the Dior couture house, the youthful Arnault (then thirty-nine) was still regarded as an *arriviste* in Paris business circles. A veteran of his family's construction business, he was a cold, aloof operator who bought, sold and restructured companies as regularly as some men washed their socks. Tennant was at last permitted to buy a 10 per cent stake in LVMH, but only through the intermediary of a new company, Jacques Rober, in which Guinness would own 40 per cent and Bernard Arnault 60 per cent. That gave Arnault control over Guinness's investment. In French financial circles, it was whispered admiringly that Arnault had contrived to have his creeping takeover of LVMH 40 per cent-financed by the British. Moreover, Tennant had to accept LVMH taking a reciprocal 12 per cent share in the British company. LVMH became the largest shareholder in Guinness, with a large enough stake to be a destabilising influence on Guinness's share price.

Tennant took the precaution of investigating the finances of Arnault and his family, concluding they did not have the resources to launch a full takeover bid for Guinness. Over the next two years, Guinness put £300 million into Jacques Rober. It was a far from riskless course, but Tennant believed that ultimately

Arnault's interest was in building the LVMH businesses, including the spirits joint ventures.

The French government kept a stern eye on Guinness's role in LVMH. It was determined to see that this great treasure chest of French luxury names remain in French ownership. 'Guinness never had a level playing field,' said Simon Duffy, Guinness's head of corporate finance. In 1988, Guinness bought some LVMH shares directly (ie not through Jacques Rober). The French *Trésor*, whose approval is required before any non-EC company can buy French shares, took ninety-five days to approve Guinness's status as an EC company. Outrageously non-*communautaire* behaviour, it was a warning shot across Guinness's bows. 'Chevalier told us the Elysée [the office of French president Mitterrand] would never let us get any more than a minority stake,' said Duffy.

In January 1989 Chevalier and Louis Vuitton chairman Henry Racamier launched a plot to oust Arnault and take back 'their' company. At a lunch at LVMH headquarters they proposed Tennant join them. They even dangled the lure of selling Moët Hennessy to Guinness. Arnault knew about the two Frenchmen's plot; midway through the lunch, two LVMH butlers in formal dress burst into the room with two long telexes addressed to Chevalier and Racamier. Arnault was suing them for alleged violations of their responsibilities. Chevalier and Tennant had known each other for more than twenty years. But Tennant no longer believed in Chevalier's personality-driven approach to business. UD and Moët Hennessy were too big and too international.

On 5 January, Tennant met Arnault and agreed to support him, in exchange for a seat on the board of LMVH and an increase in Guinness's shareholding in LVMH to 24 per cent. Chevalier resigned, telling the press rather picturesquely: 'In a battle between liberty and power, I chose liberty.' Tennant said: 'I tried to get him to stay. He made a mistake. He should have stayed.' Some were shocked that the elegant, aristocratic Tennant would make common cause with the hard-nosed Arnault against the erudite Chevalier. Beneath the bonhomie and earthy, vernacular language he cultivated to disguise his aristocratic origins, Tennant was a tough, unsentimental operator. After two years of infighting and Gallic egos, Tennant found Arnault's rationality a breath of fresh air. 'There are always people who want to be critical of someone who's risen rather sharply. As far as I'm concerned, whenever Arnault has said something clear and unequivocal, he has delivered on it.'

The joint ventures were the prize that made all the machinations in Paris worthwhile, enabling UD and Moët Hennessy to pool marketing and selling forces in more than a dozen countries. They offered the benefits of size without the costs of takeover. (Shortly after the joint ventures were first announced, Canadian drinks giant, Seagram's bought number two cognac-producer Martell for a price Seagram chairman Ed Bronfman commented he hoped his grandchildren would appreciate.) Typically joint ventures come unstuck because one partner feels the other is taking unfair advantage of the venture. The UD/Moët Hennessy joint ventures were carefully constructed to avoid such problems. The products were themselves complementary: Scotch and cognac sold in the same bars and off-licences, but not as head-on competitors. Innovatively, the relationships left control of brand marketing strategy with the parent companies. They developed the local marketing tools like advertising, and paid the local marketing costs. The profits from each brand went back to the parent company. Either one of the parent companies had the power to remove the managing director of the joint venture. 'To make sure the guy running the business is in fact mutually acceptable and does recognise that he's working for two partners and does work adequately for both partners, he knows that if he doesn't then the aggrieved partner has the right to replace him,' Tennant explained. The nature of the international brands marketing business binds the joint venture closely to each of its parents. The glue holding the joint ventures together was that both companies shared the underlying philosophy that strongly pedigreed drinks should be marketed as symbols of quality, prestige and luxury.

In five years, UD moved from controlling less than 20 per cent of its in-country distribution to controlling more than 80 per cent. By withdrawing many of its minor brands from many national markets, it increased the focus and strength of its major brands. The total number of in-country distributors fell from more than 1700 to around 250. UD applied a new, revitalised marketing push to the major brands, including redesign of everything from the shapes, labels and caps on the bottles to the advertising campaigns. Perhaps the best example of the success of the transformation was in Japan.

Before 1987, the old Distillers operated in its standard export role in Japan. It had just one employee in the world's second-largest economy. It had many in-country distribution agents, many of whom grew rich off Distillers' brands. Some of the agents did not even distribute drinks. They simply licensed distribution rights from Distillers, subcontracted the distribution to another company for a fee or royalty on each bottle sold. Their only cost of business was the three-monthly lunch they bought for the Distillers man visiting from London. The most successful Japanese distributor was a Japanese named Takahashi. By good marketing, including raising the price of a bottle to £40, Takahashi established Old Parr as Japan's leading premium Scotch. He promoted it as ideal prestige product for the gift-giving that was *de rigueur* at Japan's many family and business days of celebration. By 1987, Takahashi was a multimillionaire. UD executives who visited him at his offices were amazed to see him demonstrate his deep love for Scotland: he would push a button on his desk and a wall would slide back revealing a train-set on a fifteen-foot-wide table faithfully reproducing the Scottish rail network. Even the Forth Bridge was there in vivid detail.

Takahashi's passion for Scotland waned somewhat when he learned UD intended to take back his licence to Old Parr and distribute the brand themselves. He was over seventy and spending less time at work and more time indulging his hobby, ballroom dancing. But his sons were in the business. Reluctantly, Takahashi yielded. UD deputy managing director James Espey lured a veteran Japanese marketing man from Seagram's to run the new Old Parr Japan (OPJ). Working cautiously, patiently and following Japanese etiquette, OPJ kept nearly all its retail and bar relationships, and most of its Japanese employees, despite the changeover to the new owners.

The transition at bourbon brand IW Harper was more difficult. When Riklis sold Harper to Guinness as part of the Schenley stable, Suntory offered Tennant £30 million for the brand. They already distributed the brand in Japan. Tennant was considering the proposition until a presentation in London by Greener, Espey and Bain consultant Stan Miranda convinced him that with the Japanese market for bourbon growing at double-digit rates, Harper, number one in the market, was worth keeping – and distributing themselves. Suntory reacted angrily to losing its distribution rights to Harper in 1988. They dumped their remaining Harper stocks at discount prices to undermine the brand's image; they ordered it out of all the bars they owned; and they brought in a new bourbon, Forester, to try to take back the number one spot from Harper. UD fought back with a big advertising push for Harper, and its local joint venture with LVMH signed up dozens of new bars and retailers to replace the losses. UD won the battle. Harper widened its lead as number one, and eventually Suntory withdrew Forester from the market.

As a global company, UD was able to focus its efforts on the best brands for each national market. For example, Old Parr and White Horse were both strong in Japan. Both were damaged though by so-called parallel imports from the US and the UK where those Scotches sold for half the Japanese price. Parallel imports not only hurt UD's profits, they undermined the Scotches' all-important brand images. UD solved the problem by simply taking Old Parr off the market in those countries. White Horse had more of a following in the Anglo-Saxon world, so instead UD changed the bottle's shape in Japan, making it tall and slender. In their short, squat bottles, parallel-imported White Horse now looked to the Japanese like an inferior imitation. In the five years between 1986 and 1991 sales of Old Parr in Japan doubled to more than 200,000 cases. Sales of IW Harper bourbon *quadrupled* to 500,000 cases. Guinness was earning some £50 million a year in Japan, compared to less than £10 million in 1987. It was the most profitable British-owned company in Japan, and the second most profitable foreign-owned business there after IBM.

Bain continued to be closely involved in UD strategy in many parts of the world. With an office of forty-five professionals in Japan, Bain was especially valuable to UD there. A Harvard-educated MBA, conversant in Japanese, American-born Stan Miranda made an important contribution to UD's Far Eastern expansion. Miranda worked for a year on secondment at Guinness as an adviser to Greener on strategic issues. The secondment of Bain consultant Olivier Roux was widely criticised in the aftermath of the Guinness scandal, but Greener believed Bain consultants made a valuable strategic contribution to UD. Claiming that in 1992 Bain worked for nine of Britain's top 100 quoted companies, Miranda argued that consultants still played an important role at large companies. 'Companies like Guinness have many more middle and junior level MBAs today than they did ten years ago, so consultants' roles tend to be more at the senior strategic level where they can share experiences gained from other companies and other industries,' said Miranda.

Halfway round the world, in Greece, United Distillers pursued a different, but equally effective strategy. Greece was one of the world's top ten Scotch markets, and growing fast. But it was not a good market for the old Distillers company. Its highest-ranked Scotch in Greece scored only fourth in the country's league table.

In 1987 Andrew Morgan joined UD to spearhead a new attack on the Greek market. A mere thirty years old, Morgan came from American razor blade giant Gillette. Gillette sold fast-moving consumer goods and Scotch was a slow-moving consumer good. But Greener wanted the analytical, strategic and marketing skills that veteran multinational marketers like Gillette had turned into a science. After six months at UD's new Hammersmith head-quarters, Morgan went off to Athens as head of UD's Greek business.

In UD's new regionally based, decentralised management structure, Morgan had wide autonomy to re-invent UD's local sales and marketing strategies. Morgan studied the Greek market. The first thing he learned was that Scotch was a younger and more image-conscious business in Greece than it was in Britain. 'It was all about lifestyles and brand name and badging,' Morgan said. 'It was certainly *not* about targeting the older group as Bell's did in the UK.'

The on-trade – the bars and nightclubs of Athens and other Greek cities – was where the greatest opportunities lay. The Greek on-trade accounted for 65 per cent of the country's Scotch consumption (the comparable figure in the UK was 20 per cent). With the economic boom that followed Greece's entry into the EC, Greek nightclubs were packed every night with the newly rich, eager to display their wealth to friends, business associates and women. 'They came in there with a back-pocketful of cash thinking, Christ, what do I do with this? The solution was usually showing off by buying expensive bottles of whisky in expensive nightclubs.'

Morgan began by pulling a dozen UD brands out of Greece entirely. He chose four brands to concentrate his resources on, two standard whiskies, Johnnie Walker Red Label and Dewar's, and two deluxe whiskies, Johnnie Walker Black and Dimple. Normally, UD put all its brands into one distribution company. In a large market, they might divide their brands between two distribution companies, creating some healthy direct competition between rivals. Morgan chose a different route. He divided the market between on- and off-trade specialists. 'You needed very specialised skills to break into the on-trade,' he said. The man he found with those skills was unconventional. Owner of five night-clubs and a first division Greek football club, Nikos Kanalakis was a self-made entrepreneur. He had begun his career sweeping up broken plates in nightclubs, reconstituting them and selling them back to the nightclubs. By 1988, aged just thirty-two, sporting ample gold jewelry, a Mercedes and a personal bodyguard, he was a well-known figure in Athens. His only drinks distribution experience was as a sub-distributor for Bell's but Morgan believed he had the knowledge and the contacts to establish a new Scotch in the nightclub scene.

The old Distillers Company would scarcely have considered doing business with a man like Kanalakis. He was too unconventional, too entrepreneurial for their stuffy culture. The moment it became known Morgan was discussing a deal with him, rumours flew back to London, smearing Kanalakis's business practices and background. 'It was all inspired by his competitors,' said Morgan. There were some dramatic moments. On a visit to Athens, Anthony Tennant went to meet Kanalakis. Tennant knew his markets. Speaking through an interpreter, he mentioned that Greek suppliers encountered many bad debts and asked Kanalakis how he coped with the problem. Kanalakis's reply came back quickly: 'We do not have any bad debts.' Tennant took in the serenely smiling figure before him, flanked by his broad-shouldered bodyguard. Apparently, bar owners in Greece slept easier if they did not fall behind in their payments to Mr Kanalakis. Tennant thanked him for his time and departed.

Morgan gave Kanalakis distribution of Dewar's and Dimple. Dewar's was a new brand to Greece, trendy with the nightclub habitués. A twelve-year-old premium whisky, Dimple had a key asset: a distinctive bell-shaped bottle which meant that when a waiter brought a bottle to a nightclub table, everybody knew the customer was drinking deluxe whisky. (In an Anglo-Saxon market, premium whisky drinkers favoured Johnnie Walker Black, precisely because its discreet bottle, identical to the cheaper Red Label bottle, telegraphed the message that this consumer was sophisticated enough to recognise a good whisky without the help of a distinctive bottle. Whisky snobbery was everywhere different, but always present.)

Morgan backed Kanalakis with advertising campaigns promoting both products. The Dewar's ads spared little subtlety in linking the whisky with sex. 'If you took all the ad-speak out, what it said was beautiful women like men who drink Dewar's,' said Morgan. The ads were modifications of a campaign originally developed in Puerto Rico. On the ground, Kanalakis worked the nightclub owners. There was a tradition in the nightclubs of putting an unopened bottle of whisky on every table. The customer could send it back and order his personal favourite, but many simply chose to crack open the bottle they found there. Dewar's and Dimple began to show up on more and more nightclub tables.

In 1987, Dewar's sold just 29,000 cases in Greece. Over the next five years, it rose by more than 50 per cent *per year* to reach 360,000 cases in 1992. From being virtually unknown it went to 10 per cent of the whisky market. Morgan's other distributor, the Boutari Brothers, did an almost as impressive job with Johnnie Walker Red, trebling its sales to 440,000 cases. By 1992, Red Label was number one in the Greek off-trade, Dewar's number one in the on-trade, and United Distillers' market share was up twenty points to 50 per cent. Growing internationalisation of the Greeks and UD's marketing push combined to raise Scotch sales ahead of traditional Greek spirit ouzo. Scotch became the national drink of Greece. Morgan was promoted, to run all of UD in southern Europe. His successor had to cope with the problem of too much success: Red Label and Dewar's were so big they were now competing with each other.

Morgan attributed the success in Greece to the combination of sophisticated brand-building and marketing skills with the drive and talents of the local distributors. 'The local nous, local contacts and knowledge of the trade our partners brought to the party was invaluable.' Morgan preferred partnering with local entrepreneurs rather than other multinationals wherever possible. 'Working with another multinational, there is a danger that you both think you know it all on marketing strategy and probably neither of you knows how to do it on the ground.' Around the same time he negotiated his deals with Boutari and Kanalakis, UD competitor Grand Met bought 100 per cent of the famous Greek brandy company Metaxa. With the entrepreneurs who built Metaxa gone, Grand Met encountered local management problems which seriously set back their expansion plans in Greece.

The drinks industry was becoming more strategically oriented.

Salesmen travelling around with a bag full of samples were no longer enough. 'Now you need business managers, guys who can look at the needs of a large customer and put together a presentation consisting not only of all the terms of trade but a programme of promotions to support the product throughout the year, a complete package that benefits the retailer as well as us,' said Morgan.

Spirits has become a luxury and a prestige business. It is also increasingly a Third World business. One fact perhaps sums it up best: in 1991, Thailand surpassed the USA as the world's number one market for Johnnie Walker Black Label, the world's best-selling deluxe whisky. With 56 million people, it consumed 500,000 cases of Black Label. 'Do you know what country has the world's highest *per capita* consumption of deluxe whisky?' asked Brendan O'Neill, head of UD's international division until 1993, pausing for effect. 'Venezuela.' Working late into the night in his office on the twelfth floor of UD's Hammersmith HQ, the nerve centre where marketing strategies for the world were hammered out, O'Neill was obsessed with price points. Arranging a row of bottles, tall slender square ones, short, squat ones and elegantly pear-shaped ones on the table before him, O'Neill explained that, after raising the prices of Venezuela's best-loved Scotches by 50 per cent, he was now engaged in introducing new Scotch brands at lower prices. The enhanced prestige of Scotch raised demand among consumers who could not afford a $30 bottle of Buchanan's 18 Year Old, so O'Neill introduced new brands or spruced up venerable old names like 'Ye Monks', pricing them at an affordable $10 or $15 a bottle. A former finance man with British Leyland, O'Neill's approach to Scotch markets was cool, calculated and strategic, almost military. He was selling a growing product to a growing nation. 'It's a lot more fun working for a company making £800 million profit than trying to save the British motor industry,' he said.

Scotch whisky was centuries old, but United Distillers was a young, fresh company. In some ways it was like a start-up, constantly innovating, experimenting, restructuring. The culture of the young company was set by Tony Greener. A hard-driving sailing enthusiast, Greener was tall, slim and very fit for a man of fifty-three. On weekends he went yachting or tried new thrills like heli-skiing. He enjoyed racing his colleagues up the twelve flights of stairs to his office, and had a gym installed on the thirteenth floor of Landmark House for his early morning workout. When Greener took over as managing director of Dunhill in 1975, the company made 90 per cent of its profits on smoking-related products; when he left in 1987, 90 per cent of its £50 million profits came from other products, including menswear, leatherware, colognes, Chloë fashions and Montblanc pens. Montblanc was a particular success. Acquired in 1977 – 'it cost 10.8 million Deutschmarks when we bought it, in December of that year' – the company was relatively obscure. Outside Germany, it had less name recognition than rival pen manufacturers Cross, Waterman or Parker. By the late 1980s, Montblanc was synonymous with prestige writing instruments, the fat black *Meisterstück* a status symbol throughout Europe and gaining popularity in North America. It was an object lesson in how to build a luxury brand name. 'Tony is a fantastic manager of people and setter of goals. He believes that nothing is ever perfect. Every aspect of every brand can always be improved,' commented Brendan O'Neill.

'If you are selling a quality product, every aspect of it has got to shout quality,' he added.

When Greener arrived at UD in 1978 it was a mix of disparate cultures. There were newcomers, like him; there were people who had moved over from Guinness's beer division; the largest number were holdovers from the old Distillers Company. Many of the latter did not take kindly to the new hard-driving management style. One veteran of the old Distillers described a lunch he attended at Guinness headquarters with Bernard Arnault, LVMH chairman. Arnault asked for a glass of champagne, which duly arrived. The Frenchman looked around, hoping not to drink alone, but Greener and his colleagues studied their mineral waters. Finally, this Distillers veteran asked for some champagne and Arnault's face brightened. 'For goodness sake, UD is in the liquor business, not the Bible business!' he commented.

Another ex-Distillers executive cited Spain, where UD's efforts to change its distributions arrangements went badly wrong. Lawsuits ensued and sales of Johnnie Walker Red Label were hit. Greener admitted mistakes were made in the tumultuous early years at UD. 'Since we didn't have an established way of doing things built into the company, if you wanted to try and do something you had to follow the thing right through the piece to make sure it got implemented. When I said to somebody, OK, let's march in this direction I knew what I meant, but other people might not have had the faintest idea what I meant.'

Crispin Davis took over from Greener as managing director of United Distillers in 1992. He left Procter and Gamble in 1987 at the age of forty ('I loved P and G and I still do. It was a very hard decision.'). With brown hair hanging over his collar and a relaxed, outgoing manner, he cut a different figure from his predecessor. Greener wore Dunhill suits; Davis blazers by Hugo Boss. The relaxed Davis enjoyed joking about the subliminal message of the UD ad catchphrase, the 'whisky moment': it was the time for a knees-up, or 'in some markets, a skirts down'. It was a generational change, a young man to run a young company of young men and women.

Davis's top priority is forging a corporate culture for United Distillers. He christened it the 'UD Way'. 'It's still only a piece of paper but it gives an expression of where we want to take the company and what are our fundamental values and principles.' Davis listed four key principles that were part of the UD Way: a strong orientation to produce financial results, or constant annual profits growth; a belief in building brands; the third principle was dedication and hard work – 'People here work much longer hours than almost any other company I've come across.' Finally, there was a strong commitment to internationalism. Davis himself worked for P and G in the UK and the US and was managing director of their German business before joining UD. Internationalism was more than taking a French course at university, or running a foreign company from London: 'You have actually got to live and operate in various countries, experience the different cultures, the different marketplaces, the different trade channels and the different consumers.' People had to be adaptable, tolerant and flexible, because there were still important differences and idiosyncrasies in each local market.

United Distillers' first five years were mostly concerned with establishing the right structures in London and around the world. The next decade will be devoted to building brands. With rising affluence in so much of the Third World, there will be an ever-increasing demand for Old World statements of quality and taste. UD has the drive, flexibility and professional skills to meet the demand.

The drive to create a motivated, decentralised, *exciting* management culture also went on at UD's production operations in Scotland. One morning in 1992, production engineer Nicky Youl was examining the thermometers on the forty-foot-high fermentation vessel at the Port Dundas grain distillery outside Glasgow. Port Dundas produced 200,000 litres of 95 per cent alcohol grain whisky a day. Grain whisky went into every Scotch. It was as vital as the far more renowned malt whiskies which gave each Scotch its distinctive flavour. Youl was energy director at this distillery which employed 240 people. Reporting to the production manager, she had responsibility for Port Dundas's £1.5 million energy bill. She was just twenty-four, out of Heriot-Watt University two years earlier with a chemical engineering degree. Guinness put her through an intensive series of ten courses in management and finance at their London Park Royal training centre, before sending her up to Port Dundas. Distillery manager Jim Wilson liked Youl's energy and ambition and made her energy director. He asked her to find ways to reduce energy costs by recapturing unused energy from the distillery's electricity-generating gas turbine and the thousands of litres of waste water the plant produced.

'It's a bit daunting at first taking on so much responsibility, but everyone tells you you can do it, so you do it,' said Youl.

Asked about the Guinness scandal, Youl admitted she knew

nothing about it. 'Someone gave me a book about it when I joined the company. I didn't read it.'

An energetic girl from Northern Ireland, recently married to another Port Dundas staffer, she dashed up and down the slippery iron ladders with great enthusiasm. She loved her work. 'I never wanted to sit behind a desk. It's exciting in a distillery because you never know what will happen from one moment to the next. You're always trying to improve things.'

FOUR

TI Group

The Manufacturing Revolutionary

Bob Gibbon arrived at work early one morning in the spring of 1982. A colleague poked his head around the door: have you heard the news? The Havant factory burned down last night! 'Horrible,' Gibbon agreed. Gibbon smiled to himself. This could be the best break for Crane in years, he thought. 'We've got to get to the MD quickly,' he said. 'Somebody might tell him to rebuild it.'

Gibbon was a manufacturing revolutionary. Earlier that year, he'd been promoted to chief production engineer at John Crane's Reading factory. Despite being only twenty-five, he could not wait to overhaul the company's entire manufacturing process. He was always talking about new theories on efficiency, organisation, downtime and throughput. Tall, with straight brown hair falling across his forehead, he lacked the patience for the small talk of the office. But when somebody talked about production issues he came to life, his intense brown eyes fixing the listener in a stare that held him like a vice. From the moment he arrived, two years before, he was an unusual figure at Crane Packing. He spent hours hunched over a tiny Sinclair ZX-81 computer at a time when many were still scared of the mysterious machines.

Crane Packing was Europe's largest producer of mechanical seals. Seals had thousands of uses in industry, on land, sea and air. Every ship's propeller used one to keep water out or engine oil in while the propeller turned. Nearly every pump used one to seal gases or liquids inside rotating equipment. Oil refineries used hundreds of seals, to keep oil and gases in while pumping them through the processing plant. Mechanical seals were made of metal rings which fitted together like a sandwich or a doughnut, a hole in the middle for the shaft. A seal used the liquid it pumped as a lubricant between its moving faces. The seal had to be engineered to extremely precise tolerances. If the gap between the faces was too narrow, they would touch and the seal would wear out. Too wide, and the liquid would escape. Precision engineering was expensive. The tiny, intricate mechanical seal inside a car's water pump accounted for half the cost of the pump. A properly engineered seal could be installed in an oil pipeline in a desert to pump oil safely, day and night, for years. In a ship like the *QEII*, the Crane seals around the propeller shaft had to absorb a 'whip' of several millimetres in every direction, as the enormous forces of the sea lashed the propeller. The small quantities of water which penetrated were pumped back out again by pumps also equipped with Crane seals. Seals for car water pumps were produced in six-figure quantities. But most Crane seals were made in very small numbers, many custom-designed as a one-off for a specific purpose. Good design was crucial. So was manufacturing. A well-designed and accurately manufactured water pump seal would last the lifetime of a car.

In 1981 Crane Packing got a new managing director. His name was Mark Radcliffe. Crane was a division of Tube Investments, the Birmingham-based industrial conglomerate. With turnover of £25 million, Crane was one of TI's most consistently profitable subsidiaries. The Midlands' largest engineering group, TI liked to grant its subsidiaries great autonomy. For decades, Crane had been run by its own management, trained and promoted internally. But in 1980 recession and the growth of new competition hit Crane's profits hard. The TI board took the unprecedented step of imposing an 'outsider' on Crane Packing.

Radcliffe was one of TI's hard men. Before he joined Crane he was occupied closing down some of TI's loss-making divisions and selling off others. He found the Crane management too inward-looking, a bit tired. 'They were terribly nice people and very experienced, but there was a bit too much looking through the rear-view mirror,' he said. 'They need new blood.' He was determined to inject a new culture into the company. Radcliffe was a tough, hard-driving leader. His staff at Crane would describe him as something of an autocrat. An old Gregorian (ex-pupil of Downside public school), a former Coldstream Guard, a chain-smoker, a British gent of the old school, he was determined to make Crane a world-class company. Radcliffe started out behind a drawing board. He knew engineering from the ground up. He'd seen how some of Crane's big British pump-manufacturing customers had got into trouble when new competitors invaded their traditional Empire markets. If Crane was to avoid that fate, it needed to improve its new product development, its manufacturing and its marketing. 'The company needed a whole new level of aggression,' he declared. To inject that aggression, he announced four objectives: growth, customer service, cost efficiency and cash efficiency. Those objectives, he told his management team, should dominate every employee's thinking.

An MD from outside the company was a jolt to the proud Crane Packing. When Radcliffe first arrived, the company asked him to stay in a hotel in Burnham Beeches until each Crane director had met him. Then they agreed on the form of words for the announcement to Crane employees. Only then was Radcliffe welcome to enter Crane's Slough headquarters. Radcliffe brought Bob Gibbon into Crane as a young engineering graduate. Every year TI took around a dozen graduates straight from university. Gibbon was the first graduate at Crane who had not been to public school. He was from a South Wales coalmining family. The old Gregorian and the boy from the valleys made an unlikely team. Together, they would shake up Crane Packing dramatically.

Gibbon grew up in Mountain Ash, a mining town in the bleak South Wales valleys. He did not share much in the prosperity Britain enjoyed in the 1960s. One of Bob's childhood memories was watching England win the 1966 World Cup on a neighbour's television set at the age of nine. The Gibbon family could afford neither television nor car when Bob was growing up. His grandfather and uncle were coalminers, but Bob's father rarely kept a steady job for long. His mother held the family together. When the last of the six Gibbon children reached school age, Bob's mother began training to go back to work as a nurse. Bob had to rise early, get his brothers and sisters dressed, breakfasted and out to school. In the evenings he cooked tea for the family, washed up and put the younger ones to bed. Only after his chores did he have time for homework. Luckily, math and sciences came easily to him. Family and teachers agreed Bob would not follow his older brother down the mine, but go on instead to further education.

At the University of Manchester's Institute of Science and Technology (UMIST), Bob felt many of his fellow students were not as bright as him but earned higher marks at school. With his family responsibilities he did not have the time to do his best. With quiet determination and perhaps a certain defensiveness, the boy from the Welsh valleys pursued his own goals. First, they were limited to rugby and football. Bob played for the mechanical engineering department and for the college, six days a week, often seven. In his third year, education suddenly seized his attention. Bob did a final year project on the simulation of manufacturing systems. A manufacturing system was like a real-life game of snakes and ladders. Raw material went through any number of different processes before coming out as finished product at the other end. Each individual process had a fixed time duration and cost. Different products went through different processes, but intersecting, sharing the same machine or operation, at many points. The challenge was to achieve the maximum production in minimum time and at minimum cost. The complexity and the intellectual challenge fascinated Gibbon. He did so well on the project that his tutor suggested he stay on to do an MSc in manufacturing technology.

Bob spent most of his master's degree course working on a project in a real factory in Liverpool. It was there that he realised his calling. The challenge of manufacturing was to overcome a never-ending flow of logistical problems combined with the challenge of motivating the people in the manufacturing system who actually produced the finished products. He enjoyed the quixotic nature of the Liverpudlians. They resisted any imposition of authority or regimentation but would selflessly give their all for the common good. 'I had to talk to everybody from the shopfloor guy to the foreman, the manager and the managing director,' Gibbon recalled. 'It really crystallised everything I'd been doing and thinking up till then.'

When Gibbon joined Crane Packing UK in 1980, the company manufactured its seals in three factories – Reading, Slough and Havant. All the factories suffered from long lead times and chronically late delivery. The Crane brand name kept sales strong, even in recession. But profit margins shrunk steadily. Customers were growing disenchanted with having to wait six months for delivery of a seal no bigger than a man's fist.

Every one of the half dozen or more rings in a Crane seal had a unique set of holes, notches, grooves or other shapes machined into it. The variety of the components was almost endless. Crane had specifications to 150,000 different parts in its files. On any day hundreds of different parts were in production on one of the many machines in each of the three factories. If each component had to pass through two, three or more machines, and each machine had to work on a dozen or more different parts during a week, it was not surprising that finished seals could take months to produce. The logistical complexity of trying to produce so many different parts in volume was such that it was beyond the capacity of Gibbon's Sinclair ZX computer to evaluate the options.

The traditional solution of the factory managers was to produce everything in batches as large as possible. Typically, a component was not scheduled for production until the managers felt it was worth producing 100 or 200 of them. The factory was stuffed with work-in-progress. The managers hated to see a machine or an operator with nothing to do, even for a moment. They felt comfortable only when an operator had a great stack of uncut components sitting behind him. Gibbon believed the long lead times were due to the large batch quantities the managers insisted upon. At university he had been introduced to new theories of flexible manufacturing systems which argued that very small batches were more efficient. 'At UMIST there was quite a core of people who were at the leading edge in that technology,' Gibbon recalled. 'That was the kind of background I came from so to me it seemed logical and feasible that we should go that way. I was quite surprised really to find that at that time that knowledge was almost totally unknown in industry.'

Gibbon saw the 1982 Havant fire as his opportunity to begin implementing the fundamental changes he wanted. Putting the Havant production into Reading would require a wholesale reorganisation of the factory. Gibbon proposed cutting the batch sizes dramatically. The theory of flexible manufacturing was that small batch sizes would make the factory more flexible, better able to cope with sudden emergency orders. It was also a learning process. With small batches and heightened interdependency between each stage in the process, every delay in the production process would be exposed and the manufacturing team would have to work on reducing it. Also, cutting out the mountains of work-in-progress would save thousands of pounds on the carrying costs of the vast amounts of stock in the factory.

The drawback, said the traditionalists, was that it would involve more resetting of machines. Since it took two or three hours to set up a machine tool for each job, they said it was only good sense to cut fifty, 100, or more pieces before changing to another set-up. Gibbon's thinking went against seventy years of mass production tradition: how could it possibly be efficient to go through the laborious, expensive process of resetting a machine three or four times a day?

The materials management department, which controlled the flow of raw material into the factory and of customer orders on to the shopfloor, did not accept Gibbon's arguments. They abhorred the sight of a machine sitting idle as the resetting took place. They argued that the more hours a machine was cutting metal, the more efficient the factory. A huge stack of work-in-progress was a security blanket to them. It meant a machine would never be starved of work. If lead times were too long, they blamed the production department, including Gibbon's production engineers. Gibbon's youth and aggressive support of his ideas alienated managers of some of the other departments at Reading. 'I had a vision, I could see how to do things better. I had the passion to want to do it better. I just got frustrated and the passion came out as aggression,' Gibbon said. The older managers saw him as an impatient young man, his head stuffed with impractical ideas from university. He lost his battle to cut batch sizes.

'I needed to take a different tack,' Gibbon resolved. The new tack he hit upon was technology. Computer-numerically-controlled (CNC) machine tools would cut set-up time dramatically. If it took one hour instead of three to set up a machine for a cutting operation, then the batch sizes could be cut too. CNC tools used a computer to control the movement of the cutting tool and the workpiece. They were faster to set up, faster to operate and more flexible. They could do more operations on wider size ranges of components. They were also more accurate. Each CNC machine could replace as many as half a dozen old machines. But they were not cheap. Gibbon put forward a plan to spend £450,000 on five machines. In 1983, at a company that was stingy on capital investment, it was a considerable sum.

The investment required the approval of the TI Group (as the company was renamed in 1982). With Radcliffe's backing, Gibbon laboured for weeks preparing his presentation. He covered every detail of the proposal, including savings from the machines in money, manpower and delivery times. The board was won over by his meticulous thoroughness, and his passion. 'This was the most important thing in my life. It was the most important thing for Crane,' he said. It was still TI policy that all subsidiaries bought machine tools from TI's machine manufacturer Matrix Churchill. Matrix Churchill's CNC machines were not as versatile as Japanese models. Gibbon and his team worked for months with

Matrix Churchill engineers to customise the machines to include additional features they wanted.

Melanie Pople joined Crane as a trainee production engineer in 1983. The system she found was highly regimented and old-fashioned. Production engineers were divided up into two divisions, planning and work study. Planning engineers wrote down in detail how each job in the factory had to be done, and work study engineers went around the factory with stopwatches making sure everybody was efficient. 'Crane had been used to trading on its past successes and waiting for people to come to us for orders,' said Pople. When Gibbon was made head of production engineering at Reading, he abolished the planning and work study divisions. Instead production engineers would work on specific projects, with a specific objective. Pople was an enthusiastic supporter of Gibbon's innovations. Gibbon's obsession with detail made for hard work and late nights. But she was captivated by the challenge and by his vision that manufacturing could be a competitive edge at Crane. 'In the old days, you more or less chose a machine tool by saying this one looks big enough to do the job. With Bob, we analysed the performance envelope with respect to speeds, power, feeds and the financial aspects of each purchase.'

The shopfloor workforce at Crane was largely apathetic. They regarded the university-trained production engineers as smug and arrogant and resented their control over the factory. Gibbon's working-class origins helped him build relationships with the shopfloor workers. On Saturdays, he played football with them. All week long, he spent time on the shopfloor, trying to enlist them in his war to change manufacturing. He pumped them for their views about the strengths and weaknesses of the machines. He explained how cutting batch quantities could help eliminate their problems. 'It's like salesmanship,' said Gibbon. 'You find out where a guy is coming from, you ask a lot of questions, you listen and then you trade a bit of information that will give you credibility. You build a rapport, and at the end of the day you are building a common solution.'

After the new CNC machines arrived, Gibbon tried an experiment. He persuaded the materials department to try reducing the batch size of one frequently ordered part, a six-inch wide stainless steel retainer ring. Instead of releasing the order only when fifty or more were needed, they would release orders for the retainer as soon as they came in. It worked. In a short time, lead time for the retainer fell from six weeks to two. Gibbon began to make converts. More products were put on reduced batch sizes. By 1985, the average lead time across the whole factory was down from twenty-five weeks to seven.

It was a major achievement. But Gibbon wanted to go further. You can always improve, he said. Cellular manufacture was the key to the next breakthrough, he said. This step would transform the factory, the people in it, and the whole of John Crane. In 1985, cellular manufacture, like just-in-time production, was not widely known in Europe. Gibbon knew these ideas from his course at UMIST, where he had studied them and often seen them in operation at small, advanced factories around the UK. Gibbon studied earlier versions of cellular manufacturing which dated from well before the concept became popular in Japan. A British version, known as group technology, had enjoyed a brief vogue in the 1960s, but did not catch on. Gibbon had read and been impressed by the writings of the founder of group technology, John Burbidge. 'It was a very powerful technique, but you had to go the whole hog,' Gibbon said. 'But the British, because of the way we are, we wouldn't go the whole hog. They played at it and it didn't work, so they blamed the technology.'

Cellular manufacture meant a team or 'cell' of five or six men would take responsibility for all the operations involved in making the components of a seal. Many employees had spent twenty years operating or setting just one kind of machine. In the new system, every cell member would set and operate all the machines in his cell. The factory would be much more flexible. Once the cells mastered their tasks, they would take responsibility themselves for reducing throughput time, lead time and work-in-progress. But it was a big leap in its demands on shopfloor employees. Instead of a man sitting at a machine, a stack of rings in a bin behind him, comfortable in the knowledge that as long as he was cutting metal he was discharging his responsibilities, now everybody would be part of the challenge of hitting the weekly targets. 'People are the key,' said Gibbon. He pushed, prodded and persuaded the workers that they had the capacity to become multiskilled and handle the greater responsibilities.

The factory's foremen, called charge-hands, led the transformation. 'We handed a lot of the decision-making to the charge-hands, and they seized it with both hands,' said production engineer Melanie Pople. The results sometimes surprised even Bob Gibbon.

Steve Adkins had joined Crane from school in 1971. He had no particular interest in engineering when he took the job. When he was twenty, his mother died and Adkins had to take care of his younger brother who was still in school. So he was stuck at Crane. He drifted into union affairs. He acquired a reputation as one of the more combative, difficult men on the shopfloor. For a while he was a shop steward, but soon grew disillusioned with the hypocrisy of the union leadership. Lanky, sandy-haired, full of nervous energy, at thirty-one Adkins was ready for a change. He was bored with his monotonous job operating a machine on the night-shift.

'I suddenly realised this isn't what I want out of life,' he said. 'I didn't want to stay on the shopfloor.' He spoke to Gibbon, who promised him new opportunities were about to open up. Many of the older workers were frightened of the demands of cellular manufacture. Gibbon needed younger, intelligent men like Adkins to lead the others. Adkins became a cell supervisor.

It took Steve Adkins two weeks to learn how to operate the new CNC machine tools. With fifteen years' experience on machines, he quickly grasped how to program the computer to control the three-dimensional movements of tool and workpiece. 'It took me an afternoon to teach him trigonometry,' said Pople. Later, she asked Adkins to work with her on a machine-buying project. He was flattered at being involved in an investment decision involving

£250,000 on high-technology CNC machines. Ten years younger than Adkins and the only woman in the factory, they formed a close, mutually supportive working relationship. His practical knowledge of people and manufacturing complemented her engineering skills. 'In his own sweet way, Steve was very arrogant and self-confident. He was not afraid to tell you where you were going wrong and he was never afraid to discipline people who needed it.'

Gibbon introduced monthly review meetings, with all the cell supervisors. He gave them details of Crane's performance on sales, orders, profits, lead times, late orders and other vital numbers. They shared the data with the men. The openness helped build team spirit. Urged on by Gibbon, the men began to take the initiative. 'Bob believed everybody at work has got something to put in and they should put it in,' said Adkins. 'He didn't like you coming up with an idea and not doing anything about it. If you had an idea you had to do it, and he would back you.'

Adkins became an informal leader inside the Reading factory, passing on skills, challenging the men and motivating them. He took over the CNC course from Pople, teaching other workers how to use the machines. He was also leader of the drill-ring cell, most complex of the factory's cells. He took control over scheduling work in the factory, and took the initiative in experimenting with ever-smaller batch sizes. Seeing it as a personal challenge, be brought average batch sizes down from seventy-five pieces in 1987 to twenty-five by 1991 and fifteen in 1992. He worked on increasing the efficiency of the cell lay-out, cutting machine downtime and raising quality levels. In an old building on a Reading industrial estate, the factory was crowded and noisy. After 1987, Crane bought state-of-the-art Japanese CNC machines, but there was still a lot of older equipment on the shopfloor. The first-floor canteen was small and rudimentary. But the team spirit was palpable. On the canteen wall was a chart showing monthly sales. Adkins had many projects underway: he was aiming to cut the scrap rate to 0.3 per cent. He had plans to reduce the absentee rate. As responsibility cascaded down from management to supervisors, the distinction between management and men became ever more blurred. Blurring it further, Adkins gave up his CNC training role, transferring the responsibility for training new employees to cell members. 'You end up with a much better skilled man because those guys will not let him move on until he really is as good as they are on the machines.'

Absenteeism declined dramatically. 'If a guy is out sick, we say to him, look, it's not the company you're affecting, it's your mates,' said Adkins. 'You're letting them down because it's them who are going to have to work that much harder because you are not here.'

Adkins attributed the wholesale transformation at Reading to the cellular system giving the men a sense of 'job ownership'. In the old system, after a man performed an operation on a part he never saw the part again. In the new, U-shaped, cells, every cell member saw workpieces come in and finished components leave. 'A guy might be operating one machine today and a different one tomorrow, so if he caused a problem on one, he'd find himself having to cope with that problem the next day,' said Adkins.

Martin Smith was another cell supervisor who rose to the challenge of the new system. As tool-room supervisor, he kept the tools used by the machines and prepared them for each job. Melanie Pople wrote a computer programme to keep stock and assemble kits of tools for each job. She showed Smith how to use it. He was intrigued by the computer – he had never used one before. Smith was twenty-eight. Tall and dark-haired, with a wry sense of humour, Smith never liked school and left at sixteen with two CSEs. But he had the intuitive mathematical skills to understand computer logic. Pople taught him the d-Base language. In the evenings he took the computer manual home and studied it. 'In two weeks, he was better at it than me,' said Pople.

Soon Smith wanted a bigger challenge. He decided to learn 'C', the language most widely used by professional programmers to write custom-made programmes for business and industry. 'It was supposed to be quite clever,' said Smith. He got hold of a copy of 'C' on a floppy disk and an instruction manual. He bought himself a PC for home. 'Whenever I could sneak a bit of time at work and at home, I taught myself,' he said. He wanted to try his hand writing a programme for a real-life project. He asked around at the factory and Adkins suggested the DNC project. DNC (Direct Numerical Control) tied all the factory's computer-controlled machine tools into one network and allowed an operator to send cutting programmes from one desktop PC to any machine in the shop. A programme to manage communication between the machines and a PC was a far from simple task. But Smith decided to have a go. The programme he wrote worked so well that they decided to use it in the factory. Around the same time, production engineer Andy Caffyn was quoted an estimate for a ready-made DNC programme for Crane's Slough factory. It cost £75,000. Caffyn reckoned that Smith's programme was better. 'It's tailor-made for our factory, and when it needs to be updated, Martin does it for us,' said Caffyn. It was a classic example of how empowerment turned a semi-skilled operative into a highly-skilled professional. Smith was determined to build his computer skills further. Still based in the toolroom, Smith took on computer projects from all around John Crane. 'It's just natural that once you get involved in something you want to keep learning,' he said.

Gibbon asked Adkins to give a presentation to Crane's operations managers from all over Europe on the cell system at the Reading factory. The request set off a bout of introspection for Adkins.

'I had never given a presentation to anyone in my life and I thought: do I really want to do this?' He decided he couldn't let the opportunity pass by. He told Gibbon he would do it. It was, he said, one of the most nerve-racking moments of his life. 'My stomach was doing somersaults, but I went in there and did it.' It was such a success that Adkins was asked back to do more, for TI management and other overseas visitors.

In 1990, when Gibbon asked him to do a presentation updating the European operations managers on further progress at Reading, Adkins suggested making a video instead. 'Bob was always telling us do something different, don't have tunnel vision. So I thought, instead of just standing there doing a presentation, let's do a video.' With a colleague, Adkins created a twenty-minute video. The video explained how each of the cells at Reading worked, and how each man was trained to operate every machine in the cell. It talked about the savings in time and cost achieved by the cells. Editing it on his home VCR, Adkins backed the pictures with the old pop song 'You Ain't Seen Nothing Yet' as a soundtrack. It captured the enthusiasm and dedication of the Reading workforce. At the end of the presentation, the operations managers stood and applauded. Gibbon made an embarrassed Adkins stand up and take a bow.

Gibbon found and applied ideas from everywhere to improving manufacturing at Crane. At Toyota in Japan, an auto engineer named Shigeo Shingo pioneered a system for reducing the set-up time on machine tools. Shingo claimed that any machine could be retooled and reset in ten minutes or less. He called his technique 'Single Minute Exchange of Die', or SMED. The key lay in planning the set-up well. At Crane, set-ups on the CNC machines usually took more than an hour. Adkins went on a course to learn Shingo's method. He used the SMED techniques at Reading to cut set-up times in half.

Gibbon gave regular guest lectures in manufacturing at Brunel University. 'I don't think it's right just to take things out of the educational system,' he said. 'You have to give something back too.' He asked Adkins to give a demonstration and lecture on SMED. The cell supervisor with no O-levels was nervous at giving a lecture to a group of post-graduate engineering students. Some of the students were a little cocky when Adkins asked them to try their hand at setting a machine. They came down a peg when they discovered it took them twice as long to do what he made look easy. The lecture was a success and he was asked to return the next semester.

In 1992, Adkins enrolled in a DMS (Diploma of Management Studies) course. He wanted financial and management skills to help him move into a management position. He found being 'back at school' hard work. He studied every evening after work. His wife helped out, typing essays for him. He worked at it with the determination of someone making up for fifteen years' lost time. While working towards the DMS he was already thinking about the next stage, a Master's degree. He laughed at the contrast between the sullen shop steward of a decade before and the ambitious student of today. 'If somebody had told me ten years ago that by the end of 1993 I'd be in a position to do an MBA, I'd have told'em in no uncertain terms where to go.' He attributed the change to Bob Gibbon. He expressed his gratitude to Gibbon with an almost religious fervour.

'Bob is a motivator. He pushes people. He sets high targets and he expects you to achieve it. Most of the time you think I can't do that, but you end up achieving it.'

Adkins's enthusiasm was shared by nearly all the men at the Reading factory. They felt the steady increase in responsibility and the constant arrival of new challenges made the job more interesting and rewarding than before. Their incentives included the financial but seemed more psychological. They enjoyed being more involved in decisions. They enjoyed experimenting with new technology and new methods. They looked forward to coming to work in the mornings. It was not a feeling they remembered having in the early 1980s. 'We're just a load of guys doing the best we can and enjoying ourselves in the meantime and I think if you can enjoy yourself as well as get the work out then you are really lucky,' said Adkins.

Still another major push on the manufacturing front came from a novel. In 1984, Mark Radcliffe gave Bob Gibbon a copy of a book called *The Goal*. It was a novel written by Israeli manufacturing consultant Eli Goldratt to illustrate his theories on improving productivity. The book told the story of a plant manager threatened with the closure of his factory in six months. In a chance encounter at an airport he meets a mysterious Israeli professor who tells him the secret of manufacturing success. In a dramatic race against time in which the hero narrowly avoids losing his wife as well as his job, he implements the new theory, saves the factory and gets a promotion as well. Goldratt added a bit of sex and soap opera to liven up his story. Yet the real passion in the book is in the author's description of the innovative use of machine tools and conveyor lines. Gibbon loved the book. 'In a simple form, it related everything I was trying to do,' he said. 'It communicated what I was trying to say in a more powerful way than I could.' He bought a box of *The Goal* from the publisher and walked around the Reading shopfloor handing them out.

Goldratt's philosophy, which he christened the Theory of Constraints, focused on the bottlenecks in a factory, the crucial operations that slowed down the whole of the production process. With military-like mercilessness, Goldratt's method identified, attacked and eliminated each bottleneck. Like Goldratt, Gibbon believed that lead time – the time it took to turn an order into a finished product – was the key indicator of manufacturing success.

'If you get your lead times down it means you must have your quality improved, you must have got rid of your inefficiencies, you must have got rid of your inconsistencies and all the policies that screw you up. You have to have improved your communication, and you have to have your people involved. When all that comes together your lead time is compressed.

'It's not that it's the most important thing in itself, but it's the *manifestation* of everything that makes you better.'

On a visit to the Reading factory, TI's group managing director Sid Taylor spoke to the workforce and, citing *The Goal*, stressed the importance of eliminating bottlenecks. One of the workers responded by quoting part of the book back to him. 'That really blew his socks off,' laughed Gibbon.

By 1988, lead times at Reading had fallen to two weeks. Crane staff were studying Goldratt's follow-up to *The Goal*, which took batch manufacturing to a further stage. Goldratt called his new model Drum-Buffer-Rope. The entire production process marched to the 'drumbeat' of the slowest machine. Work was pulled through production as if on a taut rope. It was as if the entire factory pulsated to a single heartbeat.

Between 1981 and 1990, John Crane's sales in the Europe, Middle East and Africa (EMA) region more than doubled from

£28 million to £70 million. Operating profits rose from just over £1 million to £15 million and sales per employee rose by 130 per cent. The management team led by Mark Radcliffe improved sales, distribution and product design. But manufacturing made a big contribution. In those years, the UK factories increased output by more than 30 per cent to 434,000 components while cutting the inventory to sales ratio in half and cutting lead times down from twelve weeks at Reading and twenty-six weeks at Slough to two weeks at each factory. In 1991, Bob Gibbon was promoted to managing director of John Crane UK. He was the youngest managing director in John Crane, running the company's second biggest country operation.

Although Gibbon was now less involved in day-to-day manufacturing operations, his influence persisted. 'He is an inspiration to a lot of people here,' said his boss, head of the EMA region David Crofts. Operations director Mike Wooster, twenty years Gibbon's senior, started at Crane as an apprentice in 1968. In the early 1980s, when he was Gibbon's boss, he told Gibbon that one day he expected to be working for him. 'He was different to anyone we'd ever had here. You could see in his eyes that he believed in what he was trying to do.'

Gibbon was motivated by more than personal success and the success of Crane. 'I have some weird concept that I can do some social good in industry,' he said. He was indelibly affected by his childhood in a dying Welsh mining valley. As Gibbon saw it, if industry declined then life itself – social, cultural, personal and family life – suffered. 'Industry is the fundamental fabric of wealth generation and therefore stability and everything else in society,' Gibbon said. 'If you value and support industry, then you are supporting society in a broader sense and all the things that make it good.'

Gibbon had what he called a spiritual belief: the most important thing was for people to recognise and fulfil their potential. Inner satisfaction came from making the effort. Too many in industry never tried. He saw his role as engineer, manager and managing director to motivate people to recognise their own potential. That

paid dividends to the company, its shareholders, but most importantly to the individuals themselves. 'If you can get people to trust
you and really try to do their best, not because of external rewards
like money but for what they can get internally in their own mind,
then they are going to be very powerful and contributory people
and they are going to gain much more from it.'

In addition to lectures at Brunel University, Gibbon gave
monthly night classes in Goldratt's Theory of Constraints. Most
of those who came worked not at Crane but at other companies in
the Slough area. Managers, shopfloor workers, salesmen, they
came to the lonely meeting room in the deserted Crane building
late in the evening to hear Gibbon preach how this enigmatic
theory could help them realise their potential in their job and
inside themselves. 'There is so much constraint and so much
opportunity in manufacturing that everyone can be creative,
everyone can contribute, from the guy on a machine to the guy
who sweeps the floor or the managing director,' said Gibbon.
'There is more creativity in manufacturing than in most other
jobs. The only limitations are in people's minds.'

His one regret was that he sometimes alienated or frightened
people. Even some of his greatest supporters at Crane said he
could often be pushy or aggressive. Gibbon paused for a moment
to consider that. 'It's only because I have a passion to make things
better,' he replied. 'I believe if you have the potential you shouldn't
waste it. You should actively get out there and fulfil the potential
that you have, as an individual or a collectivity. It's just like
football.'

When Christopher Lewinton arrived as chief executive of crisis-
torn TI Group in 1986, he quickly seized on Crane Packing as
the model of the kind of world-class engineering company around
which he intended to rebuild the group. An engineer himself,
Lewinton's background was in razor blades and consumer appliances. The consumers of razor blades and mechanical seals could
not have been more different. But in their highly demanding
manufacture, and their market sensitivity, there was a certain

kinship between the products. In the 1970s, Lewinton built Wilkinson Sword into a major force in the US market. He ran Wilkinson's blade business and garden tool business. 'The tolerances on a razor blade are in angstroms,' said Lewinton. 'It's very high engineering. I picked up a strange combination of engineering and marketing background.'

In 1985, a tiny engineering company called Evered, led by two Asian-born entrepreneur brothers, the Abdullahs, came close to launching a hostile bid for TI. They failed only because they could not quite raise all the financing they needed. But for months, City shareholders and TI executives alike watched in horror. The greatest manufacturing name in the Midlands was under siege from two little-known entrepreneurs. It was a traumatic experience for the inhabitants of TI House who concluded that radical action was needed to solve the company's problems. In 1984, a new chairman took over. It was not enough, argued two vocal non-executive directors, Sir John Cuckney and Michael Davies. (Davies would display independence again in 1993 when as a director of British Airways he disagreed with Lord King over the Virgin dirty tricks affair.) Christopher Lewinton was invited to take over as chief executive and deputy chairman of TI. The board gave him a free hand to do whatever was necessary to turn the company around.

Founded in 1915, Tube Investments grew by acquisition into a sprawling giant. Twice it had profited from nationalisation of the steel industry, selling its steel interests to the government in the 1950s and again in the 1960s. It ploughed the profits into acquisitions of a wide variety of engineering businesses. By the 1970s TI companies produced everything 'from bikes to kettles'. Its dozens of brand names could be found everywhere from the US to India, Siberia to southern Africa. Each brand name was a separate subsidiary. TI was not so much a company as a federation of largely autonomous baronies. Crane Packing was one. From its acquisition by TI in 1947 until Mark Radcliffe's arrival in 1981, it had little involvement or interference from the parent company.

The recession of 1980 triggered a crisis at the conglomerate.

Domestic markets collapsed while the high pound wiped out many overseas markets. Many of TI's businesses were commodity products such as ordinary steel tubes or gas cylinders. They were highly sensitive to price competition. Exports could not survive the $2 pound. Forced to confront its problems, TI sold and shut down dozens of businesses. By 1983 its workforce had fallen by half to 31,000. But many of the subsidiaries were still struggling, hindered by lack of clear strategy and a woeful lack of investment. When Mark Radcliffe tried to sort out the Broadwall complex near Birmingham, he found some facilities had not been modernised since the site was built in 1870. TI bought £4 million worth of oil to power the Broadwall plant. 'The pipelines were so old and inefficient, only £2 million reached the plant,' Radcliffe recalled.

Glamorous brand names, their preservation and promotion, seemed to have replaced profitability or any other measure of performance as the TI corporate goal. Most glittering of all was Raleigh Bicyles. 'I remember after Raleigh won one Tour de France, somebody at TI House suggested we consider changing the Crane name to Raleigh,' harrumphed Mark Radcliffe, managing director of the Crane subsidiary from 1981 to 1990. 'I told him: every precision engineer in the world knew the name John Crane. What did Raleigh mean to them? Bugger-all!'

For a decade, Raleigh was the albatross around TI's neck. It drained the company of funds and nobody had an answer to its problems, which only grew worse as one former British colony after another stopped buying British bikes. 'The first three things a new nation does is design a flag, compose a national anthem and build a bike factory,' remarked TI executive James Roe. The Iranian revolution wiped out one important market, economic crisis in Nigeria another, and troubles in southern Africa a third. With a sprawling site in Nottingham with its own canal running through it, Raleigh suffered from overmanning and an antiquated product range. 'The best part of £50 million was lost in bicycles over two or three years,' recalled David Harding, who then worked in TI's corporate planning department.

By the time Christopher Lewinton arrived, radical change was long overdue. With his distinguished silver hair and a disarmingly friendly yet authoritative charm, Lewinton looked like a US Senator as cast by Hollywood. Born in London he had lived half his life in the US and spoke with a mid-Atlantic accent. At the age of twenty-eight Lewinton moved to the US to run Wilkinson Sword's US division. He spent a decade there, acquiring an open, aggressive, entrepreneurial approach to business. Lewinton saw his tasks at TI as creating a new corporate culture oriented towards growth and success, while simultaneously refocusing the company on those businesses where it could be world class. Lewinton planned to take TI out of every business where it had no competitive edge. He would use the resources freed up to concentrate on a small number of niches where the group's core strength in engineering could lift it to world leadership. 'What you have to decide in life is what you are good at, what is your strategy, and ruthlessly pursue it and execute it,' he said. 'Do not be seduced into the byways!'

Lewinton was shocked by what he found in July 1986 when he joined TI. The staff was deeply demoralised by years of staving off crisis. Management was badly paid, even by the standards of Midlands engineering. With money short, the group rewarded its people through status and perks. It was encumbered with hierarchy and class division. Finance executive Mike Robins recalled visiting the machine tools subsidiary Matrix. 'The first thing they wanted to know was what my position was at TI House so they'd know which canteen I should eat at,' Robins recalled. There were four canteens at TI Matrix. 'It was a classic example of what was wrong with British industry in the 1960s and 1970s,' said Robins.

Lewinton aimed to replace the culture of hierarchy, status and revered brand names with a new performance-oriented, meritocratic culture. The new focus was simple: management would build growing profitable businesses that would make money for shareholders and for themselves. 'TI was so diffuse, it worshipped too many different gods,' Lewinton said. 'I came in with the view that the thing that brought value was EPS [earnings per share]. If you grow EPS over time, and have strong cash flow, then you create wealth.' In his first month, he made a dramatic move to illustrate where he intended to take the company. He took out a personal loan of £100,000 and invested it in TI shares. 'It doesn't sound a lot of money now, but to me it was a lot at the time,' he recalled.

The next morning he called a meeting of senior executives and told them of his investment. 'I said to them we all have a rare chance here to make some serious money. If we adopt this strategy and work reasonably hard, and execute it ruthlessly, we can double our money. In three years.'

Lewinton's second move was as ruthless as the first was optimistic. He shut TI House. He replaced it with a lean, functional head office in London's Curzon Street. The small HQ heralded a new structure in which power and responsibility would be devolved down to the operating companies. In the summer of 1986 TI employed 400 people in its head office, including 200 at TI House and 200 on payroll in another building. They had sixty at the new head office. 'People started to say this is serious,' he said.

In addition to the financial savings, Lewinton believed that closing a corporate headquarters was an invaluable, perhaps essential, step, for creating total cultural change. He was influenced by a big mistake he had made in an earlier takeover. In 1973, Wilkinson Sword made a 'reverse takeover' of the larger British Match. Lewinton became managing director of the enlarged group and set out to reform the lacklustre culture at British Match. But he left the British Match headquarters, in London's Aldgate, untouched. 'I failed completely,' he said. 'Two years later I closed it.'

In 1990 TI moved its headquarters to a shiny new building on the outskirts of Abingdon, Oxfordshire. TI House was sold and became the Swallow Hotel, Birmingham's deluxe five-star hotel. The vast reception area of TI House became the hotel reception, its marble floors and polished mahogany columns intact. In their renovation, Swallow Hotels uncovered an old marble staircase with a balustrade in rich mahogany topped with a piece of hefty steel tubing. They kept the balustrade as a memento of the building's former occupiers. A cynic might say that the three restaurants and five boardrooms were a more appropriate memento.

David Harding was a TI veteran who became part of Lewinton's inner circle. He was impressed by Lewinton's action-orientation. When the new boss said he would do something, he did it, and quickly. 'Within hours of Lewinton arriving, things started to change,' Harding recalled. One change was in TI's stingy pay policy. Lewinton introduced higher levels of pay for managers, with a much larger component of performance-related pay. It helped him recruit the people he needed to turn the group around. It also contributed to the change of morale among depressed TI veterans. 'You had to lift them up, spark them up, enthuse them and make them feel like they were going to win,' said Lewinton. The most important element in the people who would run the new world-class engineering company Lewinton wanted to build was, he said, the knowledge of how to make money – for themselves, for the company and for the shareholders. 'There are some people in industry who are very bright yet have no idea how to make money. They think it's slightly immoral, or they think the product is an end in itself. I wanted people who were hungry, who wanted to drive the company forward, who thrived on the excitement of success.'

Once Lewinton 'ripped the lid off' the old culture, most of the people he relied on to execute the new strategy were TI veterans who became converts to the new style. The talent was always there but had not been permitted to blossom. The inner core who helped Lewinton build the new TI included divisional CEOs Mark Radcliffe and Sid Taylor, strategists David Harding and James Roe, and finance director Michael Garner. They were all with the company before Lewinton arrived. Before he joined TI, Lewinton had had an inside look at other demoralised companies. In 1978 the successful Wilkinson Sword was taken over by Allegheny International, an American conglomerate with a polyglot mixture of businesses. He believed that in the typical company with an imbedded culture of failure about half the executives would successfully make a transition to a new culture of achievement. 'A quarter become complete believers, another quarter would like to but can't quite make it, but they still add value. There's a quarter who find the whole thing a foreign language and should go on day one, and then there's another quarter who'd like to make the transition but can't.'

For years, TI management fretted over Raleigh, commissioned consultants' studies, but always backed away from radical action. The obvious solution was to sell it, but that would lead to a major write-off on TI's balance sheet, which could upset banks and shareholders. Within weeks, Lewinton decided Raleigh would go. Said Harding: 'He had done some work and found a potential purchaser. He said I don't care about the balance sheet, just sell it!' The deal was completed in March 1987. TI received £18 million from an American-backed leveraged buyout company, Derby International.

In March 1987, Lewinton announced TI's new strategy. The City of London, the financial press and not a few TI executives were shocked. It was no surprise that Lewinton wanted out of commodity businesses like plain vanilla steel tubes, or sectors like machine tools where technological progress had left TI far behind. But Lewinton also proposed to sell off TI's consumer appliance businesses. Brands like Creda, Glow-Worm, Parkray and Russell Hobbs were household names in Britain. They were the geese that laid the company's golden eggs, providing half of TI's £43 million profit in 1986. They provided *all* its profits in the early 1980s. Lewinton proposed to rebuild the company with a series of deals which were then little more than a dream in his head and a few lines on a piece of paper under the words 'TI's Mission Statement'. It was a radical and risky plan indeed.

Lewinton believed manufacturing industry was set to go increasingly global. He planned to use the resources freed up by selling businesses to move TI into global leadership in a handful of carefully chosen engineering niches. TI's appliance businesses were successful in Britain, but on the world scale they were tiny. They were mostly 'me-too' products, without a major competitive edge. In 1986, globalisation was evident only in some industries. It was underway, for instance, in the automotive industry. Lewinton believed the trend would gather force, and spread throughout the 'supply chain' in the major engineering industries.

'Over the last few years, a mutual dependency between the supplier and the customer has developed,' he said. 'The Japanese taught the world that quality sells a product. Quality, knowledge and service were becoming the critical factors. If you wanted to be a global supplier in those fields, you could not do it across a wide range of products because your pockets weren't deep enough. So you had to choose the products you could win with, the products with sufficient added value so you could compete on a global basis.' Lewinton coined the phrase *shrink, concentrate, and grow* to describe TI's strategy in the late 1980s. He wanted to be in businesses where TI could be number one or two in the world. Market leadership would translate into price leadership and strong profitability, which would finance the technological progress to maintain the leadership position.

He found two potential world leader businesses in tiny nuggets within TI. One was Crane Packing. Its turnover was around 5 per cent of TI's total 1986 turnover of £842 million, but Crane Packing was Europe's leader in sealing technology. Its relationships with tens of thousands of customers in a wide variety of industries was a further bulwark to its number one position. Crane's US counterpart, John Crane USA, enjoyed a similar role in the US. John Crane USA still owned 49 per cent of the Slough-based European business, Crane Packing. Founded in 1917 by Chicago engineer John Crane, the American company developed the original sealing technology and built a worldwide business, only to divest its Europe and Middle East arm in 1936 when war loomed. (In 1963 it bought back a 49 per cent interest in Crane Packing.) By 1986, the US Crane business was in the hands of American leveraged buyout specialists Kohlberg, Kravis, Roberts. An LBO dealer was not a long-term holder of industrial businesses, and Lewinton anticipated the possibility of combining the two halves of the Crane empire into one world leader. The combination of the two Cranes would yield a company with a 30 per cent market share in mechanical seals, four times that of its nearest rival. In many of his deals, Lewinton took shrewd advantage of the upheavals junk bonds and LBOs wrought on America's manufacturing base.

The second nugget of a world-leader business was in TI's small-diameter tube business, which subsequently became Bundy. Their major customers were the automotive and refrigeration manufacturers. Like Crane, Bundy employed sophisticated, proprietary technologies. Bundy's patented process for building double-walled tubes made them the preferred choice for brake tubing by most of the world's car-makers. Here, Lewinton was even more a visionary than at Crane, because TI's initial toehold in the industry was smaller. But buying world-leader businesses would have been too expensive. Lewinton aimed to *build* them by acquiring a series of regional 'building blocks'. 'You buy the blocks, strip out [ie sell] the bits you don't want, and create a world strategy,' he said. 'You put the management in place for a global business, you take the best practices and products from each of the blocks, and you gradually upgrade all the building blocks until you have a world-class business.'

From the beginning of 1987 to the end of 1988, TI bought and sold companies at the rate of almost one deal a month. It was the riskiest period for Lewinton's strategy. As Saunders did in the early 1980s at Guinness, Lewinton restructured the group by buying and selling companies. The support of bankers and City shareholders was critical. A missed profit forecast, an untimely departure by a member of senior management, or any one of a dozen different events could have caused the City to lose faith and desert the strategy. Lewinton did not hide his strategy behind a veil of secrecy. A mission statement issued early in 1987 made it plain that TI intended to exit its consumer businesses and build its specialised engineering businesses. Open discussion was a vital tool to help convert outsiders and insiders alike.

Some of the deals which followed were complex. When KKR refused to sell John Crane USA on its own, TI had to buy KKR's Florida-based manufacturing conglomerate Houdaille Industries (for £308 million) and then sell most of Houdaille back to a management team as a new company, Idex (for £112 million). 'For eight months I worked on that deal and did nothing else,' recalled David Harding. The deal was completed in September 1987. Lewinton enjoyed dealing with famous New York deal-maker Henry Kravis of KKR. 'He was utterly straight and charming and never failed to have a sense of humour,' said Lewinton. Kravis took a stake in Idex, making a further profit when the company was taken public in 1989. Said Lewinton: 'I always try to tell our people: you should never do one deal and walk away thinking you're a hero because you got it cheap. You should always be able to go back to the same person and do another deal.'

Lewinton admired Kravis's 'coolness' when negotiating big deals. Lewinton was not always so cool. David Harding recalled the tense period surrounding the October 1987 Crash when TI withdrew a crucial bid for American tube company Bundy, resubmitting it at a lower level in early 1988. 'Bundy were having a board meeting and we were sitting in a hotel room waiting for a phone call from them and Chris was terrified the telephone system wouldn't work.' The deal was completed for £86 million.

The two core businesses, Crane and Bundy, grew through recession, achieving 1992 profits of £47 million and £38 million, up 11 per cent and 12 per cent respectively over the previous year. TI had some rationalisation to do when it acquired Bundy. Four old plants in North America were shut down, and a new greenfield site was built in Ohio in the American Midwest. But it was a truly global business, with operations in 23 countries. In addition to its trademark 'Bundyweld' double-walled technology, the company owned industry-leading technologies in tube-bending. In the automotive market, Bundy focused its efforts on persuading customers to commission it to supply complete brake and fuel fluid-carrying systems instead of just lengths of tubing. The more advanced car-makers, recognising Bundy's expertise in designing and building complete systems, were already converted. Bundy's plant in Washington on Tyneside delivered systems to the nearby Nissan plant for both the Micra and Primera models. The Bundy so-called 'satellite plant' was an integral part of Nissan's just-in-time system. In 1993, Bundy delivered to Nissan every two hours. That was scheduled to speed up to every thirty-eight minutes in late 1993.

In 1992 Opel of Germany, a subsidiary of General Motors, stopped doing their own tube manipulation and contracted the work out to Bundy's German plant. Bundy did not win the business on price, but on quality and reliability. They had far more experience than the in-house engineers who had previously done the work at Opel. 'What's important in this business is knowledge, service and value,' said Bundy chief executive John Potter. 'Our asset base is not in hard assets, but in the knowledge, service and value our people provide.'

Outside Japan, Bundy had a market share that varied from 30 per cent to 50 per cent. It worked assiduously to build and consolidate that edge by extending the added value Bundy incorporated in its product. Ten years ago, the small TI tube business provided straight tubes to car-makers. Increasingly, Bundy coated the tubes, bent them, fixed them into systems, and fitted them with innovative 'quick-connect' connectors which allowed them to be fitted to cars with a twist of the wrist instead of a power-wrench. From its base in brake systems, the company was steadily moving on to fuel systems. It was also moving into new countries. In a 1992 coup, Bundy won an exclusive contract to supply Czech car-maker Skoda with brake systems. Bundy had never done any work in the formerly Communist country. 'Within thirty-six hours [of the Skoda approach] we had our people in Czechoslovakia,' Potter said. 'We now have a facility, we have the business, and we have taken it away from two German competitors,' said Potter.

TI strategist Harding commented: 'People move heaven and earth to make something happen at TI because we are a make-it-happen sort of company. We don't talk about doing things. It is done.'

One of the few decisions on which Lewinton hesitated was on the future of TI's research and development facility, Hinxton Hall in Cambridge. With the atmosphere of a Cambridge college, for decades it did basic research in areas related to TI businesses. From the start, Lewinton knew TI did not belong in basic research. Harding often visited the Cambridge facility to talk to the researchers about their work. 'They would tell you in great detail how to make steel tubes – God knows we'd been making them for years, but there were still problems and they were working on this little bit of the process and that bit . . . But I said to them many times, give me an example of something you have invented that is now on the market.' An awkward silence invariably followed. Still, they hesitated about closing Hinxton Hall and devolving the R&D responsibilities down to the operating companies. 'We knew that to keep our leadership positions we must be working on development,' said Harding. 'We worried [if R&D was devolved] how could we really be sure those guys will do it and won't turn off the development work and just worry about the current performance?' Finally, in 1989, the decision was taken and Hinxton Hall was shut. To ensure operating managers focused on long-term development, a large component of senior managers' bonus schemes was linked to profits growth over a rolling three-year period. But there was no getting away from the subjective processes to maintain long-term growth: hiring senior managers with a strong forward-looking vision and maintaining a constant dialogue with them on product and market strategy.

'We're in the business of applying technology, not originating it,' Lewinton said. Research and development involved much more than product development. It included better manufacturing techniques, better sales engineering and better after-sales service. Crane put sales engineers into a customer's facilities for weeks or months at a time, to work with the customer's engineers, and gain a sense of what that customer's needs might be in future. 'Then if you design for that need, you've pre-sold the product,' said Lewinton. 'And you've done it in one quarter of the time.'

Thirty years ago, an international company typically mass-produced at giant complexes in one or two countries and exported around the world. Crane and Bundy each manufactured in more than a dozen countries. Crane still did considerable exporting from its two major design and manufacturing centres in the US (at Chicago) and the UK (Slough and Reading). But with forty-two manufacturing sites in twenty-three countries, Bundy's exports were relatively small. Staying close to the customer meant producing at many medium-sized sites instead of a few large ones. It also meant a constant juggling act between worldwide standard-isation and tailoring products and methods to suit local conditions and local customers. In the local companies, TI preferred to rely on natives as managers. They understood the local culture and the local customers better than a man from head office could.

Senior managers had to have solid international experience to understand the business across its entire breadth. Bundy's Potter worked for extended periods in the US and Italy before relocating to Abingdon. John Crane chief executive Bob Fisher worked in Japan after school, moving on to Singapore, Brazil and the US. He spent more than twenty years outside the UK before coming to Abingdon. A soft-spoken Scotsman, he masterminded Crane's 1991 acquisition of Dover Japan, a Japan-based seal manufacturer. The takeover was aimed at boosting Crane's presence in the large Japanese shipbuilding industry. The Far East dominated commercial shipbuilding and on the military side the Japanese navy was a valuable potential customer, larger even than the Royal Navy. 'We supply forty-nine navies around the world,' said Fisher. (Some unlikely countries for a navy, like Switzerland, were good customers of Crane seals.) The Japanese management at Dover was left intact. Fisher's only move in the first year was to put a young British finance executive into the company – partly to bring the TI philosophy to the new subsidiary, and also to build the Briton's international management skills.

'It changes you, living abroad,' said Fisher. 'It changes your perspective on how business ticks because you appreciate what happens to your products in the supply chain and you meet other business associates in the country. It's just a completely different level of understanding.'

Some business theorists including former Harvard professor Robert Reich (Secretary of Labor in the Clinton Cabinet) have written that as companies spread across more national boundaries, corporate nationality was becoming almost meaningless. John Crane's European marketing and technical director Michael Wray's experience was that nationality still mattered. Wray quit England in 1969 and went to live in the US. After seventeen years in the US, France and Switzerland he was headhunted by John Crane and returned to the UK. He pointed out that three major American multinationals he'd worked for, Caterpillar, Cummins and United Technologies, had only Americans on their boards. French auto components company Valeo had one non-Frenchman on its board – Wray – but that was unusual for a French company. 'When you get to your mid-forties, you have to say to yourself, if you really want to contribute and move on in a company, you will probably have to come back to your home country.'

TI was no different. The executive directors boasted substantial international experience, but every one was British. Lewinton said he was eager to see some non-Britons on the TI board, especially from the US, a market which accounted for one third of TI's business (making it twice as important to the company as the UK).

In 1986, Wray took a 30 per cent pay cut to leave his job in Lausanne, Switzerland where he was working for United Technologies and come to John Crane. He gave up a beautiful apartment overlooking Lake Geneva and skiing a half-hour's drive away. Eager to leave the bureaucratic world of giant American corporations, he found the climate at John Crane exhilarating, and his country completely transformed from the Britain he'd left two decades before.

'In the US today, there are many restrictive union practices, particularly in the auto industry. They are only just beginning to break down. We went through that cycle ten years earlier and I think now we have come back to the point where there is a new pride in Britain in buying British goods.'

In 1992 TI added a third major leg to its specialised engineering strategy, with a hostile takeover of the Dowty Group. Based near Cheltenham, Gloucestershire, Dowty was a world leader in key high-technology components for the aerospace industry. Dowty's previous management lost its focus when it diversified into computer software and telecommunications. In its narrowly focused aerospace businesses, landing gear, actuation systems for giant passenger jets, and propellers for smaller civil and military craft, Dowty's technology was world-class. But it was starved of capital while Dowty management wrestled with the growing problems of their electronics business and a growing debt burden.

Dowty Aerospace business was a classic specialised engineering niche. Its technology was unique and ahead of competitors in key areas. Its customer base included the great names in aerospace, such as Boeing and Airbus. It was worldwide, with major manufacturing facilities in Gloucester and Canada. In the 1980s the business had gone through major restructuring and refocusing. In 1980, 70 per cent of Dowty's business was with military customers. By 1992, it had successfully completed the crucial conversion process out of the featherbedded military world, and did 70 per cent of its business with highly competitive civil customers. It had a new $90 million production site in Montreal, Canada. Its landing gear technology, including the innovative articulated bogie rear landing gear for the Airbus A330/340 and its lightweight carbon-fibre propellers, was widely acknowledged as world-leading.

It was also poised to profit from ongoing changes in the American economy. Dowty was number three in landing gear. But both its larger competitors were subjected to leveraged buyout in the 1980s and burdened with heavy debt repayments. Industry leader Cleveland Pneumatic Corporation (CPC) pulled out of a planned collaboration with Dowty on a project for Airbus, leaving Dowty to take on the entire commitment, ultimately worth millions in additional revenue. 'We'll be number one by the end of the century,' predicted Landing Gear managing director Graham

Lockyer with confidence. Restructuring at Boeing looked likely to lead the Washington-based aerospace giant to subcontract out more design and assembly work on aircraft components, including landing gear. Within weeks of completing the takeover, Lewinton was in Washington securing agreement to place Dowty engineers inside the Boeing plant to work with Boeing engineers. A similar trend among car-makers was enabling Bundy to increase its revenue and profit per car despite recession. Lewinton's 1986 vision of the global supply chain was bearing fruit right across TI.

In September 1992, TI Group rejoined the FTSE index as one of Britain's top 100 companies. With 1992 profits of £87.4 million, the company was once again one of Britain's most profitable engineering companies. Its profit in three relatively anonymous, medium-to-high-technology businesses exceeded the levels achieved from its halcyon stable of famous brand names. With 300 manufacturing and service facilities in 114 countries, serving every major industry in the world, it was truly global. But as tightly focused as ever. 'The secret of this company is three words: focus, focus, focus,' said James Roe.

Mark Radcliffe emphasised the crucial role Chris Lewinton played in the transformation. In 1987, Lewinton asked him to negotiate the sale of TI Matrix Churchill. Renowned as one of TI's hard men, he nevertheless found it emotionally difficult to part with Britain's largest and most historic machine tool manu-facturer. The revolution at TI could never have been achieved without the benefit of the fresh perspective of an outsider at the helm, said Radcliffe. 'An insider could not have been sufficiently detached to do what had to be done.'

'We've restored TI to its former greatness,' said Lewinton. 'I'm thrilled to have been a part of it.'

FIVE

The Virgin Group

'You worked for a guy who cared about each one, individually'

In a new quayside development tucked away in a crowded corner of residential Fulham in London, overlooking the River Thames, lie the offices of John Brown Publishing Ltd. John Brown runs a publishing empire comprising four inflight magazines, the *Fortean Times*, and *Viz* magazine. *Viz*, the bimonthly 'adult comic' with characters like Freddie Fartpants and the Fat Slags, is vulgar, juvenile, offensive ... and one of the most successful UK magazine launches of the 1980s. In 1991, John Brown Publishing, 80 per cent owned by John Brown, earned pre-tax profits of £2.26 million on turnover of £7.4 million. John Brown's office is on the third floor of the new quayside development, reached by a black steel exterior staircase which hugs the side of the building, catching the brunt of the wind whipping off the Thames. The office is long and minimalist, spare white walls broken only by a few pieces of modern art and the view of the grey Thames through the windows. At a desk at one end of the room sits John Brown. A large, affable ex-public schoolboy with a swatch of dark brown hair, Mont Blanc pen at hand, Brown scarcely looks the typical *Viz* reader. He chanced upon an issue in 1986, read it, and thought it brilliantly funny. 'I instantly thought, Jesus Christ, this will be big,' recalled Brown. He was then managing director of Virgin Books. Virgin Books published no magazines, but Brown marched into the office of Robert Devereux, head of Virgin Communications and one of the four-man inner council who with Richard Branson ran the Virgin Group. 'I said I've found this magazine called *Viz*. Can we publish it? Robert gauged my enthusiasm and said yes, do it.'

Three years later, John Brown wanted to be his own boss. He asked Devereux if he could have *Viz* magazine, then steadily growing in popularity, for his own company. Devereux agreed, and talked Richard Branson, at first reluctant to part with the successful magazine, around to the idea that *Viz* would do best with Brown at the helm. Brown went to see Branson at his Holland Park mansion to finalise the deal. He said he needed £15,000 cash to start John Brown Publishing. Branson gave him £20,000 in return for a 20 per cent stake. 'The negotiations took about twelve seconds,' said Brown. Today, *Viz* sells 1.1 million copies an issue, making it the fifth best-selling magazine in the UK. On the bare walls of Brown's office hangs a scuffed, time-worn plastic calculator, the kind that sells for £10 at WH Smith. Although framed, the calculator is not a piece of modern art, but a gift from *Viz* managing director Chris Donald. Donald used the calculator to work out how much money he and his youthful band of Geordie anarcho-vulgarian cartoonists would earn from their magazine. By 1992, Donald's original calculation was off by a couple of zeros. Virgin's initial investment in John Brown Publishing was paid back in the first year. Today Virgin's annual profit from Brown represents twenty times that initial investment. As for 'giving away' the magazine to Brown, Devereux commented: 'It's an act of generosity I don't regret for one second. It would not be selling a million copies an issue without John.'

In 1987, two video engineers in Los Angeles, an American named Steve Hendricks and an émigré Englishman, Kelvin Duckett, were seeking to open a new video editing and post-production business that would make first-class customer service as important as engineering and creative excellence. When American investors turned them down, Hendricks and Duckett approached the Virgin

Group. Within weeks, the pair reached a deal with Virgin's Robert Devereux: they had to scale down their initial ambitions for a 50 per cent stake to 15 per cent, but in return Virgin agreed to put up $2 million cash, and leave the operation of the business to Hendricks and Duckett. 'They had an amazing way of doing business. They gave us the money and said you guys know what you're doing. Go do it,' said Hendricks, a broad-shouldered, fair-haired all-American boy with a big, irrepressible smile. Within six months of the meeting, 525, as the company was named (there are 525 video lines in an American television image), was open for business, operating out of a formerly abandoned art deco building on a rundown street in a seedy part of central LA.

Producers of pop music videos, fed up with being treated as second-class citizens by most video post-production houses, flocked to 525. In 1992, for the fourth consecutive year, the video voted 'Video of the Year' by American cable network MTV was produced at 525. Virtually every megastar in the world has produced at least one video at 525. Michael Jackson, Madonna, MC Hammer, Prince, Paul McCartney and Pink Floyd were some of the personalities who spent long nights among the bare-brick walls, winding stairways and chrome-lined bathrooms of Hendricks's artfully decaying temple to the golden era of Hollywood decor. During the savage Los Angeles riots of 1992, superstar band Guns 'n' Roses were locked in the building overnight, under orders from the team of gun-toting off-duty policemen Hendricks had hired to protect his clients and his valuable equipment from the mobs.

Founded with six employees and two edit suites, 525 had grown to ninety employees with twelve suites in two buildings, offering services including video, audio, film transfer and special effects. While recession raged across most of America, 525 chalked up record 1992 turnover of $18 million, with profits of more than $1 million. Recently made president of Virgin Television, Hendricks is soon to open a second branch of 525 in Tokyo – the first such effort by a Western video house. Asked if he enjoys working for Virgin, Hendricks smiles his expansive smile. 'Hey, listen, Virgin are responsible for making me and Kelvin multimillionaires.'

In a once grand, now slightly ramshackle, pair of white-fronted Victorian Houses on a busy Kensington back street Sara Doukas sits at a large round table with a phone at each ear. From the centre of the table rises a three-foot-high pole, supporting a dozen equally tall plastic pages listing telephone numbers of fashion models, fashion and cosmetics companies, photographers and stylists. Sara and three other women seated around the table swing the pages around, looking up numbers and jotting them down as they talk on the phone. At the front of the room, a succession of models arrives. Sara prefers the bookers spend their time on the phones lining up business, so the young assistants and secretaries busy themselves with the models, making coffee and chit-chat which invariably includes a comment on how good each girl is looking that day. Easily identified by their height, perfect skin and the painstakingly planned sloppiness of their clothes, the models stagger gingerly, like young giraffes climbing a hill, through the narrow corridors, low ceilings and uneven floors of the agency's offices.

Sara quit the Laraine Ashton agency to set up Storm Model Management in 1987. Today it is one of the top three model agencies in London, with turnover of £3 million and 150 girls on its books. When Sara, forty, quit Laraine Ashton, she had neither models nor money, but she knew every client in the UK worth knowing and had a reputation as one of the top bookers in the business. Armed with a business plan, she went to see Richard Branson, who agreed to give her £200,000 in exchange for a 50 per cent stake in the business. The figure of 50 per cent puzzled Sara and her younger brother Simon Chambers, a former merchant banker who quit the City to help Sara create Storm. In the City, investors usually ask for at least 51 per cent, or else a small minority stake. A 50/50 split meant neither side held control, a recipe for a potential stalemate. 'Richard thought the personal chemistry was there. He wanted it to be a joint venture,' said

Chambers who, in addition to acting as Sara's right-hand man
and financial adviser, also manages Storm's growing business in
France, Austria and Germany. Other than Branson's penchant for
public relations and his occasional use of Storm's attractive
merchandise for fashion shows or other publicity stunts (and his
suggestion she call the agency Virgin Girls, which Sara took as a
joke), he does not interfere. 'It's like having a sleepy grandfather
who only opens an eye once every few months but when he does
he offers you some very sage advice,' said Chambers.

Small, cramped offices are a Virgin Group trademark. In the rare
instance of large offices, they are always stark and bare. Whether
this is because Virgin executives are fans of modern style or
because the company is too parsimonious to spring for furniture
and lighting is a subject for conjecture.

But there is one Virgin entrepreneur who does not even have
an office. He works from home, sitting on a big, plump, orange
sofa with the tools of the trade, a five-line telephone and a large
appointments book, on the cocktail table before him. He *used* to
have an office, on a houseboat on a canal in a distant corner of
northwest London. He used to get a secret pleasure every time
the suited, briefcased bankers, having taxied out to this remote
part of town, muddied their brogues on the deck of the boat,
suffered the dampness while sitting deep into a futon to negotiate
a deal, finally stood up to shake hands and bumped their heads on
the boat's low ceiling. When his business outgrew the tiny boat,
he moved to his home. When his girlfriend (now wife) had their
second child, she insisted they move to a bigger house in a less
dangerous neighbourhood than north Kensington. Since business
was going pretty well, he found a big house in chic Holland
Park, bought it for £5 million, and set about converting it to
serve as both home and office. To the right of the entranceway
today is a meeting room with a long mahogany table, big enough
to seat twenty. Behind is the operations centre, where two
secretaries man the phones, faxes, photocopiers and shelves of
files. To the left of the main staircase is the living room where he

works – expensive furniture, ankle-deep carpet and exotic paintings carefully selected by his wife, and mostly obscured by a clutter of white plastic model airplanes, airline award certificates on cheap plaques, and piles of paper emanating from the sofa like solar rays. Joan, his wife, tries to avoid the ground floor as much as possible, spending her time in the basement, where the kitchen and the thirty-foot-long indoor swimming pool and jacuzzi are, or on the first, second or third floor, where she and her two children Holly and Sam are safe from the constant comings and goings below.

Richard Branson does not work from home solely to thwart his wife's efforts to spend his fortune on furniture and paintings. The major reason he works at home is that Richard Branson hates being alone and working at home is the best way to ensure that there are as many people around as possible.

'You have to have an absolute passion for what you're doing,' said Branson. 'Some of my friends had a passion for music, or a passion for the airline business, but in my case it was having a passion for people, for collecting around me a bunch of friends who could try and do what they wanted.'

Some entrepreneurs deal in products; they make things or sell things. Others deal in finance; they buy and sell companies. Some deal in land; they build things. Richard Branson is perhaps unique in the world in that he is a people entrepreneur. He finds people who want to create businesses, sets them up and supports them in their efforts. In twenty years he has built an entire company of entrepreneurs. With dozens of entrepreneurs, it is, unsurprisingly, one of the most creative companies in the world. New business ideas emanate constantly from the Group. Sara Doukas's decision to hire a Paris sales rep to sell Storm's young British models to clients in the world's beauty capital is one example. ('You can tell Sara Doukas that we think we have some pretty good girls of our own in France,' exploded Gerald Marie, managing director of Elite, the world's largest model agency, when a reporter asked him about the notion of a British agency setting up in Paris.) A larger example of the same phenomenon was Virgin Music's 1986 decision to set up a subsidiary in Japan. It was the first, and still the only, wholly owned foreign record company ever set up in the fiercely protected Japanese market, and highly profitable (until 1992 when new parent Thorn EMI shut it down, transferring its business to the EMI label, a traditional 50/50 joint venture with the Japanese Toshiba group). The themes common to all the Virgin entrepreneurs are that each works within industries he/she knows well, so their ventures and innovations have a high success rate. The other theme is a distinctively British ability to bring a certain originality or flair to the businesses, and (as at Guinness) an intuitive understanding of quality. Branson maintains, 'We always tried to do everything we did with a sense of class. If you're small and need to get noticed then you ought to create the best because people will seek you out.

'There's always a market for the best.'

Branson proved that in March 1992, when he sold his Virgin Music group to Thorn EMI for £560 million cash. On the eve of that deal he presided, at the age of forty-one, over an empire with worldwide turnover of £1 billion. When the American *Fortune* magazine published its 1992 list of the world's billionaires, Branson stood out, not only as the second-youngest self-made billionaire, but as the only one to have built four world-class businesses in completely different industries. His success in music and airlines and on a slightly smaller scale in television post-production and video games, was testimony to his philosophy of building businesses organically, aiming for growth rather than profit as the ultimate target, but most of all, his people-based entrepreneurism. The concepts which dominate business organisation of the 1990s – small is beautiful, decentralisation, releasing the power of individuals – are epitomised by the Virgin Group.

Branson began his business in the late 1960s as a student collective in a borrowed London basement and was tagged hippie capitalist for years. But by the 1990s professors from the Harvard Business School were making the pilgrimage to Virgin's rag-bag collection of canalside buildings to write treatises on the Virgin philosophy. Moreover, there is only a handful of companies which can boast of owning a truly worldwide consumer brand name. Merely to list some illustrates how long it can take to establish one: Coca-Cola, Sony, Disney, Hilton, Guinness and Chanel. Yet to judge from the torrent of millions of dollars that flowed in from three continents after Branson's 1989 announcement that he wanted financial partners for his megastores, Virgin may have already entered that hallowed circle.

You climb the stairs to enter from the Champs-Elysées. As in any other record store, you are surrounded by teenagers in bright clothes, shaggy hairstyles and the other paraphernalia of youthful rebellion. Many of them clutch flimsy plastic shopping bags with the familiar red Virgin logo. The spectacle that awaits them at the top of the stairs is a surprise: a vast marble-floored mezzanine glittering beneath crystal chandeliers hanging from the vaulted dome ceiling. Beyond, floor upon floor and aisle after marble aisle of CDs, books, audio equipment and video cassettes spread upwards and outwards. Visiting the Paris Megastore is like shopping for records in a pre-war Austrian Palace.

Virgin France chairman Patrick Zelnik began looking for a site for the Paris Megastore in 1985. It took him three years to find the right one. He had a very precise concept of what the store had to look like: large, elegant, stylish, and situated at a central location where it could become a focal point for that section of the French population for whom music means a great deal, from children through to those who, like Zelnik himself (aged forty-six), grew up in the 1960s. Zelnik was determined that the store be beautiful almost to the point of extravagance to symbolise the importance music and books play, or ought to play, in people's lives. 'These are products which contain dreams and magic, and a store must be coherent with the products it sells.' Zelnik recruited Olivier Montfort from France's largest record chain, FNAC, to set up the Virgin Megastore. Youthful, hyperactive, fast-talking, a self-confessed 'music addict', Montfort embraced the task with relish. He examined site after site, but none met with Zelnik's grandiose ambitions. 'We were not getting anywhere with the agents, so I said the only way is to walk in the street. I forbade him to go to his office,' said Zelnik. For weeks Montfort trod the streets of Paris seeking the right site. One afternoon he went to a cinema in the Champs-Elysées. (Though barred from his office, the employee was permitted daytime cinema visits by the cultural Zelnik.) As he left the cinema he saw a sign across the street advertising 250,000 square feet of office space to let. A gargantuan space, an ornate white stone building, and overlooking the most famous street in Paris. 'It was perfect,' said Montfort.

Built at the turn of the century, the building originally housed the French headquarters of American bank Citibank. Marble staircases, glass chandeliers and mezzanine floors reflected the grand image that great banks once felt obliged to project. By the 1980s, the building was owned by an insurance company looking for a suitable office tenant. Zelnik guaranteed to preserve the quality and character of the architecture, and they agreed to let it to the ill-kempt Frenchman with his insane plan for Europe's largest record store on the Champs-Elysées. The conversion cost £2.5 million and produced a shop of 18,000 square feet. That wasn't big enough, Zelnik felt. 'So we rented the porno cinema next door and merged the two spaces together.' The entire basement of the former bank had been built as a vault, with four-foot-thick iron walls. To merge the two buildings, the builders needed to use military explosives, which required special permission from Paris mayor Jacques Chirac. They had to do the blasting at night so as not to disturb neighbouring businesses. In the course of the construction, a worker discovered a treasure chest full of jewels under a floor.

Midway through the conversion work, disaster struck. After Branson's experiment in taking his company public failed, he decided to take the Virgin Group plc private again with the help of a $250 million bank loan (a syndicated loan led, ironically enough, by the same Citibank whose former French HQ Zelnik and his team were daily blasting and rebuilding). With an enor-

151

mous burden of short-term debt repayments, Branson told Patrick Zelnik that the Megastore had to be abandoned immediately – unless Zelnik could find financial partners who would bear the initial investment costs. Zelnik got ten days from 'going private day', 31 July 1988, to find partners. 'We got Paribas as a minority shareholder,' Zelnik recalled. The strategy of taking in industrial investors as minority shareholders to share the cash flow demands of a new venture was a tactic Branson would use increasingly in his private businesses.

The Paris Megastore opened in November 1988. Its 35,000 square feet of selling space was large for a record store, but not entirely different in scale from some branches of Tower Records on the US West Coast. But Tower followed the American trend towards stripped-down warehouse stores, while the Virgin Store was conspicuously stylish, elegant, even showy. Every section boasted listening booths, 200 in all, where consumers could put on headphones and listen for free to selected current best-selling CDs. The video section boasted a film buff's dream selection of pre-recorded feature films in a variety of languages and versions: a hard-to-find 'classic' film like *Clockwork Orange* was not just available, but on the rack in French, British, American *and* Swedish versions. With a total stock of 200,000 items, the store fulfilled Zelnik's aim: it was a palace to culture. It boasted a wide range of the latest punk and the other varieties of metallic noise favoured by the world's young, yet one flight up shoppers browsed through the largest selection of classical music in the world, the strains of a Mozart concerto filling the chandelier-lit room. The book section was similarly all-embracing in its choice.

Three months after the opening, sales took off. They budgeted for 1990 turnover of 200 million French francs (£20 million), close to the figure for Virgin's long-established Oxford Street Megastore; they achieved 400 million FF (£40 million). Zelnik's hunch that a central location would make the store a focal point for shoppers proved exactly right. Every weekend, thousands of suburbanites and provincial French, young, old, individuals, couples and families, descended on Paris to enjoy the city's shops, cafés and street life. It was a century-old ritual and for most of them, a stroll on the Champs-Elysées was the highlight. For most their interest in the jewelry shops and couture boutiques of the Elysée quarter was limited to window-shopping. But nearly everyone can afford a record. Within months, the Virgin Megastore was not only the most visited store, but the second-most-visited site in all France. At the weekend, 40,000 daily visitors passed through the doors. Only the Notre-Dame Cathedral pulled more. (Notre-Dame's marketing team, the French priesthood, although bigger than Virgin's, was not so fanatical in support of their cause.)

Olivier Montfort was the man who put Patrick Zelnik's idea into reality. Slim, dark, fast-talking, perpetually in motion, Montfort was as much a 'music addict' in adulthood as in his teenage years, when he learned English by reading the *New Musical Express*. He rose through the ranks at FNAC, France's largest record store chain with 20 per cent of the French market. In the 1980s, he watched in despair as the music market deteriorated into an unimaginative business. France's giant supermarkets and hypermarkets took an increasing share of record sales. FNAC followed the trend in piling it high and selling it, not particularly cheaply, but coldly and without passion. 'FNAC sold music the same way they sold books, which was the same way one would sell hardware.' Montfort hankered to create a store which reflected the excitement he felt was inherent in music. He immediately recognised Zelnik's aim; to broaden the target market beyond the teenage pop fan might be the solution. 'It's easy to create hype. What we wanted was a store where grandfather can take the kids and they all enjoy it.' The essence of the strategy was the Megastore's broad and deep selection of product, including a range of classical and jazz, no less comprehensive than their pop catalogue. Montfort saw the store as a 'passport' for the consumer: it gave him entry into the entire spectrum of music with all its richness, variety and excitement. Excitement is stimulated with a constant stream of widely advertised promotional 'events': one week, a record-signing promotion with a pop star in town on a concert tour, the next week a Mozart promotion, to coincide with the release of a new boxed set of the composer's works. Said Montfort: 'We are always asking: what can we do to give the consumer more?'

The concept behind the Paris Megastore is markedly different from that of its sister store in London. One of the first things Olivier Montfort did after Zelnik hired him in 1985 was to look at the leading record stores in London. He was not impressed by what he saw, especially what he saw at Virgin UK: 'My aim was to improve on what Virgin was doing. They were still living in the 1970s.' Virgin's target consumers were too limited in age and taste, Montfort thought. 'They were too rock – they sold no classical product at all.' Montfort was more impressed by HMV, Virgin's biggest competitor, although still critical: 'It's a good store, but it is too middle-of-the-road, not sufficiently fashion-conscious.'

It says a great deal for Virgin that it had the flexibility to allow its French subsidiary to create a retail concept that was almost a repudiation of what Virgin Retail did in the UK. Zelnik attributed this to Branson's unique way of doing business, giving great autonomy to local managers, and then inspiring them to be as creative as he was. 'He is like a child, with no limit to his imagination,' said Zelnik. Zelnik is a calmer, more thoughtful figure than his boss. His office, firmly in the large, under-furnished mould, overlooks the arcaded Place des Vosges, built in the early seventeenth century by Henri IV, and widely regarded as one of France's most beautiful squares. Slumped in his corduroy jacket and puffing on a Gitane, Zelnik is the archetypal Left Bank intellectual, his 1960s passions for Sartre and socialism switching by the 1980s into a no less passionate appreciation of art, fine food and the challenge of business success. He insisted on a wide selection of fiction and non-fiction books at the Megastore, and personally chose the café's chef. Zelnik remarked that when he was with his former employer, Polygram, it would have been inconceivable for him to be granted the leeway to make all those decisions – or to have been inspired to make them as well as he has. 'I'm not an entrepreneur, but I'm not an employee anymore either. I'm halfway between the two.

'Richard's energy gets into your blood.'

The concept forged in Paris has proved a success worldwide. Since 1989, Megastores have opened in Milan, Amsterdam and Vienna. The target for Europe is twenty-five stores. In Japan, success has been greater still: eight stores will be open by the end of 1993.

If Virgin's greatest trump card is its flexibility, its outstanding weakness can be an excess of enthusiasm. In 1991, Virgin France opened two more record stores, in Marseilles and Bordeaux. Market leader FNAC fought back, opening a new, larger store in Paris, and using its nationwide network of shops to finance an aggressive price war in Bordeaux, clearly aimed at driving Virgin out of the provinces. More damagingly still, FNAC used its political clout to get a court order prohibiting Virgin from opening its shops on Sunday. In January 1991, the Megastores were ordered to shut on Sunday. Despite these problems, the Paris store's 1991 turnover rose to 550 million FF (£55 million, maintaining its position as the world's largest record store), but its operating profit of £7 million was completely wiped out by losses at the two new provincial stores. 'Two new stores in one year was too quick,' said Olivier Montfort. 'We are making many changes to improve our business and we expect to make money next year.'

Virgin's record nevertheless looks good set alongside that of its chief international competitor, HMV Records. Owned by Thorn EMI, HMV boasts what is probably London's single most profitable record shop. However the company was slow to spot the opportunity of the French market. When it did, it faithfully reproduced its UK formula in France – and met disaster. HMV opened a large store in Bordeaux three months after Virgin opened there, and just in time to feel the full weight of FNAC's price war. Within six months, the HMV store closed. 'We watch with amazement the way people give up on a business simply because of little problems,' commented Virgin's Robert Devereux. 'At Virgin, if we take the view that this is a business we want to be in, then we'll keep at it until we get it right.'

*

The entrepreneurial tradition of the Virgin Group has its roots in the unique partnership that was forged in the early 1970s between Richard Branson and Simon Draper. Branson's second business, mail-order record retailing, developed in 1968 out of the embers of *Student* magazine. Simon Draper was a second cousin of Branson's who had been raised in South Africa and travelled to England as a student out to see the world. He went to meet his cousin at the business's bohemian Bayswater headquarters. 'He turned up one day when he was eighteen and bought something like a thousand records from our tiny mail-order company so I felt, well, you know, he must know something about records,' Branson said, typically vague. Ever the deal-maker, Branson often employed vagueness to disguise what he was really thinking. In fact, Branson thought Draper was one of the most dynamic and creative people he had ever met.

The record company Branson and Draper founded in 1973 was built on the creative tension between the two. An obsessive collector, Draper was another 'music addict' who loved avant-garde, innovative music, like that emanating from 'art rock' circles in the UK and on the Continent in the early 1970s. Blustery, affable, as extroverted as Branson was shy, Draper was an athletically built, charismatic young man with a shock of blond hair who expressed his enthusiasms with machine gun-like speed. By 1992, in semi-retirement, Draper would own a collection of modern art recognised by the Tate Gallery as one of Britain's best. At Virgin Records, Draper satisfied his love for avant-garde pop music not only by signing bands many people would not give the time of day to, but by encouraging them in their eccentricities. He had the courage to back the acts over the long term, confident that they would ultimately find a market.

'Simon has changed the UK music business in the last twenty years,' said Steve Lewis, who worked for Virgin for twenty-one years, running Virgin's music publishing business from 1983 to 1992. Draper's tastes, encompassing jazz, electronic and Continental European music, proved to be ahead of the marketplace throughout that period. His determination to allow artists to package their records as they desired, and dress, tour or give interviews as they chose, common practice at most record companies today, was also ahead of the market. An early Virgin band called Henry Cow had a member who stood on stage ironing on an ironing board throughout each concert. The Sex Pistols were a flamboyant example of Virgin's ability to not only tolerate but put enthusiastic marketing support behind even the least house-trained of pop music phenomena. 'What Simon never did was try to knock the rough edges off a band,' said Lewis.

Where many record companies in the 1970s constantly searched for the 'next big thing', Draper took a much more long-term view of the music business. Under his leadership, Virgin signed long-term contracts with artists, willingly paying more if they could secure rights to a number of future records, over as many international markets as possible, and across related areas like music publishing as well. 'Simon believed the record company was there to back the judgement of the A&R department,' said Lewis. Artists and repertoire (A&R) is the talent-spotting division of a record company. At Virgin, Draper was head of A&R. In the 1990s, with stars like Mick Jagger and Eric Clapton turning fifty and perhaps giving each other gold watches to celebrate thirty years in the music business, it seems obvious that pop music acts can have great longevity (often greater than the executives who sign them), but in the 1970s most record companies were far more short-termist. Under Draper's leadership, Virgin was one of the first companies to invest in 'building' acts over years. Gary Horne illustrated the strategy. Signed in 1982 after he quit successful 1970s-era band, Thin Lizzy, Horne worked hard for ten years, releasing records and touring, building a following, before achieving a major breakthrough with 'Still Got the Blues', which sold three million copies around the world. In 1992, Horne received the ageing rocker seal of approval when ex-Beatle George Harrison invited him to join in a London concert. Said Draper: 'The success of a Gary Horne is more satisfying than a lot of our younger acts because you know it's built on more solid foundations.'

In the early years, Branson's lack of musical knowledge was a source of much humour inside the company. In 1973, Branson suggested putting vocals on 'Tubular Bells', Virgin's now legendary first release, a forty-minute long instrumental LP by hippie musician Mike Oldfield. 'Richard thought an instrumental record would never sell,' Lewis recalled. Draper overruled his cousin, and the instrumental was a major hit in the UK. When it was chosen as theme music for the film *The Exorcist*, it went multiplatinum in the US. As the record company grew, the mystery surrounding Branson's precise role in the business only increased. 'After 1979, Richard didn't even have an office at the record company,' recalled Lisa Anderson, who joined Virgin in 1977 and became head of international operations in 1983 and the fourth director of the company, the first new addition to the board after the three founders, Branson, Draper and Ken Berry. Anderson attributed the success of the company to Draper's twin talents: 'ears' (music business jargon for the ability to spot a hit act) and charismatic, inspirational leadership. 'Every Wednesday morning at nine we'd have a meeting in the dining room at Richard's house. The meeting began with an enormous English breakfast, and we'd gossip for twenty-five minutes. Then we'd settle down to business. We'd go over everything we had to do. It lasted until noon and Simon's enthusiasm for everything was so strong that when the meeting ended everybody just couldn't wait to get back to their office and hit the phones.'

Branson never attended these meetings. They were held at his house for the same reason a thousand other meetings, parties, press launches, competitions and award ceremonies happened around him: he liked to be surrounded by people. Occasionally, he joined a Wednesday morning meeting. 'Richard would come in and say you've got to sign this group I've just met, and we'd all go oh no, not again . . .'

Branson's role however was crucial. He was the deal-maker, the strategic genius behind the company's growth. The Branson/ Draper combination was one of the best examples of a creative working relationship between a chairman and chief executive in

British industry. The concept of splitting those two roles became popular among institutional investors and their friends in Establishment newspapers after the 1990 recession triggered the collapse of companies like Polly Peck or Brent Walker where one strong figure dominated. Most of the City comment at that time expressed the unrealistic dream of combining two diametrically opposed qualities, the risk-taking skills of an entrepreneurial chief executive with the caution of a conservative chairman. The Branson/Draper partnership worked because both were risk-takers, but in different areas of the business. In trying to drive the company forward, each seemed to bring the best out in the other.

Draper attributed the success of Virgin Records to Branson. 'I only ever saw a year out. He saw much further. He was always forcing the pace. I was striving to make it excellent while he wanted it bigger and bigger.'

Draper was repeatedly shocked by the scale of Branson's ambitions and the audacity of his manoeuvres. He cited an episode in 1975, one of the company's earliest shifts towards the mainstream. With hippie styles and music fading rapidly, Branson and Draper wanted to move the company towards the new trends. Draper attempted to sign 10cc, then part of the new wave and seen in the industry as poised for commercial breakthrough. The band members liked Draper and agreed to sign with Virgin for an advance of £400,000: 'For us, that was an astounding sum of money.' To Draper's fascination, Branson flew to New York and persuaded Atlantic Records to put up £300,000 in return for the US rights to the band's records. The signing never happened because their manager, preferring the comfort of a large record company, waited until the band were on holiday and signed them instead to Polygram. Many of Branson's early deals did not come off, but Draper was consistently amazed by Branson's ability to raise large sums of money, even though in those days Virgin was virtually unknown outside the UK industry. 'He is a brilliant negotiator,' said Draper of his cousin.

The most brilliant of Branson's manoeuvres was his decision to make Virgin Records an international company. Most independent record companies typically paid an advance to an act in exchange for world rights and then sought to reduce their cash outflow by licensing the act in other countries, in exchange for advances from the overseas record companies. Branson saw that as too conservative. On a hit record where margins might rise as high as 50 per cent, the overseas labels would take as much as half of that profit margin. Investing in a local record label in every important country would be expensive for Virgin, but if a big hit came along, Virgin's profit would be much greater.

In 1980, Branson flew to Paris and sought out Patrick Zelnik, then working for Polygram, which licensed Virgin's acts (releasing them on the Polygram label) in France. Zelnik was impressed that even though Virgin was in the midst of one of its perennial cash crises – suffering the after-effects of an unsuccessful effort to launch a US subsidiary – Branson was still launching more new ventures. 'Richard never gives up,' said Zelnik. On a Sunday afternoon in Zelnik's Left Bank flat, the two drew up a business plan. It took them fifteen minutes; detail was not Branson's strong suit. 'Every single number turned out wrong: we completely forgot to include VAT,' Zelnik recalled.

But almost immediately, the dexterity of tiny Virgin France became a big advantage. Virgin France's first important signing was a band called Telephone, then on EMI. A modest hit in France, the band wanted to try to break the UK market, but EMI refused to release their records in the UK. It was the classic problem of rivalry between national managing directors in one large company. Zelnik brought in Steve Lewis, then deputy MD of the UK record company, who seduced Telephone away from EMI. 'My attitude was we'd try and make it in the UK with them and even if we didn't we'd make money in France,' said Lewis. The band's first Virgin LP enjoyed slim success in the UK but sold 750,000 units in France, a fabulous figure for that country. 'It put Virgin France on the map,' commented Lewis.

In ten years, Virgin France grew from that inaccurate scrap of paper in Patrick Zelnik's flat to a company with 10 per cent of the French music market. In 1991, the company earned an operating profit of 70 million FF (£7 million) on turnover of 628 million FF. Half of that turnover came from French acts. Of France's eight best-selling local acts, Virgin France had three. By the late 1980s, Virgin's image in the UK had become relatively mainstream. In France, Zelnik and his team built a slightly more exclusive image for Virgin, playing off Britain's reputation for cutting-edge, avant-garde pop music and styles. Fabrice Nataf, Zelnik's successor as managing director of the French record company, said he has refused to sign bands if he could not see himself listening to them at home. 'If I owned a restaurant, I would make the food I want to eat, not the food I want to sell. At Virgin our philosophy is don't make the records you want to sell, make the ones you'd want to buy.' The formula worked: in one survey, Virgin scored as the second most recognised brand name among French consumers. Only Coca-Cola scored better.

Nataf has only met Branson four times, yet under his leadership Virgin France retained many of the trademarks of a Virgin company. An example is its consistent policy of recruiting novices, or people from completely different industries, to senior jobs. Nataf cited his highly successful head of television promotion as an example: her previous career was promoting the famous *bateau-mouche* boat rides on the Seine. 'When you know too much how it works, you don't take chances.' Nataf defined the key element of the Virgin culture as innocence. At Christmas 1991, he had 350 video copies made of Frank Capra's famous 1930s movie *It's a Wonderful Life*, and sent them out as Christmas gifts. 'Other record company heads send out foie gras or champagne. I chose Capra because he has the same philosophy as Virgin: he is completely innocent, generous and courageous. If you are that way, you can change things a little bit. The music business and the media may be blasé, but that is the purpose of music.'

With the French company as the model, Virgin set up national subsidiaries right across Europe in the early 1980s. Ken Berry, who started off as an accounts clerk in Virgin's original mail-order record business, managed the creation of Virgin's international network, flying from city to city negotiating local contracts with the majors for record pressing, sales and distribution services, and educating the young, enthusiastic local MDs in the art of running an independent record company. In each case, the strategy was the same: UK-signed Virgin acts provided a core sales volume, which was then supplemented by the signing of local acts discovered by local management. This was a radical departure in the music business which has been transfixed by the riches of the US market. Typically, record companies rushed to set up in the US, and fell victim to a recurrent pattern in which the US operation took over the company, stole or suffocated initiative at the company's other national units, and then failed to deliver in the US as the market grew more competitive and marketing costs (to use a polite term for the wholesale bribery and lavish entertaining necessary to break an act in the US) rose. When Branson sold Virgin Records to Thorn EMI in March 1992 for the rather staggering sum of £560 million, it had subsidiaries in twenty-eight countries. Commented Simon Draper: 'We built an international network and Chrysalis didn't. That's why we were worth five times what they were.'

When the acts Draper signed in the early 1980s began to break big around the world, the company's international network ensured that tremendous profits flowed back to the sprawling white late-Victorian mansion on the Grand Union Canal that served as Virgin Records' headquarters. In 1980, the company was struggling to break even. By 1983, the company made £11 million. Three years later it was £31 million. Nearly all the acts were signed by Draper personally. Perhaps the most enduring of all Virgin's stars proved to be Phil Collins. Steve Lewis emphasised that the credit for seeing the potential of this ageing, balding, drummer-turned-singer belonged entirely to Draper. 'Who ever heard of a drummer as a pop star?'

Following Branson's lead, the corporate culture at Virgin Records was a deal-making culture. Television executive Godfrey Pye gave an enlightening insight into Branson's deal-making style. In 1987, Pye agreed to sell his post-production and video editing company,

Rushes, to Virgin's television division, Virgin Communications, for £6 million. Pye cut the original deal with Communications chief Robert Devereux. 'I said to him, darling, let's get your suits to sit down with my suits and work out the details,' recalled Pye, a flamboyant, self-made entrepreneur who never hesitated to speak his mind. Virgin's accountants did a 'due diligence' report valuing some Rushes assets below Pye's claims. Devereux wanted to walk away from the deal. Instead, Pye got a call asking him to bring his advisers to meet with Branson at his house.

'I took along my suit [Chris Palin] and we went to the house and there were kids' panties all over the house and we sat down in the living room and pretty soon Branson comes down drying his hair. All folksy, he asked if anybody would like a cup of tea. He invited Chris to go along with him into the kitchen, making small talk as he made the tea.'

The three men sat down in Branson's cluttered living room and Branson turned to the subject of the deal: 'Six million? Call me old-fashioned, but I never thought it was six million. Five and a half million is all I offer. There it is, five and a half million, the offer's on the table. Why don't you go back to your office and think it over?'

'Then he looks at his watch and says, "Oh god, is that the time? I'm due to leave for a skiing trip in half an hour."' Branson got up and left.

Pye said: 'My suit was so impressed by the sight of this multimillionaire searching for three cups that weren't chipped and making us tea in all these odd teacups.

'I had to hand it to Richard. He spent half an hour squeezing teabags against the side of some cups and saved his company five hundred thousand pounds.'

Most deal-makers of Branson's skill became control freaks. Few reached the extremes of Robert Maxwell, who not only interfered, and undermined, but regularly even fired his own sons. But most deal-makers found it difficult to delegate to subordinates. In the music business, every entrepreneurial executive wanted to be involved in the details of every contract. Such a style necessarily put a limit on the growth possible at any one company, and also a limit on how viable it was once the entrepreneur departed. Geffen Records founder David Geffen, whose control extended [or so he told magazine *Vanity Fair*] to having sexual relationships with his stars, was perhaps the best illustration of that phenomenon. Branson's unique talent was that he was both deal-maker and delegator. He created a company with a deal-making culture and, acting almost by remote control, he tutored staff in how to make it work by becoming deal-makers, or mini-entrepreneurs, themselves. One American entertainment executive who knew Geffen described the difference this way: 'Geffen is a manager [ie artist's manager]. Richard Branson is an industrialist.'

Staff at Virgin Records spoke of being 'trained' by Branson in the deal-making style of management. Jon Webster, then managing director of Virgin's international companies, said that when in the spring of 1992 he sat down with EMI to work on combining the two companies' operations, EMI executives were shocked to discover that Virgin paid less than them for CD manufacture – even though EMI owned its own CD plants. 'Richard trained us in how to do deals,' Webster explained. 'You always shoot for the moon. If they say they'll do it for a pound, you offer ninety pence and you don't budge. Six months later you come back and say you want it for eighty pence.

'You just had to shoot for the moon, and you'd get it. Surprisingly often.'

In February 1982, an American lawyer named Randolph Fields was making himself breakfast in his Los Angeles house when he heard on the radio the news that Laker Airways had gone out of business. Aged twenty-nine, Fields had had an unusual background. Raised in California, he had lived in England from the age of nine. After qualifying as a British barrister, he'd returned to California, passed the American bar exam and worked as an American lawyer, building up an expertise in defending asbestos-related insurance claims. Travelling frequently across the Atlantic, Fields had acquired an intense dislike for the large transatlantic airlines, British Airways, Pan Am and TWA. He believed they packaged discomfort into their service to differentiate their different classes. Buttering his English muffin that morning, Fields resolved to return to the UK and begin work on a new airline to fill the void left by Laker.

On 11 December 1983, at lunch around the corner from the London headquarters of Britain's Civil Aviation Authority, CAA official Ray Colegate told Fields 'the door was open' for Fields's paper company, British Atlantic Airways, to apply for a licence to fly a daily route from London Gatwick to Newark. With a flourish, Fields pulled out a completed application form for the route. Months of informal discussions, 'clearing the ground' with dozens of interested parties in the manner preferred by British officialdom, enabled Fields to know exactly what was coming at this lunch. Rights to fly from London's second airport to New York's third airport was hardly the best business opportunity in the world, but it was a great victory in light of the conservatism of Britain's airline industry. Fields had had to appeal to the Thatcher government, which overruled the objections of BA and the hesitancy of the CAA. It had taken British Caledonian twelve years' flying as a charter airline before it won a scheduled licence. The small group of former Laker, BA and Air Florida executives working on the nascent British Atlantic were impressed by Fields's vision and implacable persistence.

But the CAA did not give the newcomer an easy lift-off. Fields was given three months, until a CAA hearing on 1 March 1984, to show British Atlantic was backed with £3 million capital. With such a huge, uncertain project, Fields needed one big investor who had money, liked airplanes and enjoyed taking a risk. On a trip to Las Vegas, Fields had admired how the MGM hotel mixed a gambling casino with the Hollywood showbiz theme to give a hotel/casino environment a whole new sense of fun and excitement. Why not an entertainment-oriented airline, he thought. He knew about the Virgin Group's record company, record stores and nightclubs. On 13 February he called Virgin Group and told the secretary he had a business proposition for an airline that might interest their chairman Richard Branson. He was put on hold and Branson came on the phone. Two days later, Fields was on Branson's houseboat outlining his scheme for a Gatwick-Newark daily 747 service offering a cut-price high-quality service built around an 'Upper Class' section in the front and upstairs lounge of the Boeing 747, a luxurious business class to which Virgin would naturally be able to give a special élan.

Almost instantly, Branson fell in love with the idea. Profits were flooding into Virgin from Boy George and other hit acts; his tax accountants were advising him that this was a good time to set up new companies. Like Fields, Branson was often disgusted with the quality of service on the large carriers and fancied he could do it better. He loved the romance of flying and he loved the idea of airplanes with VIRGIN on their side in big red letters. Branson's research of the industry could not be called deep. Rather, it was a typical Branson hunch: 'All weekend, I rang People's Express, [the American-owned cut-price carrier, soon to follow Laker into receivership] and I couldn't get through. It just kept ringing and ringing. Either they were thoroughly inefficient or else they were thoroughly busy. Either way, it seemed to make sense for us to have a go.' On Monday morning, Fields was back on the houseboat. Pointing out that the name British Atlantic lacked charisma, Branson suggested Virgin Airways; Fields offered a compromise of Virgin Atlantic. They shook hands on a deal by which Virgin Group would supply all the capital in return for 50 per cent of the airline. Fields would be executive chairman and own the other 50 per cent.

That handshake marked the beginning of a year of torment for Randolph Fields. Fields and Branson fell out almost immediately. The corporate guerrilla war ended only with Fields's ejection from Virgin Atlantic. It showed how ruthless and relentless a negotiator Branson could be when the stakes were high. Branson always maintained that Fields was not capable of running an airline. Fields claimed Branson fell so completely in love with the airline he would not stand for anything less than total control. He also believed Branson's sudden elevation to celebrity that followed their 29 February 1984 press conference announcing the launch of Virgin Atlantic left the entrepreneur (previously known only inside the music business) intoxicated by fame. Nick Alexander, a Virgin Atlantic director from 1984 to 1986 and a close colleague of Branson since 1981, believed all three claims were largely true: Branson *was* intoxicated by his newfound celebrity, he *was* set upon control, yet Branson was right that, had Fields remained in charge, the airline might not have survived. But the bitterness of the ensuing battle owed more to Fields's skills as a lawyer. 'For the first time Richard met his match contractually,' said Alexander.

On 23 March 1984, Fields and Branson signed what Fields called Deal Mark 1, the contract establishing the 50/50 ownership of Virgin Atlantic. Branson poured Fields a celebratory glass of champagne – and then told him the deal would not work. Because of pressure from Branson's bank, Coutts, they would have to renegotiate. The bank would not accept Virgin owning less than 76 per cent of the airline. Fields was devastated. Branson said he had no choice: either agree or there would be no airline. Fine, there will be no airline, said Fields. He stalked off the houseboat, his lawyer in close pursuit. Tears in his eyes, Fields asked his lawyer to lead him to the nearest pub. 'Don't be daft,' said the lawyer. 'Let's go back to my office, he's sure to call.' By the time they reached the office, Branson had rung three times. Over the next fortnight, Branson worked his unique seductive magic. Fields got handwritten notes and grovelling explanations in late-night pleading phone calls. On 4 April 1984, they signed Deal Mark 2, with Virgin owning 75 per cent and Fields 25 per cent. The extra 1 per cent was significant, because it gave Fields a legal blocking power over major decisions.

Meanwhile, a small team was setting up Virgin Atlantic in time to meet the launch of transatlantic service, announced for 22 June. As chairman, Fields had taken responsibility for Virgin Atlantic's reservation system. Virgin had no computer, no machines to print tickets and no licence to sell tickets in the US. Its team of executives, some of them former pilots, were much stronger on operations, safety and maintenance than on earning the revenue.

Fields's choice as head of Virgin's ticketing and reservations hardly increased their expertise: she was his law clerk who had never worked for an airline before. They decided Virgin would not seek accreditation for ticket sales through US travel agents. Instead, they would sell tickets through Ticketron, a New York telephone service selling seats for Broadway plays and pop concerts. Until that was organised, American passengers wanting to buy a Virgin ticket had to ring the UK at their own expense and pay by credit card. Virgin's head of US operations, David Tait, found himself flying to London regularly and returning with shoeboxes full of tickets for US passengers.

Fields reached a deal with Air Florida to use their computer for Virgin's bookings. But, suffering from disastrous publicity following the crash of an Air Florida jet into a bridge in Washington DC, Air Florida were in a financial nosedive. At the beginning of June, they went into receivership. Behind the scenes at Virgin Atlantic, it was chaos. The computer system was not working. Nobody had any idea how many passengers were booked on each flight, or how many had paid. 'Anybody who presented himself at Newark and said "my name is Smith and I've paid for two tickets" was immediately issued with tickets,' recalled Tait. A week before the launch, Branson was told the launch would have to be postponed – or cancelled. With Virgin Group guarantees underwriting the airline's liabilities, disaster loomed for Virgin's finances and reputation. 'It was one of those moments in your life when you feel your heart turn over,' the Virgin chairman recalled.

The 22 June launch looked fine on the television. At the ticket desk it was a different story. Several times that first week, 800 people turned up with confirmed bookings for the 450 seats on the flight. Then, suddenly and inexplicably, it changed. In early July, only 100 people were turning up for flights which Virgin's computers showed as fully booked. Some Virgin executives now believe this was a first wave of 'dirty tricks' carried out by a rival airline. Whatever the cause, Branson was horrified. The airline had rushed to launch in June to enjoy the peak travel summer period. To reach its first year load target of 75 per cent, the summer period had to score well above that figure.

Branson blamed Fields for the problems. He became increasingly involved in managing the airline, going around Fields to deal directly with the airline's staffers, themselves growing increasingly hostile to Fields. With fifteen years' experience in the airline business, Tait believed the Ticketron strategy was fatal. When Fields insisted that he drop plans for a Virgin Atlantic ticket office in the US, Tait quit. When Branson heard, he begged Tait to take the next plane to London and, when he arrived, persuaded him to resume his job.

Fields told Branson he would step back from management duties and even find a new chief executive. 'I never intended to run the airline,' Fields claimed. Convinced the airline was inches from disaster, Branson would not settle for half-measures. 'He went ballistic,' was how Fields saw it. Fields was frozen out of all management duties. He was not invited to the airline's inaugural flight to Maastricht, a typical Virgin-style jamboree including pop stars, models and stewardesses pouring an endless supply of champagne from coffee and tea jugs. 'I was the chairman and I was barred from the inaugural flights of my own airline!' wailed Fields. Far from denying these stories, Branson smiled at the memory, adding: 'We changed the locks on the office doors to keep him out.'

Branson reckoned without Fields's legal skills. Fields's position in Deal Mark 2 was secured not only by his 25 per cent shareholding, but also by the company's board which limited the directors to two Virgin men and two from Fields's side. There was a fairly standard clause allowing Virgin to appoint a fifth director in the event of deadlock but when Branson moved to appoint himself a director, Fields obtained a court injunction blocking the appointment and blocking any change in the chairmanship until various other matters were resolved. 'For most of the summer, TV viewers watching Branson parading around on his airplane didn't know that he was under an injunction keeping him off the board of his own airline,' remarked Fields. Branson abhorred board meetings, especially these where he had to follow time-consuming procedures to the letter. Fields forced him to attend board meetings two or three times a week. In September 1984, a truce was reached: Fields resigned as chairman in return for cash compensation of £200,000 and a lifetime Upper Class ticket on Virgin Atlantic. 'I'd had a virtual nervous breakdown, I was completely worn down by the stress of fighting Richard Branson, and my law practice was dying from neglect,' said Fields.

Even this deal could not last. Branson could not stand having Fields as a non-executive director and shareholder, while Fields found his lifetime ticket unsatisfactory. 'They made me fly standby!' In May 1985, they reached Deal Mark 4: Fields sold his shareholding of the now profitable airline for £1 million cash, and got a new lifetime ticket. The ironclad rules for the new ticket entitled him to tickets on Virgin Upper Class on request for himself, his 'deemed' wife (he was then not married) and two friends. The two friends were required to fly with him. 'We have a side letter where I avoid flying Fridays and Sundays and in return my two guests only have to fly with me one way,' said Fields. Branson remained deeply unhappy with Fields's free flight privileges: 'He seems to live on our airplanes.'

Eight years later, the dispute still rumbled quietly on. Deal Mark 3 required that when dividends paid by Virgin Atlantic to Virgin Group passed the £250,000 mark, Fields would receive a payment of £100,000, his first and only cut of the airline's profits. Fields claimed that to avoid making this payment, Virgin Atlantic had paid its dividends not to Virgin Group but to another Virgin company, Voyager Holdings. Branson declined to comment on the £100,000 dispute.

The Branson/Fields dispute revealed how much Branson's business style rested on his personal charisma. Branson's instinctive use of charm and seduction, combined with a wily grasp of the minutest details of a deal, met their comeuppance with Fields's legal skills. Branson once said: 'Deals are like buses. Another one always comes along.' This meant that he would always walk away from one he did not like, but it also suggested he would sign one and not shrink from hopping off it and on to another as soon as necessary. 'He negotiates by inches,' commented Fields. Branson did not hide his disgust at being forced to pay Fields £1.2 million. Citing Storm Models and other examples, he stressed that other partners/chief executives with whom he has set up companies have enjoyed amicable relationships and enormous autonomy. Fields remained, strangely, more bitter over falling out with Branson than over losing a stake in an airline which today would have made him a multimillionaire. With genuine emotion, Fields repeatedly returned to the hurt he suffered at being shut out of Branson's confidence in the hectic months of 1984. 'Even after June, I still hoped I could repair the relationship,' Fields said. Like the Vicomte de Valmont, the greatest testament to Branson's charms was the pain suffered by those who resisted them.

The most remarkable thing about the £1.2 million that Branson paid out to Fields was that it was the *only* cash investment Branson ever made in Virgin Atlantic Airways, a business whose value he put at over £300 million by 1993. From the day the airline opened for business, Branson was financing its activities from the cash earned from ticket sales for that summer. Soon after, he opened package holiday company Virgin Holidays, whose cash generating capabilities offset the terrific cash demands of the airline. It took incredible skill, and courage, to build companies while skating on the thinnest financial ice. 'Twice every year, when royalty payments had to be made to [Virgin recording] artists, no cheques could be written anywhere else,' recalled Nick Alexander. In 1989, when Virgin Atlantic's expansion plans required cash, Branson took in Japanese conglomerate Seibu Saison as a partner, giving them 10 per cent of the equity (plus options for more shares in future) for £40 million. In 1993, when Branson decided that an air service from London to Athens would open new growth possibilities for his package holiday company, he struck a deal with a small Greek airline where they would finance and own the air service, paying him a six-figure fee for the rights to use the Virgin Atlantic name. One of the motivations behind his obsession with the quality image of the Virgin name is that it can be a cash-free passport into new business.

Branson applied the deal-making skills honed in the record business to airlines. The first airplane Virgin bought was leased on a ten-year lease wih a complex arrangement which entitled him to sell the plane back to Boeing at his cost if the airline failed, but to pocket the profit if he sold the plane for more than he paid for it. In 1993, he negotiated a similar deal, but much bigger, for fifteen airplanes. 'We will have the world's youngest fleet,' he said proudly of the small, but growing, flock. Taking advantage of the slump in the aerospace business, he negotiated leases at a monthly rate of $750,000 for a 747-400, the world's largest plane, seating 500. 'The big airlines are paying $1.2 million a month.'

Virgin Atlantic's appeal rested on Upper Class, a business class service comparable to other airlines' first class, at business class prices. A revolutionary extra that won consumers' attention was a free limousine service for Upper Class passengers from anywhere in mainland Britain to the airport, and in the US to anywhere within fifty miles of the airport. Branson threw himself with gusto into the marketing side of the airline, constantly proposing new ways to improve the service. As a service-oriented private company in a world where most of his publicly owned competitors were ruthlessly cutting costs, Virgin Atlantic stood out from the crowd. Branson remarked: 'So many airlines are always thinking, if we cut food costs by a pound and we've got ten million passengers, then that's ten million pounds saved. At Virgin Atlantic, we think well if we put seat-back videos in all our seats, OK, it's going to cost us eleven million pounds, but the word of mouth of being the first to do that, of offering customers something that is really appreciated, in the long term it will be worth it.' Charles Levison, Branson's former lawyer who ran Virgin companies for fifteen years, compared Branson's keen interest in the airline with his activity at Virgin's early retail stores, where he used to prowl around asking customers what they liked and disliked about the shops. 'What fascinates Richard about the airline is that it is the perfect captive atmosphere for finding out what your customers want. But in the record stores you didn't have them trapped in there for anything like as long as on a transatlantic flight.'

'The lazy approach would be just to ask a few questions and nod politely,' Branson added. 'You've got to talk to them with a notepad and pencil in your hand and make sure you write everything down and then make sure you go and get the things sorted out that they bring up.'

Virgin Atlantic marketing director, Chris Moss, played a vital role in establishing Virgin Atlantic's reputation for innovation and luxury in the air. Seat-back videos, ice cream as part of in-flight meals, aromatherapy kits to combat jet lag, magicians and live musicians entertaining in the aisles: no idea was too bizarre for Moss to give it the go-ahead for at least a trial run on board. Moss was scornful of the traditional airline's attitude to new ideas, which he described as seeking problems rather than solutions. When he developed the idea of seat-back videos, colleagues at other airlines assured him it would never work technically: there would be electronic interference with the controls, it would be too expensive to install electric power at every seat, and so on. 'If you tackle each problem in bite-size chunks, you solve it,' said Moss, adding: 'Within a few months of doing it, we started to get calls from other airlines saying exactly how did you do that and where did you get the units from?'

Moss had no formal marketing experience yet Virgin Atlantic has won more marketing awards than most airlines in the world. A wiry greying thirty-eight-year-old, Moss was a PR man before joining Virgin with a company that built Formula One cars and racing boats. Behind the exuberant go-getter image, he was thoughtful and reflective. 'People from the conventional blue-chip marketing background often seem to lose a certain spontaneity or the ability to think laterally,' he said. Moss credited the creativity of Virgin Atlantic to Branson, describing him as a superb 'conduit' for new ideas. 'Often in organisations you have great ideas and they come up against a brick wall because the MD or somebody hasn't got the necessary vision. Richard encourages everyone from the very bottom of the company right to the top to come up with fresh ideas.'

Moss described Branson's penchant for impromptu brainstorming sessions where everyone in earshot was roped in for a discussion on a new initiative and urged to let their imaginations run wild. An example in 1992 involved plans for Virgin's Business Class Lounge at Heathrow. Led by Branson, a group of employees considered ideas including a hot tub on the Lounge roof, a 'weather-wall' of TV screens linked to satellites and radar, a miniature train set snaking through the Lounge to deliver cocktails, and more. 'Somebody said maybe we could go to the Russians and see if they've got one of their old subs, we could get the periscope and put it out the top so you could scan around he airport and watch while you're waiting for your plane to take off,' said Moss. 'Some of the older brigade do look at you a bit strangely, but it's an idea.'

At Virgin Atlantic it was Branson's first chance in years to be a hands-on chief executive. He threw himself into the role with gusto. A believer in MBWA (Management by Walking Around), Branson was constantly at Gatwick chatting to ticketing staff, flight crew, engineers and other employees, enquiring after their needs, complaints, suggestions or opinions on what was right or wrong. Nick Alexander found Branson's ease in talking to junior Virgin employees contrasted strangely with his inarticulacy when it came to explaining 'gut feeling' strategic decisions to senior executives. 'It can be difficult for MDs because he attaches as much weight to the office boy's views as he does to the MD's.'

Romance continued to be one of Branson's themes. 'Big airlines have taken the romance out of flying. But if we make sure at Virgin Atlantic that it *is* romantic, if we make sure the uniform they wear is attractive, and the crew choose it themselves, if we make sure that when they fly to a city the hotels they stay in are nice and friendly, if we take care of little things like arranging entry into nightclubs so they can have a good time out, and basically make sure it's great fun to work for our company, then I think ultimately it's the customers who benefit.'

The hierarchy of values Branson set at Virgin, staff first, customers second, and shareholders third, was similar to that he observed at the Japanese companies he was increasingly involved with after 1988, when the Fujisankei communications group bought a 25 per cent interest in his record company. 'Western companies do not concentrate enough on looking after their staff and making sure they're satisfied with their job,' Branson said. Branson was always quick to promote, and over-promote, people. 'If you promote somebody above what they'd expect, they will be determined to give their all and prove that you've made the right decision.'

He compared dealing with employees to raising children. Quoting his father, he said the ideal way to bring up children was to lavish them with praise and, unless personal safety was endangered, encourage them to experiment. 'The same applies to staff. If you lavish people with praise and look for the good things that they do, then people will know when they've made a mistake, they won't need someone to remind them of it.' One of many cases of Branson's readiness to reach for the promotion was Syd Pennington. Pennington worked for 23 years for Marks and Spencer, where he was one of the architects of M&S's food-only shops, one of the retailer's most successful innovations of the 1980s. He was headhunted to Virgin in 1989, to lead the growing pan-European chain of Virgin Megastores. In May 1990, Branson asked him to write a report on the potential for increasing Virgin Atlanic's revenue from duty-free sales. Demand was strong for Virgin's logo-bearing duty-free goods and Branson sensed potential to expand the business. Pennington recalled: 'That was a Tuesday. On the Thursday he came into my office and said is your report finished? I said it will take a bit of time, and I'm still trying to run a Megastore business. He said, this is too important to me. Have the report ready by breakfast on Monday.

'I had to go to Milan for the weekend because we were negotiating for a site for a Megastore. I came into the office on Monday morning and my secretary said: "Congratulations. You're joint managing director of the airline."'

Branson put great emphasis on the importance of fun as a

motivational factor for employees, a philosophy developed in his years in the entertainment industry. He constantly threw parties, in the large garden of his Oxfordshire country home, at hotels, or at nightclubs, where Virgin staff were treated to free food, drink and entertainment. Typically, the parties climaxed with everybody immersed in the nearest swimming pool. Godfrey Pye, MD of Virgin Television between 1988 and 1990, offered a cynical appreciation of Virgin's unique motivational activities, as observed at one such party at a Devon hotel, attended by 200 Virgin employees: 'Richard flew in on the Friday evening. He comes down to dinner, slapping everybody on the back, shouting "free champagne for everybody". After dinner, somebody throws Branson into the swimming pool, he throws somebody else in, and on it goes. Then he comes out dressed in women's silk underwear. What I always wanted to know was who remembers to pack the bra and panties for him every time he goes on a trip.' Pye's alienation from the company began almost immediately after the £2.5 million of Virgin shares he received for selling his company began to fall in value, and he never bought into the Virgin culture: 'It's like moonie-ism. They believe Virgin is the greatest place anybody could ever work.'

Countered Branson: 'Most jobs in life are boring and dull. Ideally in life, people want to have a bit of fun and enjoy life, and if you can create an environment which *is* fun, where the people working together enjoy each other's company, socially as well as at work, then everybody benefits.'

Airline consultant Hugh Welbon, a former BA executive, played a key role in measuring and guiding Virgin Atlantic's quality-led strategy. His market research demonstrated that Virgin Atlantic scored above every other European carrier in areas including the quality of food, in-cabin service and service in the airport. Welbon attributed the quality of service directly to Branson's personal motivational activities: 'At BA, the average flight attendant has never met Lord King or Colin Marshall. Once a year she gets an assessment from the head of cabin crews. At Virgin Atlantic, every flight attendant has met Richard Branson many times. The effect of that shows up directly in how they do their jobs.' Welbon's surveys indicated that a Virgin Atlantic flight attendant answered a passenger call on average within forty-five seconds. 'I recently flew a US carrier to the States and a steward came to my seat forty minutes after I rang the call button.'

Welbon's research showed that while only 10 per cent of transatlantic travellers have flown with Virgin, the airline's image was much higher among those who had flown with them than those who had not. The reverse was the case with the once respected US carriers TWA and Pan Am who, after thirteen years of American so-called 'deregulation', scored below Aeroflot and Balkan Bulgarian in overall quality, according to an independent survey by *Which?* magazine in 1991. The more Virgin could get people to try its airline, the more converts it would make among the 90 per cent of non-flyers. Hence the high priority for advertising to reach the *non*-flyers.

It could be argued that the effect of Virgin Atlantic's success has yet to translate through to the bottom line. In 1991, the airline chalked up pre-tax profits of £6.16 million, a far from overwhelming figure on a turnover of £383 million. Chris Moss argued that Virgin Atlantic's strength came from making its product its first priority rather than profit. Moss viewed profit as a constraint: the airline had to live within its financial guidelines, but as long as it made ends meet, every investment in product and reputation was worthwhile: 'We want the flight to be enjoyable, we want passengers to come back again, we want to offer an on-board lounge, we want to provide a limo service. All of these things are a way of us saying we're not the biggest but we want to be the best, and they all add up to a package that is unbeatable in terms of value.'

Virgin's group financial director Trevor Abbott reinforced Moss's view of Virgin's priorities: 'We're all in business to make a profit. But I don't give a shit, to be colloquial, about the profit and loss statement. What I'm interested in is capital profit, and growth over the long term which you can see on the balance sheet.'

Branson agreed that short-term profit was a low priority for Virgin Atlantic. He pointed to Virgin Music, which despite modest profits was sold for £560 million because of its 'great credibility and excellent artists'. That deal dashed British Airways' hopes that Branson might exit the airline business due to lack of financial resources. But it pointed also to something else: Branson's eye for building a business in a strategic position in an evolving industry. After years of fighting against Air France's near-monopoly of French air traffic, tiny French airline UTA sold itself in 1991 to Air France for $1 billion (coincidentally, a similar price to that Branson received for his music business). In 1993, ongoing European deregulation of airlines allowed Branson to sell Virgin Atlantic to any Community-based airline. After the 'dirty tricks' affair with British Airways in 1992–3, Branson's first aim was to win flying rights and landing slots from the British government to enable Virgin Atlantic to grow. But if that did not happen, selling Virgin Atlantic was a potentially profitable option. Given the bitterness of the 'dirty tricks' war, British Airways was perhaps an unlikely buyer ('as likely as me and Lord King having a gay marriage' joked Branson). But by the mid-1990s other continental airlines would be in expansion mode. 'If you create something that is unique and special and you are flying on prime routes, then there is always a market for that.'

Most airline strategies of the 1980s, like Lord King's at BA or Carl Icahn's at TWA, were based on the twin touchstones of the industry: size and experience. By defying the herd, by starting small and focusing on offering quality to the customer, Branson turned an initial investment of £1.2 million into a £300 million company. Branson attributed his success to building the business from scratch: 'You go through all the pain, like that of the first three months when I learned about ticketing and reservations the hard way, and sweating it out that way through those long nights, almost like a university education, you learn the ins and outs of the industry, and you collect around you a team of survivors who are the best people.

'You end up with real people in a real company who are proud of what they are building instead of when you buy a company and end up with a bunch of people sitting in a boardroom.'

SIX

Virgin II

The Entrepreneur as Industrialist

Virgin Atlantic was an example of Branson's long-termist approach to building a business. His activities in television illustrated the other side of his business personality, the wily, short-term deal-maker. Branson never succeeded in bulding a television empire on a scale to rival Britain's other media entrepreneurs, but out of the glare of public attention he made millions of pounds for Virgin. The occasion was the creation of an obscure satellite televison channel called Superchannel.

The birth of Superchannel went back to July 1986, when Thorn EMI sold a stake in a new satellite television channel, Music Box, to Virgin for £1. Under the leadership of new chief executive, Colin Southgate, Thorn was keen to exit the entertainment industry. When Virgin Communications chief Robert Devereux negotiated the purchase of Thorn's share in Music Box, he knew ITV companies Granada and Yorkshire were keen to be more involved in the satellite channel. The Thorn man who stayed up until 3.30 a.m. negotiating the deal headed a Thorn engineering division and was unaware of moves in the television industry. A week later, Devereux sold 35 per cent of Music Box to Yorkshire and Granada Television. Price: £1 million. Not bad for a week's work. Better was to come.

Also in July, the regional independent television companies

formed a new company called ITV Superchannel Ltd, jointly owned by fourteen of the fifteen companies. The company's avowed aim was to use the new, exciting medium of satellite television to transmit British television programmes to a new 'pan-European' audience. 'Pan-European' was the voguish concept describing the single audience that potentially existed across Europe. With cable and satellite television, it was possible to reach millions of homes across Europe from one satellite transmitter floating high above Europe. Advertisers of soft drinks, personal care products and even consumer electronics were increasingly launching and promoting products in a single pan-European marketing campaign. All it would take was the right television progammes to create a single, profitable pan-European audience. The ITV executives were sure this would be British programmes, especially those made by themselves. This piece of hubris was the fundamental mistake that would cost them millions. There was no evidence that the largely Belgian, Swiss, Dutch and German audience which in 1986 had cable or satellite television wanted to watch British programming; their traditional national television channels had never shown much interest in buying British pro-gramming. But ITV executives like Brian Tesler of London Weekend and David Plowright at Granada, the two driving forces behind Superchannel, believed British television was the best in the world and therefore, as night follows day, Europeans would queue up to watch it. Thames Television was the only ITV company which refused to join the Superchannel consortium; Thames was also the only ITV company which had produced a programme, the *Benny Hill Show*, where the pound notes from sales to overseas broadcasters might have stacked higher than a pile of positive reviews from the critics.

In an early morning meeting in the bathroom at Branson's Notting Hill home, Branson and Devereux plotted strategy for Music Box. Branson was in the bath and Devereux sat on the lavatory. With the slow development of pan-European advertising, Music Box might lose money for years to come. To offset their losses, Branson suggested selling Music Box's (largely pop-video) programming to ITV for late night broadcast in the UK. Devereux wanted to sell Music Box's programming to Superchannel for daytime broadcast. They agreed that Branson would pursue the ITV option while Devereux approached Superchannel.

Superchannel embraced Music Box eagerly. They wanted its programming, but needed its satellite transmitter. Quickly, Devereux opened a second set of negotiations with American channel MTV, creating competition for his property. The result was that in August 1986 Superchannel purchased Music Box for £17.5 million cash. At that point, Virgin owned 60 per cent of Music Box. In one summer, Virgin had turned £1 into nearly £9 million. Never did Simon Draper's assessment of Branson seem more accurate: 'He is not an entrepreneur, he's an opportunist. He sees opportunities and he grabs them.'

Although Virgin owned just 15 per cent of the new Superchannel, it was agreed by the ITV executives on the Superchannel board that Virgin would play a large role in managing the channel since its people had experience of satellite television, a highly competitive, shoestring-budget business. But the ITV group did not want to lose control. A system of joint managing directors was devised. Virgin veteran Charles Levison and Richard Hooper, recruited by ITV from British Telecom, shared the top job. The new management prepared for the January 1987 launch by negotiating a succession of sweetheart deals: a new Virgin-owned company named Music Box was contracted to make six hours a day of pop music programming for Superchannel; the video editing and other technical services were contracted to Virgin's facilities company West One Television; finally, Superchannel paid rent for its premises in London's Rathbone Place, to Virgin who owned the building. ITV had one sweetheart deal of its own, providing news to Superchannel via ITN, the ITV-owned news broadcaster. ITV agreed to waive all fees it was entitled to from the broadcast of ITV-owned dramas and comedies until Superchannel was in profit. Virgin did not make any such charitable move.

Beginning in 1986, West One Television made an annual profit

181

of some £1 million, nearly all attributable to work done for Superchannel, recalled Virgin Television deputy MD Chris Palin. Music Box MD Mike Hollingsworth put his company's annual profit at £2 million during those three years. 'Richard set up Music Box with £750,000 of capital and I never had to touch a penny of it. We were cash-positive from day one.' One of Britain's best-known television journalists, Hollingsworth turned down the offer of a job as Superchannel's programme director for the editorially less interesting job at Music Box, largely because he saw the financial and business possibilities of the latter. 'I became a classic Virgin entrepreneur with a large slice of the action, running a small company staffed by low-paid eighteen-year-olds,' Hollingsworth recalled. A boyish-looking blond with the straight-talking style of a man raised in the newsroom, Hollingsworth smiled wryly as he related the story of Virgin and Superchannel. As he saw it, the Rathbone Place building, divided by a central corridor between Superchannel and the Virgin companies, was like a funnel. Money poured in on one side and left through the other. At the lushly appointed Superchannel, portly ITV executives visited regularly, their chauffeured cars idling patiently outside. Across the corridor, the Virgin companies were furnished and serviced much more austerely, but earned enormous profits. Hollingsworth's biggest problem was figuring out what to do with his cash mountain before other parts of the Virgin empire could claim it. At its peak, it reached £3 million cash, all in the Regent Street branch of Lloyds Bank. Commented Hollingsworth: 'I am convinced that early on in Richard Branson's career he recognised that if you could get a foothold in a company using services and resources you could influence that company's outgoing contracts and sell to it. It's not corrupt. On the contrary, it's totally overt. If anyone confronted him over it, he just grinned and admitted it.'

Within weeks of joining Superchannel, joint MD Richard Hooper took a long break, suffering from nervous exhaustion. ITV's man in the company was out of action for the three most crucial months in the station's life. Among the many tasks Charles Levison accomplished in Hooper's absence was devising the

Superchannel office plan. Levison's office took up most of the length of the rear wall of the building. 'Hooper was in the cupboard area at the corner,' recalled one executive. To many it would have been obvious the company was firmly in Virgin's grip and the lemon was about to be squeezed. But ITV executives had little experience of the harsh world of competitive business. One Superchannel executive remarks: 'People like Plowright and [programme director] Carole Haslam were into big ideas and public service television. It was very impressive to listen to but it wasn't business.' An advertising executive who served briefly at Superchannel was more blunt: 'They thought they would colonise Europe with the best of British broadcasting. It was the crudest piece of misdirected jingoism.'

Richard Hooper returned to work in January 1987, days before Superchannel's launch. Prime Minister Margaret Thatcher, no less, attended the launch party at Rathbone Place on 29 January. At 6 p.m. on 30 January, Superchannel began broadcasting. Within a half hour, despair set in, 'Faxes began to arrive from BBC saying we couldn't broadcast this programme and that programme because they hadn't obtained consents from the artists. By the end of the evening the entire schedule was shot to bits.' Superchannel had failed to conclude union agreements with either Equity or the Musicians' Union to determine a pay scale of fees to artists for satellite broadcasts. Not only programmes but adverts too were pulled. The small number of so-called pan-European viewers who tuned in, curious about what 'Best of British' television might mean, saw a large number of repeats of a Pond's Cold Cream advert. In the US, where scarcely a soul had ever heard the term 'pan-European', the advertisers had been foresighted enough to secure worldwide satellite and cable right from their artists.

Legally blocked from broadcasting most of their ads and with the BBC unable or unwilling to deliver broadcast rights on many of the programmes in their schedule, Superchannel was losing £4 million a month. By July 1987 they would be out of cash. Yet, for the first few weeks, the ex-ITV executives seemed to believe it would all come right in the end. 'We had meetings where topics on the agenda were the quality of the office plants and whether the carpet had thick enough pile,' recalled the executive. He said he did not know whether to laugh or cry when Virgin's Robert Devereux turned up one morning to negotiate a new deal on office furnishings. 'We were burning up millions a month and choosing new potted plants. It was the original Comedy Channel.'

In the midst of these corporate machinations, an event occurred which displayed Branson's unique charm. A call came through to Virgin Television from a client in Turkey saying a minister of the Turkish goverment was coming to London to see Mrs Thatcher and he wanted to see a modern television facility. Could Virgin oblige? West One boss Chris Palin immediately saw the business opportunities and arranged for a full tour of the Rathbone Place premises. The puckish Godfrey Pye took an especial delight in making the arrangements: 'I told Richard: this is great! We've got a minister coming, albeit a Turk. We must roll out the red carpet! You may even pick up something for your holiday company.'

As Pye related it, on the appointed afternoon several black cars slid to a halt at Rathbone Place and a group of men in dark suits with bulges under their left arm emerged. 'Mr Titiz was quickly bored with the walls of TV monitors and wanted to talk to Richard Branson.' They were shown to a boardroom where a smiling Branson joined them. Speaking through an interpreter, Mr Titiz said: 'Have you visited our country?'

Branson replied: 'My plane stopped over there briefly on my way back from visiting with Intourist in Moscow. I must say, I think you're doing marvellous things in Greece.'

The entire room fell silent. Branson had committed the worst *faux pas* imaginable, confusing Turkey with its 4000-year-old rival. After a few moments the Turks abruptly stood up, muttered their goodbyes and left. As Pye explained about Alexander The Great, Kemal Atatürk and Cyprus, Branson shook his head: 'Boy, I really blew it didn't I?' To Pye and Palin's amazement, Branson went on an immediate walkabout through Virgin's offices telling all and sundry the story of how he'd 'blown it'. Even the cynical Pye was impressed by Branson's modesty, lack of embarrassment, and sheer determination to maintain the camaraderie which was part of the Virgin corporate spirit. 'You just couldn't help but love a guy who could make a terrific balls-up like that and then go around enjoying a laugh at his own expense with his own employees,' said Palin.

In August 1987, cracks began to appear in Superchannel's support when the station asked for more capital from its ITV shareholders. The initial capital of £40 million was close to exhaustion. Eager to keep the gravy train rolling, Virgin offered to contribute its full 15 per cent. Grudgingly, ITV agreed to kick in another £20 million.

Six months later, that too was gone. The final bust-up occurred in April 1988, when Central Television and London Weekend Television refused to put in any more money. 'It was like a Feydeau farce,' commented one board member, recalling how Superchannel chairman Brian Tesler insisted Central's represent-ative on the Superchannel board leave the room when Central refused to put in more cash. Minutes later, the phone rung for Tesler. It was his boss, London Weekend Holdings chairman Christopher Bland. LWT's board had decided not to put in more money. Tesler had no choice but to eject himself from the room, with Robert Devereux taking over as chairman. 'I came into the reception area and found the chairman of LWT skulking around like a naughty schoolboy out of class,' said one Superchannel executive. For Tesler this was a painful moment. The 'Best of British' crusade was close to his heart. But LWT's loss on Superchannel was already £5 million and the hardheaded Bland had had enough.

ITV's travails were not yet over. They needed a buyer to take the 85 per cent of the channel off their hands. Virgin had got them coming; now Virgin would get them going. At a May 1988 television trade show in Cannes, Levison met Marielena Marcucci of Beta Television, Italy's second largest private broadcaster. Keen to expand beyond Italy, Marcucci leapt at the chance to become partners with Virgin in Superchannel. This discussion took place on a Friday evening at the bar of Levison's Cannes hotel; he would have an answer before the weekend was over, the vivacious Italian assured him.

On the Saturday morning, Marielena called Levison at his hotel room in Cannes: could he come to Lucca on Sunday? Marielena's father Guelfo Marcucci ruled Beta Television and the Marcucci pharmaceutical empire from the beautiful walled Tuscan city of Lucca. The city was virtually a personal fief of the super-rich family. Marcucci dispatched his personal helicopter to take Levison from Cannes to Lucca. A tentative deal was struck for 50 per cent of Superchannel at a low price, reflecting the business's lack of profit.

Back in London, Levison came up with a clever wheeze: if Virgin could buy out ITV at an even lower price it could turn a profit selling 50 per cent to the Marcuccis. At a London hotel, Levison made his offer: £1 for ITV's 85 per cent interest in Superchannel . . . plus a payment of £3 million to Virgin to cover Superchannel's considerable debts. ITV were desperate to get out. With the 1991 franchise renewal round approaching, they were concerned that too much Superchannel publicity could hurt their image. By September, the ITV negotiating team, led by Anglia's Tim Wooton and Yorkshire's Andy Hardy, agreed to meet Levison's price. At an evening meeting at Anglia Television's London offices, they sat down to finalise the deal. But Marielena Marcucci had got wind of the meeting. She turned up at Anglia's Mayfair offices, only to find the doors locked. 'I threw stones at the windows until somebody finally heard,' Marielena recalled. She claimed Levison saw her and tried to distract the ITV men in the hope she would go away. (Levison doesn't remember this meeting.) After securing entry, Marielena announced she would take the ITV shares for nothing. For ITV, raising the sale price from minus £3 million to zero was no small achievement. On 1 Novmember 1988 Marielena Marcucci took over as managing director and majority shareholder of Superchannel.

Twenty-one days later, she put Superchannel into administration – effectively bankruptcy. She spent the next few months tearing up the sweetheart deals, negotiating down the amounts owed to creditors (the largest was of course Virgin), and when the differences arose with Branson, increasing Beta Television's stake in the company to maintain effective control. The Channel continued to lose money, but was for the first time efficiently run, and with the Marcuccis' goal of building a network in western and eastern Europe (Superchannel was the first western broadcaster to establish an audience in Moscow), it has what may prove to be a realistic business plan.

Richard Branson often talked of 'limiting the downside' as a fundamental principle in his business philosophy. The Super-channel affair gave a good view of how this philosophy can operate: by finding partners sufficiently naive or slow-witted to foot the bill while an army of Virgin companies pass money around via a blizzard of deals while, under the watchful eyes of Branson and Devereux, a net profit ultimately returned to Virgin. A study of the history of Virgin's deals reveals a surprisingly large number of companies who enter willingly into such partnerships, often prompted by a need to fulfil public pledges to shareholders, or grandiose statements of strategy or principle, or just an irrational desire to be in the glamorous world of entertainment which Virgin made its natural habitat.

In just over two years, fourteen ITV companies had lost some £50 million on Superchannel. Virgin had invested some £5.5 million in the channel, but earned far more than that in profits from the various share sales and 'sweetheart' deals. In addition they came out with two intact businesses, West One Television and Music Box, and a large shareholding in Superchannel. At the end of his eighteen months as Superchannel MD, Richard Hooper gave a neat summation of the affair from the ITV point of view: 'This is the first time in history that anybody has ever been raped by a Virgin.'

Branson declined to discuss Superchannel in detail, but he did not hide his disdain for much of ITV's management in the late 1980s; 'They were big boys, very big boys. Not very commercial boys, but they knew what was happening and they went into it with their eyes open.' Branson said that he preferred deals from which all sides emerged happy, a situation he claimed was more common than the Superchannel variety. 'I've been a street-fighter since the age of fifteen and for the first fifteen years of this company's existence there was only one word that mattered and that was survival.'

He added: 'I think I know my subjects fairly well and if I see an opportunity I will leap in there. But it's a small world and you are always having to come back and deal again with the same people and I learned early on that you need to try to strike deals whereby there is a bit in it for both sides, with perhaps a few exceptions –

'A bit of a contradiction there, I suppose,' he said, breaking into his boyish grin.

Many deal-makers build businesses in order to deal; they labour for ten or twenty years to build a large, successful business, which then languishes as their attention turns to the red-blooded excitement of power-breakfasting with obsequious merchant bankers, launching dawn raids, buying and selling companies, and the other melodramatic pantomimes of finance that create shareholder value without increasing national wealth. Branson took the reverse course: he dealt in order to build businesses. When the American magazine *Fortune* published its 1992 list of the world's billionaires, Richard Branson was the only name on the list to have built two world-class businesses. That he had done this by the age of forty-two made the feat only more impressive. It was testament that Branson's 'staff first' philosophy paid big dividends.

'I believe companies should be run from the bottom up, because the people at the bottom are in the front line. It's the engineers that make sure the planes get away properly, it's the air hostesses that customers are in contact with for several hours each trip, and it's the people at the airports they deal with every time they fly.'

He added: 'Too many companies put shareholders first, customers second and their staff third. Virgin's philosophy has been very much staff first, and if you put your staff first then your customers effectively also come first, and your shareholders sort of catch up.'

In the 1980s, as Virgin Music's profits skyrocketed and Branson became a celebrity, many Virgin employees grumbled that the hippie capitalist had become entirely capitalist and not at all hippie. 'Poster boy for Mrs Thatcher's capitalism,' grumbled one ex-Virgin employee, while another commented: 'We were supposed to be different from the breadheads.' The spirit of teenage rebellion that nourished Branson's enthusiasm in its early days matured into a business instinct for challenging companies he perceived as big, slow, flabby or profiting from a protected monopoly. His deal-making often succeeded because he was driven, like a bird with an uncanny homing instinct, towards sectors where fat, lazy companies made easy prey. Like most entrepreneurs, Branson was uncomfortable with introspection. When asked if he was on something of a crusade to out-compete or out-manoeuvre those fat and lazy companies, he seemed shocked at first but soon embraced the idea.

He described his excitement in 1992 when he negotiated a route to South Africa, breaking the sixty-year monopoly of South African Airways and British Airways.

'It is more than just business, it is almost a crusade. You know, it's nice to be popular, it's nice to be liked, and when you know that everybody in South Africa desperately wants some competition, some lower fares and better quality service, you want to get in and offer them that.' Branson went on to relate how he had met with the South African minister of transport to try and get a commitment on opening up the route to Virgin Atlantic: 'It was enormous fun because I sat opposite this man and he started talking the way a politician talks. He didn't say anything at all.

'So straight afterwards I held a press conference outside his building praising him for an hour, wonderful that he's finally agreed to break the monopoly, etc. etc. I wasn't quite sure whether it was what he'd actually said but by the end of the day he hadn't contradicted it, and very soon we'll be up and flying to Johannesburg and it is tremendously rewarding and satisfying. It's great for the staff, it's great for our other routes, and one feels that we've actually done a service and helped the profits of the company.

'Our next battle now is Australia.'

Virgin Records International MD Jon Webster offered an amusing snapshot anecdote of Branson the business crusader a decade earlier: 'When I was at Virgin Retail, A&M Records came to London once a year and held a dinner each night for the major record retailers. We were the last night. It was not to talk about trading or anything, it was just "thank you we've had a great year". So about twenty of us sat down in a big alcove in a stuffy restaurant, everybody in suits except our crowd. All the A&M guys ordered Perrier. Our lot ordered wine, but it's all very boring and then we're on the brandies by now and suddenly Richard says let's talk about discounts.

'The A&M guys say: come on Richard, now is not the time.

'Richard says: Fuck off, c'mon, you're giving us twelve and a half per cent and we want more!

'Richard climbs up on to the table and says: I'm going to take my clothes off one by one until you give me more fucking discounts.

'He got down to his underpants before he was dragged off the table.'

While Virgin's rebellious streak makes good copy for newspapers, it has also had a positive effect on many of the monopolistic industries which it has shaken up. As managing director of Island Records, David Betteridge gave Branson his start in the record business when he agreed to distribute Virgin's first releases in 1973. Betteridge credited Virgin with revolutionising record retailing in the UK: 'He was the first to go for stack 'em high and sell 'em cheap. There was a fair amount of outrage from the Establishment at the time – the same as what he's trying to do now with the airline.'

Betteridge attributed Virgin's success to Branson's persistent ability to keep in touch with his business at the sharp end. 'A lot of men put the trappings of their wealth around them. They lose the shape of their business because they miss the ability to see what's going on on the ground. Richard is not like that. He's extremely wealthy yet he's still got that hunger to succeed. He's still a street-fighter.'

*

In 1986, Richard Branson made the worst mistake of his career, when he decided to take Virgin Group public on the London Stock Exchange. He had good reasons to take the company public, both negative and positive. On the negative side, he had repeatedly come up against resistance from his main bankers, Coutts (part of National Westminster). They had been his bankers since he was a teenager and Branson felt they had failed to grow with his company. 'There's a danger sometimes that you treat your bank like your parents,' he said.

The flotation started off badly. On 13 November 1986, Virgin Group plc went public with a valuation of £240 million. But the City of London's institutional investing community largely ignored the issue. 'We had 60,000 small shareholders, the largest of any offer outside of privatisation, but it wasn't underpinned by institutional support,' said Branson.

For Branson, a strong share price was especially essential in 1987. Branson had a secret master plan: a hostile takeover bid for Thorn EMI. Branson's plan was to use Virgin's shares to acquire Thorn EMI, selling off Thorn's television rental business to property and retail group Mountleigh, then led by the expansionist Tony Clegg. 'The plan was to do a Hanson: sell off all Thorn's other businesses and end up with the music business, debt-free,' recalled Trevor Abbott, Virgin's group financial director.

The lack of institutional investors' support was a serious problem for a new public company facing what was likely to have been a hostile takeover war against Thorn. Although Thorn had a very chequered record on the stock market, it had a long history in the City and close links with powerful City investing institutions. It would certainly be able to put up a strong fight if it chose to. Virgin Group had just begun quietly accumulating Thorn shares when the Crash of 19 October 1987 struck.

'I thought we should average down but the non-executives disagreed,' said Branson. 'Average down' was market terminology for continuing to buy the shares at the new lower price, bringing down the average purchase price of the shares. It is the lingo of the risk-taker, but the non-executive directors who had joined

Virgin when the company went public were not risk-takers. Led by Don Cruickshank, veteran of the old money Pearson newspapers-to-wax-museum group, the non-executives saw their role as putting a check on Branson's wilder schemes. The Thorn takeover was abandoned.

It is impossible to know how Virgin Group might have developed had it succeeded with what Branson called the 'Big One'. However, it performed surprisingly badly with many of the smaller investments it made during its thirty-three months as a public company. In 1986, Virgin plunged into the property business, with a subsidiary called Vanson Developments (the name a melding of Virgin and Branson). Branson was renowned for insisting on cheapness when it came to offices and had always resisted the temptation to branch out into property. 'My office had four buckets and we needed every one of them when it rained,' recalled former Virgin Records senior executive Lisa Anderson. Spare cash at Virgin always went into new acts or new companies. But after Virgin went public, Vanson ploughed millions into the property market, buying several large tracts in Crawley, home of Virgin Atlantic's headquarters. Even before the 1989–90 collapse of property values, several of Vanson's largest investments went sour. In 1989, the company chalked up a staggering pre-tax loss of £5.7 million.

Virgin also established a publishing, broadcasting, video and television group, under the umbrella company Virgin Communications, and led by the ambitious Robert Devereux. Married to Branson's sister, Vanessa, Devereux was the most intellectual of the Virgin inner circle. More articulate than his brother-in-law, he was far better at expressing and explaining the principles behind Virgin's business strategies or management philosophies. Like Branson, he was a deal-maker, enjoying nothing more than working out the hundreds of fine points, subclauses and options that are attached to the dozens of possible outcomes contained in any major deal. But Devereux's business objectives were more conventional than Branson's. Branson's new initiatives were typically in obscure byways of the business world (model agencies, catering services, vintage airplane rides) or what colleagues considered outright crazy like Virgin Atlantic Airline. Devereux was attracted by the cut and thrust of City deals: acquisitions, joint ventures, earn-outs, and other manoeuvres made possible by the smoke and mirrors of 'paper' transactions (ie payment in shares) and acquisition accounting. Branson shared Devereux's media ambitions, especially if it led to a Virgin television channel beaming the name into British homes every evening.

By 1991, Devereux was a convential Virgin entrepreneur – that is, an entirely unconventional businessman by City standards. In that year, Devereux's most successful business was in computer video games, their creation, distribution and retailing. Like most Virgin businesses, it had been started from scratch in an industry the 'suits' did not understand or dismissed as dominated by Japanese giants Nintendo and Sega. Yet by 1991, video games were the hottest item with teenagers and Devereux's Virgin Communications earned £10 million operating profit.

In the 1980s though, two of Virgin's worst deals ever occurred as part of Devereux's efforts to buy and build a media empire. The acquisition of London video editing company Rushes for £5.3 million from Godfrey Pye, the largest acquisition in Virgin's history, turned out to be far more expensive than Virgin planned after the company proved to need significant investment in a new generation of editing equipment. Pye did not take to the Virgin culture. His relations with Devereux deteriorated steadily until he quit in 1988. Another, more complicated, deal, in which Virgin took a minority shareholding in long-established best-seller publisher WH Allen and attempted to merge it with its Virgin Books, publisher of pop music books, also went badly wrong. Said Robert Devereux: 'It was one of the worst business decisions ever. We acquired a controlling interest at far too high a price and, taking the view it wasn't part of the Virgin family, we let the management get on with it without enough involvement.'

Branson was personally chagrined when the situation deteriorated to the point where Virgin Group plc had to buy out the other shareholders in WH Allen, and embark on a rationalisation which, for one of the few times in Virgin's history, involved forced redundancies. 'WH Allen was basically bankrupt and, as a public company, we couldn't be involved with anything on the brink of bankruptcy, so we had to put more money in and lay people off and break contracts with authors. The whole thing was just a nightmare,' Branson recalled.

In the acquisition of Rushes and WH Allen, Virgin fell into the same trap as many other public companies in the 1980s. Buying a 'people business' from its founders was always likely to create problems: it immediately enriched the founders, robbing them of part of their incentive to make the company succeed. Turning people who were previously their own bosses into employees was a transition almost guaranteed to demotivate and often create outright resentment, especially in the sort of people strong-willed enough to have created their own successful company.

Devereux claimed that with the aid of new management, both companies had since been sorted out. Devereux did not abandon WH Allen. He downsized it, focused it on non-fiction, and made it profitable again. 'One of the reasons for Virgin's success is its tenacity and never-say-die attitude,' he believed. Rushes regained its reputation as one of London's three most prestigious video-editing houses, its quality image reflected in the high prices it charges. 'Rushes is today worth twice what we invested in it,' Devereux said. But he added: 'In retrospect, if we hadn't been a public company we definitely wouldn't have done either of those acquisitions.'

More serious than the small acquisitions that went wrong was the corrosive effect that going public had on Virgin's core business, the UK record label, and especially on company chairman Simon Draper.

To visit Draper at his Virgin office in 1992 was to see a man surrounded by the rewards of building one of the most successful, creative, and innovative record companies in the history of the industry. Behind his large desk hung what some might call a painting. It was a wooden barn-door split in half, stuck on to a canvas, and splotched with dark streaks of colour. Other bizarre and intimidating pieces of art hung from Draper's walls, threatening to attack the unwary visitor or misbehaving rock star at any moment. One wall was reserved for pictures of Draper's car collection, which included his 30 Aston-Martins. Worth more than £3 million, and probably the world's largest collection of the marque, there were several classic 1960s-era 'James Bond' Astons, a red 1992 6.3 litre Virage, and a silver convertible 1992 Volante. The location of Virgin Records' headquarters, sandwiched between the busy Harrow Road and a disused canal in a grotty corner of northwest London, reflected Branson's obsession with cheap offices, but the building reflected Draper's tastes. A bold, stately, late-Victorian mansion painted bright white, it was attached, via a tall, slender glass atrium, to a modern, brightly sunlit new wing. The matt-black reception area was coldly minimalist. Even the sleek, smiling receptionist, black-haired and dressed entirely in black, looked as if she might be automated, controlled from some invisible figure behind one of the high black metal panels surrounding the reception area. Another 'painting' in the reception area bore the intriguing quote from Lenin, perhaps directed at Virgin's new owners, Thorn EMI: 'Liberty is precious. So precious that it must be rationed.'

On the telephone Draper wrestled with the director of the World Pheasant Protection Society, slithering out of a charity fund-raising auction. Draper kept over 100 varieties of pheasant in an aviary at his Sussex mansion. 'I'm motoring all day at Goodwood, then I have a dinner party at home, so the likelihood of making my way back into London for an auction is pretty low, I'm afraid . . .'

After Branson, Draper was the most important individual in the entire Virgin Group. His musical and entrepreneurial instincts had shaped the company, and his leadership was admired and respected throughout the organisation. But by 1986, before Virgin's flotation, Draper was disgruntled. Record company profits had soared to £15 million. Branson had taken those profits and invested them in a large number of other ventures, including Virgin Atlantic Airways, which Draper saw as an expensive, highly risky business in a field where Virgin had no expertise. In additon Virgin profits paid for Branson's increasingly expensive lifestyle. By 1986, he had a sprawling home in Oxfordshire, his Necker Island estate in the Caribbean, and was about to move from a large home in Ladbroke Grove to an even larger home in Holland Park. Branson's lifestyle could not be called lavish: in 1986, he rode around in a chauffeur-driven Ford Escort. Branson's houses, like virtually everything else his money went into, were used as much for business as for pleasure; for Branson his business was his pleasure which was his life. But from Simon Draper's point of view the crucial difference was that as owner of 80 per cent of the Virgin Group, Branson had total discretion over how to spend all the money.

Draper owned 20 per cent of Virgin Records, but saw little benefit from that shareholding. In 1986, he still lived, with his wife Françoise, in the same basement/ground floor Ladbroke Grove flat he'd lived in for years. 'I didn't like being a minority shareholder. I needed a way to realise my assets, so naturally I was in favour of going public,' Draper recalled.

'It was the very day the company floated,' recalled Steve Lewis, then running Virgin Music Publishing. 'Simon came into my office with a set of keys in his hand, and said: come for a drive in my new Aston-Martin.' Worth some £20 million in Virgin shares after the company hit the stock market, Draper became alienated from the business. He discovered he hated being a public company: 'We'd always run the business for the long-term and suddenly it was all turned right round. It was so uncomfortable.' All five members of the Virgin inner circle hated the laborious time-consuming process of lunching City investors, meeting with bankers, brokers and accountants, to discuss annual results, semi-annual results, formulate public statements on strategy, and so on. But none hated it more than Simon Draper. Steve Lewis recalled: 'Simon would come back from a meeting in the City, and I'd say Simon how'd it go, and he'd say: "Great! I met a guy who knew all about Miles Davis and we spent the whole lunch talking about his old records."'

Draper was disillusioned by the contrast between the dull, unimaginative demands of the City, and the exciting prospect of Virgin's expansionist dreams. The needs of the City were twofold: first, a public company had to issue a statement of long-term business strategy, preferably a clear and easy-to-understand one; secondly, and more importantly, it must deliver annual increase in profit every year, equal or slightly above the targets it set for itself via the City's analysts who acted as its jungle drums to the shareholding community. A cynic would say that the strategy was often so much window-dressing and behind the scenes many public companies ignored it and focused on keeping profits rising each year. With its tradition of open discussion of everything and family-style management, Virgin was more sincere, and perhaps more naive, about its long-term strategy. When Branson said he had gone public to build Virgin into a worldwide record business, he meant it. Virgin financial director Trevor Abbott said the company earmarked an investment of at least $30 million to build a record company in the United States. Each year some of that investment had to come out of Virgin's annual profits. Ironically, if Branson had decided to buy an existing American record company, he could have deployed accounting techniques to put the cost of the investment through the balance sheet and leave Virgin's annual profits unaffected. These accounting techniques, known officially as acquisition accounting, and less officially as 'the Indian rope trick', were used by hundreds of British public companies in the 1980s and, to a lesser extent, in the 1990s. But acquisition of a record business was anathema to Branson, who thought he could organically build a record company as well as anyone in the world.

Following the model pioneered on the Continent, in 1986 Branson, Draper and Berry recruited two top American record executives they knew well (Jordan Harris and Jeff Ayeroff), gave them 10 per cent equity in Virgin Records USA, invested in a modest infrastructure in Los Angeles and in the multi-million dollar signing of ageing rocker Stevie Winwood, who was again hot in the US, to give the label some pizazz. The results were little short of amazing. Virgin's first release in the US, by a band called Cutting Crew, went to number one (duplicating the experience of their first release thirteen years earlier in the UK). Over the next three years hit acts including Soul 2 Soul, Lenny Kravitz and Paula Abdul emerged from the label at a rate out of all proportion to its size. As Virgin's British acts came free from their commitments to other US labels and returned to Virgin, the US label could only grow in size and profitability.

But while the news from the US was overwhelmingly good, all was not well at home. For the first time, Draper felt out of touch with the increasingly fragmented musical tastes of the teenage generation. 'I found it hard to get the enthusiasms of a nineteen-year-old,' he admitted. In 1988, Draper 'semi-retired' from the business, handing over to Jon Webster who became MD of the UK record company. But Draper retained control of A&R which included the signing of all new artists. The result was a damaging division of responsibilities at the core of the business. Said Webster: 'We had a situation where A&R were saying this is brilliant, go, go, go, and the rest of the company were saying no, maybe it's not brilliant. As a company we weren't really being led by A&R and we weren't as focused as we should have been.' The real criticism was with Branson, who should have moved more aggressively to augment, or replace, Draper with other artist-orientated executives, a move Draper would scarcely have objected to. Absorbed with his airline, Branson took far less interest in management of the record company than before.

Costs escalated with the growing artist roster, UK profits declined, and the Virgin label broke few new acts after 1988. After the October 1987 Crash, the Thorn takeover plan had to be abandoned. In 1988, financial director Trevor Abbott devised a plan to extricate Virgin from this uncomfortable situation. He proposed the company return to private status by buying itself back from the public shareholders with the aid of a £180 million bank loan from a syndicate of banks led by the American Citibank. The bank loan would mean a heavy schedule of repayments, but Abbott had a menu of options to show the debt could be repaid.

One option was selling the record company. 'When I first went to them [Virgin's directors], they were aghast. The non-executives thought I was crazy. But I was fanatical about wanting to do it. I was more certain of that decision than of anything else in my entire business career.'

Branson was quickly converted to Abbott's scheme. Typically impatient, Branson was now just as contemptuous of the gyrations of the stock market as he had been of the timidity of bankers five years earlier. 'In 1988 our profits doubled from fifteen to thirty-one million pounds, yet because the market crashed our stock price went down,' he said with a touch of bitterness. In addition, Branson hated spending time working the City, repeating platitudes to brokers and bankers with scant understanding of the entertainment industry. Privately, he was slightly pleased Virgin's non-executive directors were against the idea. Their presence had made the Virgin board into yet another talking shop. 'I don't agree with the idea of non-execs on a board. I think everybody on a board should have something to do, a company to run,' Branson said.

On 30 July 1989, Abbott's scheme took effect. Virgin Group plc was replaced with four new holding companies: Virgin Music, Virgin Retail (the Megastores), Virgin Communications (embracing television, video, books and computer games) and Virgin Holdings (the airline and travel agency, as well as assorted other businesses including nightclubs, balloons and property).

Virgin Music chairman Simon Draper was characteristically blunt in his diagnosis of Virgin's experiment in going public: 'I think Richard did it because, in the 1980s, it was the badge of success of the triumphant entrepreneur.'

Branson rejected the idea that personal glory was behind his decision, but conceded: 'For just a brief part of our life we mistakenly thought that it would be great to go public and use your shares to acquire other companies. It was the way things were done at the time and perhaps there was a bit of "everybody was doing it".

'The upside was that we showed people we were worth £250

million and that enabled us to go on and do other things. I think we underestimated the downsides.'

All five members of Virgin's inner cabinet (Branson, Abbott, Berry, Devereux, Draper) claimed that no major decisions were ever taken without unanimous agreement. Relations remained friendly, but the previous intimacy between Branson and Draper waned as their interests grew apart, Branson's towards airlines and Draper's towards art and his other hobbies. One former Virgin executive comments: 'Simon and Richard didn't fall out, but they did stop playing tennis together.' The obvious solution to the problem of asset sales required by the bank loan was now to sell the record company. 'You have to have a passion for what you're doing and I could see that Simon was beginning to lose interest, and in a sense it was time to move on to your next passion,' said Branson. 'Everything pointed to the sale of the record company,' commented Draper, ready to exchange his semi-detached position for a fully detached one. Abbott stressed that the sale was not required to meet the debt. 'If we had not sold, we would have been a £1.25 billion company [turnover] in 1992, and we could have easily carried the £200 million debt.' Devereux was worried about narrowing the base of Virgin's entertainments interests, but liked the big prices competitors were offering for the last big independent record company. Only Ken Berry resisted the idea. He feared the Virgin culture would not survive a sale to a new owner.

On 6 March 1992, Virgin Group announced it was selling Virgin Music to Thorn EMI for £560 million. As usual, Branson had played it long, dangling the company in front of potential buyers for well over a year. There were a couple of hiccups along the way: when the board of Hollywood entertainment conglomerate MCA decided against bidding for Virgin, MCA shareholder David Geffen called to tell not Branson but Thorn executive Colin Southgate, effectively suggesting that Thorn lower *its* bid for Virgin, in what looked to Branson like a gratuitous effort by Geffen to torpedo the sale, or at least bring the price down, preserving Geffen's reputation as the entrepreneur who built the world's most valuable record company (Geffen Records had gone to MCA for £320 million in 1990). Branson's comment was 'Over the years I'd met Geffen a few times and never thought there was any problem in our relationship.' Branson added that Thorn's Southgate was immediately suspicious of Geffen's motives and probably jumped to the conclusion that Geffen was plotting another manoeuvre to buy Virgin. The price Thorn paid, 1.7 times Virgin Music's turnover, was not unreasonable by comparison with previous deals. It looked high by comparison with Virgin's 1991 profits of only £21 million, but insiders expected that figure would double within a year as the US moved into profit, adding a net $15 million to the bottom line, and as rationalisation of Draper's over-heavy artist roster cut UK costs. 'We would have made economies ourselves if we hadn't sold,' Draper admitted.

As usual in a Branson deal, there was a last-minute stinger. Throughout the negotiations, the discussions included Branson's taking either cash or Thorn shares for Virgin. Thorn wanted to pay less if it paid cash; Branson insisted on the same £510 million. Twelve hours before the deal was done, Southgate relented, offering Branson the same £510 million in cash. 'I suspect Colin wasn't quite sure that he fancied me as the largest shareholder on his board,' said Branson. Perhaps more to the point, Thorn had had a fabulous 1991 in music and, subject to the City's need for annual profit increases, were licking their lips over Virgin's attractive 1992 schedule of record releases.

For Branson the decision to sell was not an easy one. The record company was the start of his business and right up to the sale always the most certain provider of profits. Branson had close personal relationships with many executives on the record company, some going back twenty years. Robert Devereux had dinner with his brother-in-law only a week before the deal was announced and even then Branson was anguished about selling: 'For Richard, it was like marrying off a daughter. You know she's got to get married, but you never stop having doubts and regrets.'

'There are lots of ways to look at it,' Branson commented later, still struggling with his feelings over the sale almost a year afterwards. 'I've always admired and believed in the Japanese philosophy of never selling anything, they just collected, collected, collected, never sold, and built up massive debt, and with the recession going on over there now I'm sure a lot of them wish they'd sold some of their assets before the market dropped completely.' Branson's voice trailed off as he pondered the issue. Selling the record company was the clearest case of the clash between his deal-making style and the family-business culture of long-term teamwork and mutual dedication he fostered at all his companies. One by one he rehearsed the arguments for selling: the boom in the prices achieved for record companies was probably at its peak; since he and Draper had lost interest, Thorn were better placed to move the record company forward and help it grow; selling out and investing in other businesses he would create more jobs and more wealth than not selling. 'If you do run a company where, hopefully, you care about individuals and where people are all-important and you do try to run it like you run your family, then obviously if you sell it's going to be far tougher for all concerned than if you are a normal company.' Branson broke off again, staring at the swans swimming lazily under the dull autumn sunshine in the pond behind his Oxfordshire home. 'You know, one day one's going to die anyway, and that's another way you can look at it. You don't live forever and you can't take anything with you, and perhaps the best thing you can do is to pass a company on to another company who can get all the benefits from it.'

On the morning of Friday 6 March 1992, Jon Webster's phone got him out of bed at 6 a.m., an unheard-of hour for a record company executive. Ken Berry told him the record company had been sold. Only weeks before Webster had moved sideways to run Virgin Records International, after Berry recruited Chrysalis man Paul Conroy to give the UK label a much-needed reorientation in its A&R policy. He had heard rumours since the previous Christmas that Richard might sell the record company to Thorn, so he was not surprised. But he was saddened. Like many at Virgin, his admiration for Branson bordered on idolisation. In his car en route to his office, Webster picked up the carphone and

one by one called every Virgin employee he could think of to warn
them of the press announcement coming later that morning. Most
simply said thank you and rung off, too lost for words to say
anything else. When Webster got to the office, he continued his
calls.

After lunch, the entire staff at the Virgin Records headquarters
gathered in the auditorium. The mood was sombre. For many,
Virgin was the only company they had ever worked for. Even those
who had never spoken more than two words to Branson or Draper
believed Virgin was a special place to work. They were worried
about the future. Many were also worried about their jobs.
Branson, Draper and Berry were at the front of the room, not
exactly on the stage but hovering around it. Jet-lagged from his
overnight return from Tokyo where he had gone to negotiate
agreement to the sale from Virgin's Japanese partner Fujisankei,
the slim, bearded Ken Berry stood wearily on the stage. Simon
Draper sat on the steps at one side while Branson, tired but full
as ever of nervous energy, paced around at the side. Branson
began to speak: he explained that the company had been sold to
Thorn EMI, but that there were guarantees that Virgin's autonomy inside Thorn would be preserved, under the leadership of
Ken as Virgin chief executive. He said there would be some
rationalisation, and said that for anybody who lost a job as a result
there would always be a job with him at Virgin Atlantic. It was the
wrong thing to say. Branson's off-the-cuff, obviously impractical
offer only reminded them of their fears. Sensing this, Branson
stopped. Draper broke the awkward silence. He began strongly,
characteristically going right to the point. 'Today I am very sad,
but I'm very rich. You probably don't feel sorry for me,' Draper
continued, trying to explain how much the company meant to him,
but he too found the words stuck in his throat. With 200 stunned
friends and colleagues staring at him he could not go on. Ken
Berry leapt into the breach, taking the discussion back towards
the details of the deal, leaving unanswered the big questions
surrounding the future.

Jon Webster thought the conversation was too trivial for such an occasion. When Berry asked questions, Webster stood up. Tall, gangly, exuberant, everybody knew Webster as one of the most dedicated members of the company. He looked across the room at Branson. 'Speaking entirely personally, I'd just like to thank Richard, Simon and Ken for the past seventeen years. Whatever happens in the future, it's been the happiest time of my life.' Webster sat down. Heads swivelled and stared at Branson who was crying. Branson looked up at the faces and bolted from the room. He ran all the way down Ladbroke Grove to his home in Holland Park.

'As I was running, I passed a sign saying "Branson sells for £500 million", and there I was, tears streaming down my face, and I thought: people are probably looking at me saying what the fuck has he got to cry about?'

He added: 'We'd been doing something since we were teenagers, and it was a difficult moment for everybody, especially me.'

Later Webster said: 'Richard always cries at occasions like that, which I think is a good thing, men *should* cry. That didn't surprise me. What surprised me was Simon. That was the first time I'd ever seen him at a complete loss for words.'

It took three months for executives to see what the future might hold. On 1 June, the sale became final. The next morning, Thorn announced eighty redundancies inside Virgin. Most of them were inside the Virgin Music Publishing Division and they included the MD of Publishing, Steve Lewis. Lewis had joined Virgin in 1969, leaving university before sitting his finals because a scruffy, intense teenager named Richard Branson promised him greater excitement with an organisation – it was more a student collective than a company then – called Virgin. The day Lewis's departure from Virgin was announced, Virgin Music Publishing had eight songs in the top 40, including the number one. Lewis had been managing director of Virgin Music Publishing Worldwide for eight years and raised profits every year. By 1991, Virgin Music Publishing had fourteen subsidiaries around the world, earning profits of £3.9 million on £30 million turnover. Steve Lewis was walking evidence of Jon Webster's dictum that 'the success of

Virgin was built on the willingness of every single person in this building to work their ass off for Richard'. In those eight years, Lewis turned down job offers from many other record companies, some of them offering to double his salary. As a director of Virgin Records, Lewis knew that Simon owned 20 per cent of Virgin Records, and he had himself owned 20 per cent of a Virgin artists' management company (which never made any profit). But he was never offered, nor asked for, share options, or an equity stake in the publishing business. 'In these cynical, post-Thatcher times, you could say I was dumb. But who else would make you MD of an important publishing company when you had absolutely no experience of publishing, and then give you the time to learn?' Lewis asked.

As 1992 wore on, Virgin executives had an object lesson in the difference between an entrepreneurial, family-style record company, and a large public company. One Virgin executive was shocked to be summoned to a meeting with a senior EMI executive at London's new luxury hotel, the Lanesborough. The EMI man's rooms, the Royal Suite (cost: £2500 per night), were festooned with flowers and butlers stood by to serve drinks, light cigarettes and hand ringing telephones to the record men as they lounged in sofas and chatted. Before its demise, Virgin Music Publishing had run 200 'live' UK publishing contracts (ie with artists actively writing new songs, as opposed to old copyrights which made up the bulk of a publishing company's catalogue). EMI Music Publishing UK had only sixty live contracts, yet employed sixty staff, twice the number at Virgin. 'At Virgin, the company was run in the interest of the shareholders, which meant Richard. Thorn seemed to be run in the interests of the senior management,' commented one former Virgin man.

When it came to compensation for laid-off Virgin executives, Thorn management were generous with their shareholders' money. The law set a minimum compensation term of one week's salary per year of service for each employee laid off. Ken Berry fought hard for a better deal for his colleagues. Thorn agreed compensation of one month's salary for every year of service. The wonders of acquisition accounting, where all the onetime costs of the Virgin takeover could be 'written off' without affecting Thorn's annual profits (the vital number for Thorn's investors and share price) smoothed the path for Thorn's generosity. 'I learnt a new word: "blackholing" an expenditure,' commented one longtime Virgin executive wryly.

Some of the promises about Virgin autonomy under the EMI umbrella would also vanish into thin air. Superstar Tina Turner was dissatisfied with her record label, EMI's Capitol division. So late in 1992, EMI chief executive Jim Fifield transferred her to the Virgin label. This neat solution kept the ageing soul singer happy and will probably help Virgin meet the demanding target of quadrupling profit Thorn EMI set at the time of the takeover. But it made a mockery of Virgin's traditional culture of building a close long-term relationship with its artists. It could be argued that Virgin's unique culture or musical philosophy was first undermined by Branson himself, when (with one eye on buyer-presumptive Thorn's hunger for market share) he signed ageing acts like the Rolling Stones and Janet Jackson. Ironically, the artist-sensitive philosophy survived more strongly at some of Virgin's non-UK subsidiaries. It will be difficult for this philosophy to survive Thorn's need for a quick boost to profits in 1993 and steady increases thereafter. If the Virgin culture of intense employee commitment and dedication is to survive, Thorn may also have to relax its strong management centralisation. By late 1992, several key Virgin employees voted with their feet. In November 1992, Jon Webster was one of those who announced his resignation.

Also in November 1992, Steve Lewis announced his new job. After turning down offers from most of Britain's large record companies, Lewis signed on as chief executive of Chrysalis Music Worldwide. Run by independent entrepreneur Chris Wright, Chrysalis had the same family-style, go-getting company culture Lewis had enjoyed at Virgin. Like Branson, Wright had sold his record company to the omnivorous EMI monolith. Lewis's job would be to lead Wright's effort to build a new record company (in direct competition with the label he had sold to EMI). Lewis pointed out that the week he announced his new job the number one and number two slots in the British singles chart were held by songs whose publishing rights he'd signed to Virgin. 'There has not been a new act out of Britain with global, long-term appeal since Simply Red. There's a tremendous opportunity right now for an independent label which believes in building artists,' said Lewis. In woolly jumper and with irrepressible enthusiasm, he sounded like a younger Simon Draper.

Lewis grew sad when he talked about Branson. He remarked that for all Branson's talk about the importance of people, it was Ken Berry and the Thorn staff who had dealt with the aftermath of the 6 March upheaval. Branson was scarcely involved. In March, Lewis phoned his old friend and they discussed their feelings about the sale. But over the following weeks and months, Lewis heard not one word from Branson, not even when Thorn announced Lewis's departure from the company. Lewis had received a seven-figure compensation package from Thorn; his disappointment wasn't over money, but over a friendship that seemed to have disappeared. The man Lewis had admired, perhaps idealised, more than any other in the world had lost some of his glitter. He was melancholy rather than angry.

'I'm trying to keep some perspective on this. The thing you can never take away from Richard is that he created a great working environment. You didn't work for a faceless corporation. You worked for a guy who cared about each one, individually. But he's not the same person as he was twenty years ago.'

When Branson learned of the redundancies, he set aside part of his profit from the sale for the victims. The sums ranged as high as £75,000, he said, and covered those who had been made redundant without compensation from Thorn and hadn't found other jobs. But some in the record industry were surprised. When in 1989 Island Records was sold to Polygram, every single employee down to the maintenance staff had had a small share in the profit.

*

Thanks to Thorn EMI's shareholders, by late 1992 Richard Branson had more cash in the bank than most people in the world. He still did not have an office. He still wore the same baggy sweaters, although he was showing a new willingness to wear the blazers in fine Italian wool that his wife bought for him. He still spent his weekends in the same rambling Cotswold farmhouse at the edge of the busy Cotswold town of Kidlington. One autumn afternoon, he held a meeting at the farmhouse with two investment bankers representing Japanese investors who wanted to participate in the fast-growing chain of record Megastores in Japan. The drive outside the house was full of Jaguars. A small, older Ford Escort, Branson's car, squatted by the front door. The walkway around the house to the back door was littered with children's bicycles and badminton rackets. In the sunken living room, washed by the sunshine streaming in from three sides, Branson and finance director Abbott slumped into soft, squishy sofas, drinking tea. Across from them, two suited bankers did not look terribly comfortable on their sofa. In the next room, Branson's children Holly and Sam watched television cartoons with their nanny.

Although the conversation with the bankers involved tens of millions of dollars, Branson asked them to wait when a reporter arrived to discuss the unpleasant subject of the future of Virgin Records and its employees. Leaping up the three steps through the patio doors, Branson walked silently across the vast garden, soon to be converted into a cricket pitch, to a large wooden gazebo, capped with an intricately painted ceiling on the high, pointed roof, in the same Indo-Chinese style as the beachside shelters on his Necker Island. Slumping in another soft, squishy sofa, he gazed at the swans which populated his private inlet of the River Windrush, and agonised over the question of the future of Virgin Records, the Virgin Group, and the people involved. He was as concerned with each individual as he was with the large financial issues. Trying to sum up the reasons for selling the record company and what it meant for everybody, the thoughts crowded in on him and he started, stopped and paused for long periods of thought. This was the Richard Branson the City had dismissed as inarticulate: options, explanations and a thousand possible outcomes flowed though his head like the currents in the Windrush, and he lacked the oratorial skill to express them. Yet actions spoke louder than words, and the sixth largest record company in the world, the highest-quality long-haul airline in the west, and the fastest-growing chain of record stores in the world were eloquent enough. The Virgin image – what Branson called doing everything with a sense of class – was appreciated around the world: in 1989, an American company had upped its offer by $5 million simply to keep the name 'Virgin' on a video company it bought from Branson.

'There is a sense of guilt involved here. It's a horrible feeling to think that somebody you know is looking for a job as a result of a decision you've made, and the only way I can defend that to myself morally is to say that fortunately it's very few people, and that Thorn has looked after them well, and that we will look after those that Thorn has not looked after. And that the end result, I think, will be that many, many more people will be employed than otherwise.

'That billion dollars, you know, it's not going to be left in a bank account. It's going to create quite a few new companies.'

SEVEN

ICL

Knocking out the World Champ

Dawn was breaking as Peter Frank warmed his car against the chilly January air. He cruised slowly down the hill, looking at the quiet little seventeenth-century houses that lined the main road of the old village where he lived. When he reached the Coventry ring road, he pointed his car towards the motorway and put his foot down. Got to allow plenty of time for London traffic, he thought. It was 9.15 a.m. on another grey, cloudy winter's day by the time Frank reached his destination, British Gas headquarters in London's High Holborn. He drove through the warren of tiny side streets to find the entrance to the underground car park. The security guard at the main reception smiled through the plastic window as he passed the sign-in book across. 'How are you today, Mr Frank?' Frank returned the smile. 'Not so bad, and yourself?' A large, fair-haired man, who looked more like a rugby player than a computer salesman, Frank always had a friendly greeting and never forgot a face. He took the lift to the fifth floor and walked quickly down the corridor to John Allan's office. He was two minutes early.

Allan's secretary took his coat and showed him into the office. Frank almost froze in mid-step. Sitting on the sofa was his archrival, Martin Goodman. Frank was the British Gas account director for British computer company ICL. Goodman did the

same job for American computer giant IBM. British Gas was one
of the largest users of computers and computing services in
Europe, spending over £100 million every year on information
technology. With its aggressive post-privatisation management, it
was growing, seeking out new markets at home and abroad. ICL
and IBM competed vigorously for every last crumb of computer
spending from British Gas. IBM was famous for its aggressive
sales force and Goodman fitted the mould. He was a wily
character, a charmer and a hard worker who had snatched his
share of big pieces of business from Frank.

'How're the wife and children, Martin?' said Frank with a big
smile.

Goodman rose and took the proffered hand. 'Great. And your
family is well?' His small hand almost vanished in Frank's beefy
grasp. Frank squeezed just a bit harder than was necessary. The
two men sat down, at opposite ends of the sofa.

From behind his desk, John Allan admired the charade and
suppressed a smile. A pugnacious Geordie, British Gas's director
of information technology enjoyed provoking these two consum-
mate salesmen every now and again. Allan kicked off the meeting.
'Gentlemen, as you know we've been talking to McKinsey for
some time about our IT strategy and we've made a decision which
could have major implications for both of you. So I thought it only
fair to get you both in and tell you at the same time.'

At the mention of management consultants McKinsey, Goodman's face brightened. The American consulting firm was a keen
supporter of IBM. Allan went on to explain that British Gas
wanted to rationalise, centralise and increase the efficiency of its
IT operations. With twelve Gas regions in the UK, each acting as
autonomous businesses, British Gas was doing many computing
jobs twelve times over. McKinsey's advice was that British Gas
choose one IT supplier and ask him to build a single computer
system to handle all British Gas's IT needs. Allan accepted their
advice that that was the target to aim for – provided of course that
British Gas's suppliers thought it was achievable. Allan wanted
Frank and Goodman to provide written documents within two

weeks with their view on whether a single company-wide IT system was a good solution to British Gas's IT needs. Frank and Goodman exchanged glances. That was typical of Allan. He was very fair and methodical. He obviously had a well-developed scheme in his mind for this marathon IT reorganisation, but he wanted to give the two computer companies a chance to put their thoughts in early on. As for whether it was a good solution, obviously it would save British Gas tens of millions of pounds. Frank and Goodman shared the same thought: it was a massive job, designing and building a single computer system to handle 90 per cent of the households in the UK, transferring the relevant data from twelve regions to the new system, getting the new system up and running, training British Gas personnel in all twelve regions to use the new system. It would be the deal of the century . . . for the winner.

The plan, said Allan, was to look at two Gas regions whose IT systems were 'best of breed' and ask those two suppliers to submit tender bids explaining how their system could be expanded to cover all twelve Gas regions. The two 'best of breed' regions were British Gas West Midlands and British Gas South Eastern. West Midlands was ICL and South Eastern was an IBM computer system. Allan wanted one bid from IBM and another from ICL.

McKinsey's study, Allan continued, showed that British Gas's computing needs could be fulfilled by one giant computer system tied into all their regional and district offices by telephone link. This computer system would require four central data centres. Allan would like IBM and ICL each to draft a bid outlining a structure for the new centralised system, a time frame for the transition, and of course estimate the costs involved. That price would be an awfully big number. Allan and his staff would evaluate the two bids carefully. Cost was important but only one consideration. The merits of the two existing regional computer systems would be analysed, along with the proposed nationwide expanded versions, for reliability, security, efficiency and the improved customer services they should enable British Gas to deliver to *its* customers. Allan intended the most thorough evaluation in British

Gas's history. Twelve committees would be set up to look at the bids and every region and every department of British Gas would be involved.

'What do the regions think of this move?' asked Goodman. It was a good question. More than 2000 people worked on IT in British Gas's twelve regions. Seven of those regions used ICL computer systems and five IBM. Many of those people would probably lose their jobs and others would have to convert from a familiar computer system to the new regime. ICL and IBM computers were incompatible. They used different hardware, different data storage systems, and, crucially, different computer languages.

They won't like it one bit, but they won't have any choice, thought Frank.

'The change will be gradual and there will be plenty of retraining to move people on to the new computer system,' said Allan.

In addition to the 'best of breed' comparison, said Allan, British Gas would evaluate the two suppliers as well. It would look at the quality of ICL and IBM, now and going forward into the next century: their customer support, their commitment to future product development, their financial stability and more. Goodman was smiling. He's eating this up, Frank noticed. It was hardly surprising IBM was the computer industry's Rock of Gibraltar, the sun around which every computer company revolved. As for ICL . . . well, it was a modest-sized British company with some interesting products and a very chequered past. Frank stopped taking notes now and listened attentively, his brow furrowed.

British Gas would be heavily dependent on the chosen company, Allan was saying. It was essential that it feel confident this company had the resources, the skills, the technology and the management, to deliver quality services not just today but for years to come. So Allan hoped both men would not mind his team asking some probing questions about their respective companies. 'This is going to be a long-term relationship for both sides, and we want to make sure we choose the company we feel most comfortable going forward with over the next decade and beyond,' said Allan. Rising from behind his desk to signal the end of the meeting, Allan finished by saying he hoped the two men would do what they could to help the British Gas team make a fair and thorough analysis. They nodded. The final bids would be due on 31 May 1991 and British Gas would make a decision in July.

'I'm sure it's going to be an interesting six months for all of us,' said Allan.

Frank and Goodman walked silently down the corridor to the lifts, each absorbed in his own thoughts. In the lift, Goodman turned to Frank, a smile on his face.

'Don't worry, Peter. I'm sure you'll pick up some pretty good pieces of business during the changeover to an all-IBM British Gas.'

As soon as he was settled in his car, Frank seized the carphone and punched the number of ICL's Slough office. 'Is John Jones about?' he asked, slipping instinctively into his usual bonhomie when the secretary answered. His tone changed when Jones came on the line. 'John, whatever you're doing, drop it. It's on. The big one. We need a meeting now. I'm on my way over to you. Call everybody on the team and tell 'em to be at Slough by the afternoon.'

Martin Goodman had good reason to be optimistic. IBM was probably the most outstanding example of corporate success in the twentieth century. From the moment computers became a serious international business, IBM dominated the industry. Throughout the 1960s and 1970s, IBM's sales grew by billions of dollars each year. Its 1990 sales of $69 billion were larger than the gross domestic product of four members of the European Community. In the 1960s, its domination of the industry grew so overwhelming that the US government filed a lawsuit against IBM in 1969 charging it with monopoly power over the US computing industry. From the point of view of the economists advising the US Justice Department, IBM was the textbook case of a monopoly. It accounted for more than 60 per cent of the industry's revenue.

It had extremely high profit margins. It kept the important computer languages its machines used secret, so its customers were reliant on its service personnel, and it was always a few jumps ahead of competitors. It gave away computers to strategic customers like universities, so when American companies considered buying a computer they had to consider the fact that most of the young engineers just out of college knew only IBM's programming languages. Its nastiest tactic was so-called 'pre-announcing'. If a competitor had a technological breakthrough computer, IBM would announce a faster, better model of its own. The competitor's orders would dry up while customers waited to see what IBM's new offer looked like. Strangely, it repeatedly took more than a year until the new model surfaced.

But IBM's ruthlessness with competitors was not the reason for its success. The secret of IBM's success was its obsession with customer service.

> At IBM, everybody sells! That's not a slogan or a gimmick. It's a fact. Walk into the IBM building in New York or into any of its offices throughout the world and you'll get the idea. Every employee has been trained to think that the customer comes first – everybody from the CEO to the people in finance, to the receptionists, to those who work in manufacturing.

That was IBM marketing vice-president 'Buck' Rodgers's view in his book *The IBM Way*.* The company philosophy hadn't changed since it was founded in 1914 by the hard-driving Tom Watson Sr. IBM veterans told the story of how Watson walked in once on a sales meeting where salesmen were assessing various problems they had with customers. Several piles of papers were stacked on a desk at the front of the room under signs reading

* Rodgers, FG 'Buck', with Robert Shook, *The IBM Way*, Fontana/Collins, 1986, p. 62.

'Manufacturing problems', 'Engineering problems', and so on. Watson listened for a bit, walked up to the front of the room and, with a sweep of his hand, sent the piles of papers flying. 'There aren't any categories of problems here. There's just one problem. Some of us aren't paying enough attention to our customers,' he stormed and walked out.

Up to the 1950s, IBM salesmen sang the company song at annual meetings ('We know and we love you Thomas Watson/We know you have our welfare in your heart'). Way before the invention of the computer, IBM was massively successful with adding machines, typewriters and other office products. The introduction of the IBM System/360 computer in 1964 made computing economical for every medium and large company in the world and transformed IBM into a global powerhouse. Technologically, it was not the most advanced computer in the world; in that same year ICL introduced the ICL 1900 Series which ICL engineers believed was ahead of IBM in some respects. But it did not matter. IBM's sales force went forth with the fervour of Christian missionaries and their gospel of customer service and conquered the world. Under Tom Watson Jr (who took over from his father in 1956), IBM created a vertically integrated machine. In an ever growing network of factories, IBM made almost every component and wrote almost every line of software used on its computers.

The vertically integrated vision was common to pioneers in a new industry. Sixty years earlier, Henry Ford bought forests, built steel mills and bought up scrapped Model Ts so he could control every step in the production of his cars. The onslaught of competition from General Motors taught him that Ford was a company, not an ecosystem, and he had to cut back on his grandiose vision. But the computer industry was different. By its nature it was vertically integrated. Making first thousands and then millions of calculations per second, a computer could function efficiently only if its hardware – the thousands of tiny circuits etched into each silicon chip – worked in tune with its software. The data had to be arranged in a specific way ('formatted' in the jargon) so the computer language could use it efficiently. Printers, keyboards or smaller computers hooked up to the central computer also had to speak the same language.

The complexity of computer languages also meant that once a customer had arranged all his data and written all his application programmes for one computer system, it was incredibly expensive and time-consuming to move to a competitor's system. A large company might have data on 100,000 employees and programmes to print monthly paycheques in an IBM language. IBM products were typically 30–50 per cent more expensive than the competition. But was it really worth changing to the competition if the changeover would take months, require dozens of programmers working night and day, and it might be a year before the new system worked absolutely error-free? And, if the new computer system crashed (ie suddenly stopped working as all systems did from time to time), there was no guarantee that the competitor would be able to offer a service as quick and reliable as IBM. According to 'Buck' Rodgers, IBM customers 'are not looking for the cheapest solutions to their problems . . . They're buying peace of mind and a good night's sleep.'*

In 1977, Jimmy Carter took over as US president. His cabinet included three IBM non-executive directors. The man who had been elected to represent the 'little guy' gave more cabinet-level representation to one corporation than to trade unionists or any other traditional Democratic constituencies. Like the Labour Party in Britain, America's Democrats were more impressed with high-tech growth companies than hardheaded Republicans who tended to see high-tech as just another word for high profit margins. The anti-monopoly lawsuit was dropped.

But almost immediately, IBM's monopoly began to be eroded by technology. The dramatic fall in the price of silicon microchips gave birth to smaller, cheaper computers. By the mid-1980s, IBM's declining grip on the market was clear for all to see. There were now three distinct segments of the industry: mainframes (the

* Rodgers, op. cit., p. 175.

traditional big computers), mid-range computers and personal computers (PCs). In all three sectors, IBM was the largest supplier. But its market share was smallest in the segment that was growing the fastest, PCs. For the first time ever, IBM was forced to cut prices on its mainframes. In 1992, the scale of IBM's problems became bitterly apparent, when the company announced the first operating loss in its history, major restructuring including cuts of more than 40,000 in its workforce, and the resignation of chairman John Akers.

IBM's crisis was severe and dramatic, but its position remained very strong. Sales of mainframe computer systems may have been flat worldwide but it was still a $50 billion industry and IBM still accounted for 40 per cent of it. In the UK, it was undisputed market leader, with a 14 per cent market share of the entire IT industry (which included all computer systems, software and back-up services). In the so-called 'Top Ten' market of the ten largest IT companies, who focused on the high-profit customers, the large corporate users of computers, IBM held a formidable 33 per cent market share. And IBM still had its impeccable reputation for quality and customer service. For a director of information technology at a large company who liked to sleep well at night, there was a slogan: 'Nobody every got fired for buying IBM.'

'A lot of the older generation of managers have got a very poor image of ICL. They don't trust us. They don't trust our products, they think our service is unreliable, and they don't know us as a company.

'We've got to do something to change their perception of ICL. We've got to convince them that we're no longer the old-style dinosaur-type supplier, that we've changed.

'It's not enough to just tell'em we've changed. We've got to show them. We've got to demonstrate it. We've go to *do* something different. We have to deliver some achievement, some piece of business that is so big, so visible, so *unexpected*, that everybody at British Gas sits up and says: "Wow, how did boring old ICL manage to achieve *that*?"

'Only then will they look at us again and see how much we've changed.'

It was October 1989. Peter Frank had taken his sales force away to the quiet De Montfort Hotel in the ancient Warwickshire town of Kenilworth for an intensive two-day rethink of ICL's business with British Gas. In the late 1980s, ICL's position with the giant gas company, one of ICL's top ten customers worldwide, had gone from bad to worse to catastrophic. In 1987, the company's largest regional division, British Gas North Thames, broke a decades-old relationship with ICL when it commissioned IBM to provide it with a new mainframe computer system. A year later, British Gas asked American minicomputer giant Digital Equipment (DEC), to provide a new system of office computer for all its UK offices. And a year later, British Gas's retail showrooms asked German computer manufacturer Nixdorf to supply a retail computing system for the utility's 500 retail outlets. Each contract was a multimillion-pound piece of business lost. The North Thames loss was particualrly catastrophic. The main-frame computers which controlled the billing and customer service for the 2 million customers spread along the Thames valley from High Wycombe to Southend was a massive – and highly remuner-ative – IT system, accounting for as much as a quarter of ICL's revenue from British Gas in some years. Still worse was the damage to ICL's image inside British Gas. IBM now held five Gas regions, compared to seven for ICL. The American giant looked as if it was on the brink of becoming British Gas's largest IT supplier while ICL appeared the defensive old-timer, its position a relic of the days when British companies, especially nationalised companies, always bought British.

Since its privatisation in 1986, British Gas had been going through major changes. With 18 million customers, turnover of £10 billion a year and profits of £1.5 billion, it was in the top rank of global energy companies. It was the only fully vertically integrated gas supplier in the west. It pumped gas out of the North Sea, operated a pipeline network throughout the UK, supplied consumers and serviced facilities, which often included not only the supply network but residential appliances and central heating systems. A monopolist in the supply of gas, it was a large competitive operator in retailing domestic appliances and heating systems. This massive operation required 80,000 employees, making British Gas one of the nation's largest employers. Privatisation brought in a new price control regime administered by Ofgas, a government agency and self-proclaimed champion of the public interest. Ofgas restricted British Gas to annual price rises below the rate of inflation. Between 1986 and 1992, average gas prices fell by 20 per cent in real (ie inflation-adjusted) terms.

Caught in a vice between private shareholders looking for growing profits and strict price controls on their home market, British Gas management needed a new management style, new objectives, in short a new corporate mission. The solution it moved towards in the late 1980s involved expanding their overseas business, applying their UK expertise to gas exploration, supply and consultancy in global markets. At home, the only way to increase profits was through greater efficiency and cost-effectiveness. In an organisation that before 1986 was run like the civil service, there was plenty of room to increase efficiency. The historic division of British Gas into twelve regional 'Gas boards', dating from nationalisation in 1948, had led to the duplication of many tasks. Beginning before privatisation, and gathering speed afterwards, the new management team at British Gas head office centralised activities, cutting down on duplication, making the company less bureaucratic and better able to respond to change. Like many British companies in the 1980s, tumultuous change and ferment followed decades of in-bred routine. Even while functions were being centralised at head office, British Gas management laid plans to move the head office to the more central and cost-effective location of Solihull in the West Midlands.

ICL's big losses of British Gas business were partly due to the change in the management style. The new British Gas management was based at the head office. 'We had always focused on the Gas regions, never on the headquarters,' said Peter Frank. Frank took his team to Kenilworth to discuss the new style at British

Gas and plot how ICL could recapture its previous strength with the utility. The De Montfort was an ideal place to escape from day-to-day office pressures and formulate strategy. It was a comfortable little hotel looking out on the green common, split by the River Avon, which made up the centre of the old castle town.

Rain beat on the hotel windows and water swept down the town's steep high street, turning the common into a squelchy, damp carpet under the feet of the few dogs and dog-walkers venturing outside. Frank and three of his colleagues on the British Gas account team sat on easy chairs in the hotel meeting room and analysed their problem. As if to compensate for the imposing height and railroad-car shoulders which made him a commanding presence in any room, Frank was always unassuming, keenly attentive to others, the proverbial gentle bear. 'I'm just a hairy-assed salesman,' he liked to say. Yet the jovial camaraderie hid a calculating mind. After a childhood in what he called the 'one-horse town' of Northwich, Cheshire, he left school at eighteen. Three years later, he joined ICL in sales. With a keen intuition for people, enormous energy and a strong work ethic, Frank acquired a thorough understanding of electronics and computer software. Working almost exclusively on government agency and utility accounts, he learnt to understand the aims, routines and thought processes of those giant organisations. He broadened his experience with two overseas stints for ICL in the 1970s. In Russia he saw a different kind of giant organisation, state-owned ministries where computer systems were purchased less for their performance than their impact on the purchasing executive's position in the vast web of Soviet bureaucratic intrigue. He found Australia a refreshing and liberating experience. Business was almost unbelievably informal. Everybody was approachable. Company presidents answered their own phone. In 1987, aged forty-one, Frank was moved from a line management position to take over the British Gas account, and asked to try to salvage a desperate situation.

After ensuring room service had taken care of everybody, Frank kicked off a no-holds-barred discussion of where ICL had gone wrong with British Gas. They agreed they had two sets of problems: first, they hadn't kept in touch with the rapid changes at British Gas. Many of their best contacts in the organisation were part of the older generation at the company, now nearing retirement or shifted aside as a new generation of managers took control of the company. Their second problem was ICL's poor image, legacy of its past. In the late 1970s, ICL had not devoted enough time or money to customer support. Their reliability, and the support offered when problems arose, were far below the standards set by IBM and other American and Japanese competitors. British Gas suffered badly from teething problems, 'crashes', 'bugs', and other breakdowns. Bill collection, customer services, even safety, could be affected by the breakdown of a vital computer system. By the mid-1980s the problems had been resolved, but some senior British Gas executives retained a distrust of ICL. 'We had got to a point where they were pleasant to us but we could see that they were never really going to buy from us,' said Frank. It was like Alfa Romeo, he said. Over a decade ago, they had conquered their rust problem, but many consumers still immediately thought 'rust' at the mention of the Italian marque.

Since then, British Gas and ICL had both changed radically. New management had come in at ICL in 1981 and completely transformed the company. One product of the new emphasis on customer care was ICL chairman Peter Bonfield's 80/20 principle. It stated that 80 per cent of a company's business came from 20 per cent of its customers. Those customers had to be given intense marketing attention. It was under the aegis of that principle that Frank called his major strategic rethink at the De Montfort.

'Change equals opportunity,' he said. By the early evening, the group of four ICL salesmen hammered out a seven-point plan to rebuild ICL's position with British Gas. It was a long-term, ambitious and risky plan. The first step was to identify 'rising stars' among British Gas management, build relationships with them and convince them of ICL's merits.

'How are we going to identify these rising stars?' asked a salesman.

'What we're looking for is somebody who all of a sudden gets promoted out of his peer group and gets put into an important job at a relatively younger age, say late thirties or early forties,' Frank replied. 'That's still quite unusual at British Gas. Anybody who when you go to see them has got some revolutionary ideas, is prepared to challenge the consensus, will stand up and say I don't agree with some of the cultures and attitudes within this organisation.

'People who are prepared to be a little bit maverick are going to do well in British Gas in the years ahead.

'Last, but by no means least, when you look in their eye, is there that glint in their eye? Do you get that gut feeling that tells you: this guy is going to go places.'

Between them, the four ICL salesmen had half a century's experience selling to British Gas. They knew hundreds of British Gas executives. They knew how the informal network operated. Potential high-flyers at British Gas spotted each other early on, and built up informal contacts and relationships which became increasingly important as they rose to senior positions. By the time they broke for dinner they'd compiled a list of forty rising stars at British Gas. They divided the names between them. It was to be a hard sell not of products, but of ICL itself. IT decisions were so important to a large company that every sale was more than a sale of a computer and software. It was a sale of the company supplying the IT. Most of the rising stars had nothing to do with IT directly. But at some point in their career, they would have input into IT decisions.

Frank turned to ICL's biggest problem, its poor image. The ICL of 1989 was radically different from a decade earlier. It was leaner and more aggressive. Its product range was narrower and boasted superb quality. Frank argued they needed to do something radical, dramatic and unexpected to convey to British Gas that ICL had changed. Probably, it would involve winning a major piece of business outside ICL's traditional area of mainframe computers. 'It's not going to happen overnight, but we have to look out for it. Whatever it is, it's going to have to make a big impression. It has to be something so big and so visible that people say: wow, how have ICL managed to achieve that?'

Another bold point in the plan was to create a small team charged with building relationships with the increasingly powerful team at British Gas head office in London. This team would have no immediate responsibility for generating revenues: most IT purchase decisions were still made in the regions. It was another long-term investment. Soon, many IT decisions would be made at High Holborn. Frank put his right-hand man, John Jones, in charge of the new head office team.

Jones, then aged forty, had taken over as account manager for the southern England portion of the British Gas account in 1986. Within months of his arrival, ICL suffered the devastating loss of the North Thames mainframe business. Jones took the loss personally.

'I felt very motivated by what happened at North Thames,' he said. 'Because I damn well knew that ICL were superb. We had superb products, we had leadership and we were a very dramatic organisation. We talked all the time about the pace of change in our industry and ICL was able to change incredibly fast to meet the demands of the customers and the marketplace and I really wanted to show British Gas that we were as good as I knew we were.'

Jones had two passions in life: ICL, and the Irish draft horses he raised on his small farm in Northamptonshire. Both offered an exciting challenge. At ICL, the job and the company changed so rapidly that he was always learning and adapting. Breeding the perfect Irish draft horse similarly captivated him. He took pride in both activities. He was convinced ICL products were among the world's best and he had similar admiration for the ten heavyweight hunters he exercised every weekend at his farm. Quiet and introspective by comparison with the gregarious Frank, Jones had started at ICL (then ICT) as an eighteen-year-old apprentice in their Croydon factory, before moving on to work as a field engineer. The industry was booming then and Jones worked night and day repairing computers with screwdriver and soldering iron. Computers were still relatively new and computer engineering was a glamourous occupation. Five years later, he moved again, into sales support, because he wanted more direct dealings with customers. 'I enjoy people and I enjoy a bit of the banter,' he said. When a salesman on the British Gas account left ICL in 1979, Jones, who knew more than anyone else in the company about that region's IT system, was made the salesman.

Early in 1990, Jones was in a meeting with two planning managers from British Gas's information technology department. They were part of the growing cadre of head office executives playing an increasing role in making company policy at the gas giant. Jones was not selling anything: in keeping with the Kenilworth strategy of the previous autumn, he was simply getting to know the executives at British Gas head office, listening to them talk about the problems and issues they faced in their business. They told Jones about ideas they were working on for increasing the efficiency of their IT operations. The previous year, they said British Gas bought desktop PCs from at least a dozen different suppliers, everybody from Compaq to Amstrad. British Gas's purchasing departments were enjoying the constant price-cutting in the PC industry, leaping into the market to buy a few dozen PCs here and a few dozen there every week or two. But the administrative complexities were beginning to outweigh the cost savings. And though all the PCs British Gas bought were the industry standard 'IBM-compatible' model, they were still not completely compatible. Often a systems engineer had to be dispatched to make some programme which ran on somebody's desk run on somebody else's. What BG needed, said the planning manager, thinking out loud, was one supplier who could supply every PC the company needed to every one of their dozen regions, making them all mutually compatible – and doing it at a competitive price.

'We could do that for you,' said Jones.

The planning manager looked up from his cup of tea.
'Really, John? Does ICL make PCs?'

The burden of ICL's heritage as so-called national champion of Britain's computer industry had almost destroyed the company. From the birth of the computer industry in the early 1950s until 1981, ICL and its predecessor companies' history was marked by an obsession with engineering and technology, to the exclusion of the business issues vital to the success of the technology. Repeatedly, Britain's major computer-makers struck financial crisis when sales failed to arrive in time to pay for ambitious research and development programmes. Each time, the leaders of the industry or meddling government ministers responded with 'solutions' in the form of mergers or takeovers. In theory, a bigger company would spread its costs out over a larger revenue base and take advantage of economies of scale. A larger company could distribute rationalisation over a larger number of employees or factories, sharing the pain of cutbacks more widely, an option always attractive to politicians. Tony Benn, Labour technology minister from 1966 to 1970 and one of the most active proponents of computer mergers, said, 'When one looked at industry, it was about the difference between big industry and small industry.'* With his involvement, and the sweetener of several million pounds of government monies, a series of mergers led to the creation of International Computers Ltd in 1968.

Socialism had little to do with this policy; the love affair with industrial bigness was pursued at the same time by right-wing governments on the Continent, and later on by the Heath Conservative government. Indeed, to find true socialism in the computer industry, one had to look in another direction: at IBM, which took world leadership of the industry by the straightforward stratagem of winning huge American Defence Department contracts (principally for the design of America's early warning

* Campbell-Kelly. *ICL, A Business and Technical History*, Clarendon Press, Oxford, 1989, p. 257.

defence systems against Russian air and missile attacks), and then quickly redesigning those products to sell to the commercial market. As late as 1960, the Pentagon was paying for more than a third of IBM's R&D expenditure. Government support for R&D and the presence of a large home market (another American advantage) were important for success in computers: but more important was the skill of professional businessmen. American 'socialism' (President Eisenhower christened it the 'military-industrial complex') worked because it took taxpayers' billions and put them under the control of businessmen in a competitive environment where the pressure was constantly applied to turn military *projects* into civilian *products* customers wanted and would pay for.

The problem with bigness was that it took a company further away from the marketplace. It removed the spur of competition. It encouraged the growth of bureaucracy. Before 1980, promotions at ICL depended on seniority, status and the old boy network. Every merger broadened the base of products and markets the company was supposed to tackle, diluting its resources. It lost focus and commercial drive. Every merger led to the resignation of good, commercial managers and their replacement with con-servative, visionless executives, usually technologists. The com-pany was managed by committee.

At the very top, every merger or crisis led to the arrival of another eminence from the Establishment, typically unqualified, to lead the company. Computers were just too glamorous. In his official history of ICL, Martin Campbell-Kelly breaks from his dry, academic tone to remark that ICL had an unfortunate habit of taking the wrong chairman every time a choice was offered. (Campbell-Kelly cites one 1960s-era computer company chair-man remarking that the chairman of English Electric 'going into computers was reminiscent of a gentleman going into farming.') In Parliamentary hearings on the future of the industry, American computer-leasing financier Saul Steinberg responded to question-ing on ICL's strategy by stressing the lack of the right sort of top managers: '[ICL] should decide on which IBM executive it wanted and then go out and pinch him.'*

Today's ICL was formed by the 1968 merger of ICT (itself the product of an earlier merger of Ferranti and EMI with the old ICT) and English Electric Computers. Both companies had a wide range of mainstream computer products (ICT's 1900 series and English Electric's System 4) developed to compete head-on with IBM's System/360. The computer companies who did best in the 1960s did it by nibbling chunks of the business around the edges of IBM domination, attacking specialised users like banks (Burroughs) or real-time airline reservations systems (Univac). Rejecting a 'niche' strategy as beneath them, the newborn ICL wanted to continue making a full frontal challenge to IBM. But, like the mothers of bride and groom bickering over the decor at the wedding, neither of ICL's two parents would accept the other's system as the basis for the next generation of computers. The result was an all-new, heinously expensive system (known as the New Range or System 2900). The New Range's design, or architecture, was based on a new operating system (the master software programmes controlling the computer's operation) called VME. According to Campbell-Kelly, 'the new range architecture was masterly. It was elegant, efficient, not in the least baroque, and in advance of anything offered by any other manufacturer (and this arguably remains true in the late 1980s).' Because it was incompatible with either of its predecessor systems though, the New Range alienated dozens of customers. And its development costs, which carried on throughout the 1970s, plunged the company into two financial crises, first in 1971, and finally in 1981, when ICL came near to bankruptcy.

The crisis was triggered, characteristically, by IBM. In 1979, IBM brought out its own range of new computers, the 4300 Series. Responding to the incursion of the Japanese into the industry and the American Amdahl Corporation producing 'copy-cat' IBM computers, Big Blue (the American company's nick-

* Campbell-Kelly, op. cit. p. 284.

name, after the colour of the steel on its mainframes) cut prices by effectively 75 per cent (as measured by dollar per million computer instructions per second or MIPS, the standard measure of computer speed). A year later, Britain entered its worst recession since the Second World War. The entire industry was traumatised, but the effects were especially bad at ICL. Unsold computers piled up in the warehouses at Manchester and bank debt rose to danger levels. ICL went (again) to the government, cap-in-hand. Influenced in part by horror at the prospect of replacing the government's own massive computer systems at the Inland Revenue and many other departments, and by the foresight of junior industry minister Kenneth Baker, who believed in ICL's potential if it was well-managed, the Thatcher government agreed to guarantee £200 million of ICL bank loans. The price for this generosity was acceptance of a new team of top management.

ICL's new chairman was former BP board member Christopher Laidlaw. The new managing director was Robb Wilmot, previously managing director of Texas Instruments' UK business. Laidlaw saw to relations with City, government, and bankers, while Wilmot set about revolutionising the company. Only thirty-six when he joined ICL in May 1981 Wilmot was a commercially astute engineer, a short-tempered iconoclast, and a visionary. In his years at TI, he imbibed the American company's culture and attitudes. TI was a famous technological innovator (it invented the microchip in 1959), but the company was focused equally on market success. Management was decentralised and individual businesses, typically run by engineers, were responsible for their own profit and loss figures.

Before Wilmot's arrival, ICL was organised on functional lines. One hierarchy controlled product development, another manufacturing, another marketing. Policy was made 'across the top' via a series of committees. A computer system was too complex a product and customers' needs too broad and varied simply to break the organisation into autonomous business units and leave them to it. But Wilmot began the process of making employees feel a sense of accountability for the profitability of whatever they were working on. Some referred to it as an American style of management. So-called American style management was most visible in the small, flexible, entrepreneurial companies born in Silicon Valley, just then beginning to dominate the American computer industry. Wilmot favoured open management and direct face-to-face discussion. He hated long meetings and committees. For ICL it was a blast of fresh air. Gordon Shortreed was a young field engineer based in Edinburgh at the time. 'I remember Robb Wilmot coming up to the Royal Scot Hotel for a meeting, leaning back in a sofa, putting his feet up on the table, and talking to everybody from the local office, asking for their criticisms and thoughts.' Previously, it was unheard of for senior management, let alone the managing director, to mix so informally with junior employees. 'I was so gobsmacked I couldn't ask any questions,' said Shortreed.

Two decades of mergers had crowded the senior management of ICL with factions, ancient loyalties and time-servers. Wilmot scythed through the logjam, bringing in young people with new ideas. Their youth alone was a radical change. Wilmot appointed Chris Gent managing director of ICL service subsidiary Baric at the age of thirty-four. 'Robb re-energised the company with his enthusiasm and his profound understanding of new technologies and new markets,' said Gent, now managing director of Vodaphone, the UK cellular telephone network. Ray Piggott was a forty-seven-year-old engineer working in Hong Kong when he read an article in the *South China Morning Post* which described how Wilmot intended to change ICL. Born and raised in southeast London, Piggott moved to the US in the 1960s to work in the American computer industry. In 1981 he was running the Far Eastern division of minicomputer-maker Data General. He wrote to Wilmot offering to contribute in any way to the revival of ICL. In 1982 he signed on as managing director of Traderpoint, a new ICL subsidiary working with independent software companies to develop a portfolio of application software packages to run on ICL computers. Working with outside software companies was another Wilmot innovation. 'In his vision and creativity, Robb was years

ahead of many of the large American companies, including IBM,'
said Piggott. In 1992, as managing director of Cray Communications, a fast-growing high-tech electronics company, Piggott still
kept a 1983 photo of the ICL senior management team on his
office wall. Piggott left school at sixteen and put himself through
engineering college at night. 'I was very proud that I was made a
divisional director of ICL even though I never went to university,'
he said.

Many of the changes made by Wilmot and his team were
painful. In just one year, staff numbers were cut by 7000 to
28,000. Losses in 1981 totalled £130 million. It was a crisis and
radical measures were necessary. Robin Biggam joined from ICI
as finance director in December 1981. Every month he travelled
up to London to update the Department of Industry officials and
ICL's bankers on the progress. 'When I joined, it was so uncertain.
I spent at least one third of my time going around ICL customers,
reassuring them the company would survive,' Biggam recalled.

'Costs and huge amounts of bureaucracy were just ripped out
of the organisation,' recalled Piggott. A large part of the reduction
was in manufacturing. Previously, ICL engineers designed and
produced every aspect of their product, virtually to the last screw.
Wilmot took the company out of most of the metal-bashing
operations. The company needed to focus on its core businesses,
computer hardware and software. It was a far-sighted move. A
decade later IBM finally began to look at the vast fixed costs sunk
into the concrete and steel of its dozens of factories.

Wilmot streamlined the software engineering, based at ICL's
West Gorton, Manchester, complex. Snug inside their fortress-
like campus, engineers ran West Gorton like an extension of
nearby Manchester University. Research and development projects were initiated and then ran on for years, scarcely accountable
to anyone. Little thought was given to their ultimate commercial
value. 'It was like an academic institution. Everybody was in it for
the sheer enjoyment of it,' commented one engineer. Wilmot
stopped major language-writing projects and disbanded entire
software teams. Field engineer Shortreed recalled the trauma of

the economies and cutbacks of the early 1980s. 'When you saw the good people going along with the deadwood, that's what really hurt.'

Wilmot felt ICL was more like a postgraduate university in computer science than a company, with no business culture at all. Virgin territory, he called it. He sought to instil throughout the company a new focus on market and customer. 'Technical people tend to think that it's the product that sells the product. It's not. Organisations sell products, not products,' he said. To drive the message home, Wilmot told senior ICL engineers that a company's business practices were like the operating system on a computer. ICL needed a new 'operating system', one which included awareness of the market, customer-sensitivity and a stress on the importance of profitability. 'They were very bright, capable people, and when challenged in the right way, they quickly grasped the fundamental business concepts.' Younger engineers in particular quickly adapted to a culture where projects were judged on their likely profitability rather than on technical merits alone. 'We moved from being product-led and technology-led to being customer and market-led,' recalled Shortreed. Wilmot instilled the idea that by being lean and aggressive and increasing productivity every year by more than the rate of inflation, ICL would begin to win market share from competitors. The 1981 crisis played an enduring role in keeping ICL lean and mean throughout the good times of the late 1980s. In 1993, ICL engineers still talked about the 'permanent scar tissue' of the 1981 traumas making them sensitive to cost control even on minor areas like corporate entertainment.

Wilmot's success proved that when a company needed really radical change, it almost inevitably had to turn to an outsider. Aside from the cultural change, his two major strategic contributions were getting ICL to focus on smaller computer systems and building a partnership with Japanese computer manufacturer Fujitsu. Both changes were revolutionary for ICL. An insider would probably not have been able to contemplate them. Large mainframes were the essence of the company. ICL men were passionate about their mainframes. They simply could not imagine that these products to which they had devoted their lives, and which had been a growth industry since the early 1950s, could go into decline. Yet Wilmot foresaw the fate of the mainframe. At Texas Instruments, he had seen early models of desktop computers. He believed the tumbling price of microchips would soon make small computers powerful enough for many more business tasks. 'It was quite clear to me that ten years out, 80 per cent of the industry would be built around microprocessors,' Wilmot recalled. At one point he actually suggested ICL abandon mainframes. 'We convinced him to stick with mainframes and he convinced us that smaller systems and open systems were important,' recalled Roger Wood, then a senior ICL engineer. Teams of engineers involved in the design of mainframes were redeployed to work on 'minicomputers' and distributed processing, a system where small user-friendly computers fed off one large central computer and data bank. 'By offloading the tremendous costs of mainframe development, we were able to refocus our intellectual energy on distributed systems,' said Wilmot. By 1984, two thirds of ICL's investment resources went into smaller computers. In that year, the company brought out the DRS line of desktop computers, making it one of the first mainframe giants with a distributed-processing, desktop system ideal for the office.

At Tube Investments, it took a veteran appliance manufacturer, Christopher Lewinton, to take the company out of appliances. At ICL, it took a veteran microchip man to see ICL needed to get out of microchip manufacture. The complexity of computer production sprang from the fact that every computer is really two separate products working in close harmony: the hardware, essentially the microchips which contain the data and the 'brain' processing the data, and the software, the language telling the hardware what to do. To obtain speed and efficiency, hardware and software had to work in conjunction. Like two legs, they had to move together.

Both hardware and software had tremendously high fixed costs. But they were *different* costs. Software involved hundreds (or in

IBM's case, thousands) of men and women – the proverbial computer nerds – sitting around typing into screens day and night writing millions of lines of computer code. The production of computer hardware was essentially a manufacturing race, a competition to put more and more tiny circuits on to flat squares of silicon which were then layered together like a club sandwich.

When Wilmot arrived at ICL, he saw that the R&D demands of a broad range of general purpose business mainframe computers was too great for the company's relatively slender foothold in the market (its 1980 turnover was £716 million compared to IBM's of $26 billion). At TI, Wilmot competed against the Japanese for a decade. He knew their skills at chip manufacture. Within months, he signed a deal with Fujitsu for the Japanese company to manufacture the chips for ICL computers. ICL would design the chips, the computers and write the software. Manufacture of the chips would be subcontracted to Fujitsu. The world's second-largest computer manufacturer, Fujitsu was eager for ICL's business as expanded production would help the Japanese company drive its unit costs down.

The unprecedented deal with Fujitsu was attacked by some as giving away the heart of the British computer industry to the Japanese. The Fujitsu relationship was misunderstood and criticised throughout the 1980s. The attacks redoubled in 1990, when Fujitsu bought an 80 per cent stake in ICL. Here again, Wilmot was years ahead of commentators and the competition. He knew that software and services were already more important than the stacks of silicon and the big steel boxes that made up a computer. 'What you sell when you sell a mainframe is architecture and software. It just happens to sit on chips and circuit boards,' he said. During the 1980s, the importance of software and support services increased. ICL's great asset was its understanding of its customers' needs and its skills at designing and implementing systems to solve their problems. Fujitsu's ability to make very powerful chips and ICL's fast and efficient operating system language, VME, made a formidable combination.

By the early 1990s, ICL's Series 39SX large mainframes

delivered slightly more power than IBM's comparable ES/9000 System from a box one sixth the size and using one sixth the amount of power. The Series 39SX contained 120 different chips, every one of them designed by ICL engineers at West Gorton, Manchester. Its speed, relatively small size, and cost efficiency was due partly to Fujitsu's advanced chip technology. Equally important was the innovative architecture and design concepts in VME. VME stood for Virtual Machine Environment. It allowed hundreds of users to use a system at the same time and gave each user the feeling that he had continuous access to the entire computer; it gave him a *virtual machine*. VME represented a massive investment. By the 1990s, the operating system contained ten million lines of code. If its entire contents were printed out in one run on single-spaced tractor paper, the print-out would stand as high as a twelve-storey office block.

ICL's critics assumed that because there were fewer shiny assembly lines stamping circuit boards, Britain was losing the computer industry. But under Wilmot's perspicacious guidance, ICL was focusing on the more valuable part of the industry. By the 1990s, the thriving activity at West Gorton, Bracknell, and the fast-growing ICL sites studded along the M4 corridor proved that. In the early 1980s, cynics predicted ICL would abandon its own products and end up just selling Fujitsu mainframes in Europe. In 1981, Wilmot did agree to sell Fujitsu mainframes in Europe. 'We sold three,' recalled ICL's Roger Wood, 'and then we dropped them.' Basically copies of IBM designs, Fujitsu mainframes were less innovative than ICL designs. By 1992, ICL was selling $50 million worth of computer sytems into Japan. Commentators in Parliament were reworking their classical metaphor: who was playing the Trojan horse for whom?

The transformation of ICL was one of the more difficult corporate revolutions. Finance director Robin Biggam reflected that the intelligence and independent-mindedness of ICL employees made it all the more difficult to effect a change in culture, behaviour and mindset. After three years of preaching the message, he felt that two levels down into the organisation the cultural change remained superficial. 'Intelligent people need far more convincing,' he said. Many ICL veterans felt they had seen it all before: several times in the past, new senior management teams were 'parachuted' into the company with bold new ideas. In the 1970s another British-born veteran of an American computer company (Jeff Cross from Univac) had sounded some of the same themes as Wilmot. Many staffers kept their heads down, believing the new management would move on and the familiar, comfortable ambience of university-like rumination would quickly return. Ray Piggott and Peter Bonfield had both spent most of their working lives with American electronics companies. Piggott recalled a discussion in which Bonfield told him that, at Texas Instruments, he felt that if the boss told the employees to lie down in the middle of the freeway they would have done it. 'Peter said when he announced a new ICL policy, he often felt that 20,000 people went away and asked themselves: do I really want to do that?'

The cultural change was finally achieved, only because Wilmot and Bonfield after him devoted constant, unrelenting attention to it. They buttressed their efforts inside the company with a core of senior executives who had a clear vision, usually gained in the US, of how properly commercial electronics companies should operate. They devoted as much time to the cultural and management issues as the strategic questions of what products to develop. It took years to push the sense of commercialism down to every layer of the organisation. In 1984 the process was almost halted in its tracks, when an unwelcome takeover intervened. The shareholders in the City of London were still susceptible to the siren song that 'big is beautiful', which emerged suddenly from telecommunications company STC.

ICL was on its way to chalking up a third consecutive year of profits over £40 million, when STC launched its takeover bid. The billion-pound telecommunications equipment manufacturer told the City it foresaw great opportunities in the coming convergence between computing and telecoms. ICL senior management were uniformly against the takeover, but powerless. Chris Gent did a study of the STC bid for Wilmot. 'I told Robb they were the wrong partner. They didn't have global ambitions, they didn't have deep pockets, and unlike ICL which was very tightly managed, there was loads of overhead in STC.' The cultures of the two companies were different: ICL sold to hundreds of customers in a highly competitive marketplace and was trying to establish a market-sensitive and customer-sensitive culture. STC had few customers (principally British Telecom) and operated in the cosy world of state-owned telephone monopolies. The STC takeover threatened to undo all the work Wilmot and his team had achieved in three years.

ICL management were not opposed to a new owner. One with the resources to finance international growth, especially on the European continent, was a logical next step for ICL. The most logical owner would have been its number one supplier, Fujitsu. 'We sent Robb off to Tokyo to talk to [Fujitsu chairman] Yamamoto, but they weren't yet ready for that sort of move,' said Biggam. In September 1984, STC's offer of 90 pence an ICL share (valuing ICL at £411 million) was accepted by shareholders. Biggam was categorical in denouncing their acceptance of the bid as blatant financial short-termism. 'STC management was very poor and the reality was that they were thrown out of System X [the GEC-led telephone network consortium],' said Biggam, adding: 'If they had waited one or two years we would have found the right technical partner.' STC's futuristic promises of convergence were little more than window-dressing for an acquisition that was designed to cover up STC's own problems, which became painfully apparent a year later when STC profits collapsed.

'The day STC took over, I became non-executive chairman,' said Wilmot. A year later he resigned. Biggam quit to join Dunlop. From there he went on to become chairman of £3 billion cable company BICC. It was left to new ICL managing director Peter Bonfield to fight a rearguard campaign to keep STC's hands off his business. Over the next five years, more than £200 million of ICL cash was transferred to STC. ICL was fortunate that Bonfield had the political skills to keep ICL's autonomy intact. In a sense, ICL had a lucky break when STC's profits crisis led to the replacement of chairman Kenneth Corfield, chief architect of the takeover. In the late 1980s several senior ICL executives were poached by STC. One of these was Roger Wood, who from 1988 ran STC's transmission business. He was not impressed by the company he found. 'There was little depth of management. Whenever a senior post came up, they were always scratching around to find somebody suitable.' As profits from STC's own business sagged, STC senior management tried to boost cash flow by interfering in ICL. 'Bonfield defended ICL from being penetrated and robbed of its investment programmes to boost STC's group profits,' said Wood. STC also tried to integrate its and ICL's sales and marketing operations. STC did not appreciate the important role a large sales force played in the computer industry. 'They had an engineering culture, a cost-plus culture,' said Wood. In 1987 Bonfield took on the additional title of deputy chief executive of STC and ICL's position was safe.

This uneasy situation finally ended in 1990, when STC sold 80 per cent of ICL to Fujitsu for £742 million. (Four months later, STC was acquired by Canadian telecommunications giant Northern Telecom.) While six years' ownership by STC was a difficult experience, the transition from managing director Robb Wilmot to Peter Bonfield in 1984 was in many respects the best thing that could have happened to ICL. The contrast between the two men was not unlike the contrast between Ernest Saunders and Anthony Tennant, the managing directors who achieved such spectacular results at Guinness during the 1980s. At the drinks giant, Saunders was the visionary. Ruthless, impatient, respected more than loved by his management team, he tore apart the old, failed Guinness culture and put in place the building blocks of a world-class brands marketing company. Tennant was the implementer with the charisma to build loyalty and the perserverance to put the new principles into action throughout the organisation.

A brilliant technologist, Wilmot was often appallingly bad with people. Nearly every ICL staffer had a story about his unusual management style. He always did several things at once. If guests or employees were disconcerted (almost always) or insulted (regularly), as far as Wilmot was concerned, that was their problem. One former ICL director recalled a lunch with a man they had invited to join the board as a non-executive director. 'Throughout the lunch, Robb went through his mail. The man wrote to us the next day thanking us for our interest and declining our offer.' John Jones, then a young salesman, once had to brief Wilmot on a customer on a Saturday morning. 'He was running three meetings simultaneously, popping into one meeting, seeing where they had got to, giving them a few more objectives, going into the next one, doing the same, and then the next. It was unbelievable.' Ray Piggott, a people-sensitive manager, saw Wilmot's personal style as demotivating, especially for junior managers. 'A young guy might spend weeks preparing a presentation and then he'd go give it to the managing director who wouldn't look at him once in an hour,' said Piggott. He added: 'Robb had brilliant ideas but he didn't appreciate that 20,000 ordinary mortals had to make it happen.'

Wilmot was well aware of his lack in people skills. 'I am a technologist. We were a team and other members of the team had those skills,' he said. In his last year at ICL, Wilmot spent most of his time at ICL's Reading development centre, leaving much of the management to Bonfield and Biggam. He believed a technologist had to stay in close touch with the ever changing technology. New ideas and projects continued to flow from his fertile mind. But by 1984, ICL had its new strategy and a full complement of new products. The time had come to consolidate the company into a united, aggressive organisation pushing the strategy on to greater success in the marketplace. Those were Bonfield's skills.

'Wilmot threw a lot of balls into the air. Bonfield caught the balls and put them into the appropriate slots,' said Roger Wood. Bonfield joined ICL in October 1981, aged thirty-seven, as an executive director in charge of worldwide marketing. He was born and raised in Baldock, Hertfordshire. His father was an engineer who worked for ICT, an ICL predecessor company. With a small pointy beard, elegant silver-grey hair and sharply-pressed suits, he had a dapper foxlike charm. Years of living in the US gave him a distinct Texan drawl, which mixed incongruously with his Hertfordshire accent. He looked more like a stockbroker, the sort who might sell an obscure financial instrument out of an office in Zug or Liechtenstein, than a computer nerd. He was however a seasoned electronics engineer. Like Wilmot, he spent his early career at Texas Instruments, in the US and the UK. He had even won a patent in the US for the design of a chip for a 1970s-era TI pocket calculator. TI corporate policy required him to sell the patent rights to the company for $1. He kept the framed patent certificate with a dollar bill stapled to it in a box at home. Since joining ICL, his interests had focused on marketing, and changing the company's culture and its people to keep pace with one of the world's fastest-moving industries. As marketing director, he restructured ICL's marketing effort into vertical industry segments. The first three segments were retail, public administration (principally local government) and financial services. ICL computers naturally lent themselves to those markets. But the key contribution of the industry verticals contribution concept was that it shifted the company towards thinking of its business as selling information technology *solutions* to business problems instead of information technology products.

As chairman and chief executive of ICL, Bonfield was relentless in his determination to remake, remould and refocus the company to keep it abreast of the incessant changes in the IT industry.

'The thing with a lot of companies is that if they actually took out a clean sheet of paper and said, "Now, what is going to happen in our industry in the next ten years?", I think many of them would get it quite right. But they don't do that because there are always entrenched positions and reasons like it will upset their existing market or customers. They are constrained by history.

'But if you say: let's not be constrained by any of that because it's now do-or-die time; if you say, we *need* the right answer, you will come up with something which feels reasonably credible. We've always tried to force ourselves to say what are the trends, and then force ourselves to do something about them.'

The late 1980s saw the most tumultuous changes in the computer industry since IBM established its domination in the 1960s. Building on Wilmot's earlier moves, Bonfield kept ICL growing throughout the period. It was the only major European computer company to come through the late 1980s with a record of consistent profits. Between 1984 and 1992 the company more than doubled in size, with turnover rising from £1.1 billion to £2.48 billion. As corporate users of computers moved increasingly to smaller computers and distributed processing, Bonfield expanded ICL's range of mid-range computers, signing a partnership deal with America's Sun Microsystems and Texas Instruments, who supplied the microprocessors driving ICL's DRS computers. The deal with Sun, like the success of ICL's Office-power and Teamware software, used on more than 500,000 desks worldwide, proved that software skills were the most important in the industry. ICL parlayed its recognised software products and capabilities into partnerships with many of the important entrants into the industry. In the so-called 'computer wars' in which rival computer architectures fought for dominance (Microsoft vs Unix, Sun vs HP vs IBM, etc.), ICL was on all sides. 'We spread the risk so we're not dependent on any one technology or one product,' said Bonfield.

In 1988, ICL decided on a major assault of the desktop personal computer (PC) market – aimed primarily at its traditional customers, medium and large companies. It doubled its PC production with the 1990 acquisition of Helsinki-based Nokia Data, and then the combined ICL–Nokia PC business doubled its output in a year, selling 220,000 PCs for revenue of £350 million in 1992, making ICL Europe's sixth largest supplier of PCs. It was astonishing evidence of the flexibility of a company that only three years earlier had been routinely described as one of the 'mainframe dinosaurs' which might not survive the transition to smaller processors.

The changes in strategy and product achieved under Bonfield's leadership were important. But more important was the change in culture he achieved. As Wilmot recognised, products do not sell products, organisations sell products. The computer industry was changing so fast that a new product could never be a permanent solution. But an organisation that knew what its competitive strengths were, and was prepared to change itself to follow and anticipate the market, could thrive. 'In this industry, which is so changeable, my gut feeling is that if you aren't changing so fast that it really feels painful and is just about on the edge of being do-able, then you aren't changing fast enough,' Bonfield said. Bonfield observed that the crisis of 1981 in which ICL flirted with bankruptcy had a marvellous effect in terms of inducing change, re-energising people, and bringing a new creativity to the company. He set his sights on bringing a major new catalyst for change into the company at least every two years. 'It doesn't work to invent artificial crises, but I tried overtly to go out and bring in a catalyst for change so that you can talk to people and they will not only listen and nod, but they will actually change.'

In 1987, Bonfield hired Joe Goasdoué from British Airways as ICL director of quality. It was the first time a major computer manufacturer had taken a quality expert from outside the industry and given him a board-level job. With his Italian suits, swarthy complexion and floral ties, Goasdoué looked even less of a computer nerd than Bonfield. But there was much more to Goasdoué than a well-dressed marketing man. In his twenty-year career at BA, he had been instrumental in bringing in the quality programmes which had made that airline world-famous for customer service.

Goasdoué's methods were far more sophisticated than simple exhortation. He developed a rolling five-year plan to get all ICL staff to focus on serving the customer. He established eight distinct quality programmes, including monthly Recognition of Excellence awards for employees achieving high-quality standards and the goal of winning official quality certification BS 5750 in Britain and overseas, not just for manufacturing operations but for the entire company. ICL became the first company to win the company-wide certification in the UK. Its certificate, Number 0001, hung in the main reception at ICL's headquarters. He set up ninety quality improvement teams to transmit the quality message throughout the 20,000-strong organisation. Regular education, training and presentational sessions explained the findings of reams of independent market research on what customers thought of ICL. In 1992, Roger Wood commented that ICL was seen as a pacesetter in the quality movement by the entire European electronics industry. 'The quality culture is like a stick of rock running right through that organisation,' said Wood, who moved to Ferney Voltaire in the French Alps as Northern Telecom's group vice president, Europe, after the Canadian company's takeover of STC in 1990.

Goasdoué stressed that the most important factor in the success of a quality programme was the commitment of the most senior management. 'The first person who gets any education or training programme is Peter Bonfield,' he said. Relentless in his pursuit of quality to the least detail, Goasdoué made presentations to the board on how many telephone calls to the company were answered within the first six rings. Every senior executive 'adopted' two large customers whom he saw regularly. Bonfield himself saw two major customers a week. Computer companies always faced the choice for a chief executive between a marketing man whose grasp of the technology could only be tenuous (the IBM way) or a technologist who risked losing touch with the changing needs of customers. Bonfield's solution was to give Goasdoué enough clout to force the ICL technologists to see, touch and get a feel for the marketplace and the customers so often that they would never miss new developments. 'We have been, and will always try to be, religious about following the market,' said Bonfield. He believed that technologists made better leaders of IT companies than marketers. 'This is such a complex business that you have to have a very deep understanding of the business, the products and the technology. You can't just bring in a standard business manager and apply standard principles. It won't work.'

Under Bonfield, ICL moved to a comprehensive system of performance-related pay for all ICL employees. Everybody from office secretaries to board members was eligible for annual bonuses rising to 30 per cent or even 50 per cent of their salary in some cases. Bonfield used the bonus system ruthlessly to force employees to change. An early problem with implementing performance-related pay was that not every manager completed annual appraisals for the employees reporting to him (appraising their performance in relation to objectives agreed and set down in a meeting with the employee a year earlier). Only about one quarter of the required appraisals got completed in the first year. Executives were just too busy, they protested. Bonfield wanted at least 90 per cent of appraisals done each year. 'I came up with the idea to make the whole of the year's bonus scheme trigger only above 90 per cent of appraisals completed properly, so if you did below 90 per cent it would wipe out your entire bonus. My god, did that focus everyone's head on it!'

In the 1990s, Bonfield used acquisitions as catalysts for change. Normally, an acquisition by a large profitable company of a small, troubled company is the occasion for empire-building at the acquiring company, and drastic changes and often rolling heads at the acquired. At Bonfield's ICL, it was virtually the other way round. As margins fell in the personal computer industry, ICL used the skills of the companies it acquired to remake its own PC business in their image. Helsinki-based Nokia Data was taken over by ICL in 1991. The Nokia senior executives were not only left in place, but many had their responsibilities enlarged as ICL's PC division was put under their control. 'We all knew that the shift in the [PC] marketplace was in time to market, and whoever won the time-to-market battle was more likely to win than the person who designed the most elegant electronics,' said Bonfield. In spite of their cash flow problems in 1991, Nokia Data was a faster-moving designer and manufacturer of PCs than ICL, 'so instead of merging Nokia into ICL, we merged ICL's PC operations into Nokia and drove the whole thing out of Scandinavia.' The payoff was that ICL learned quicker than any other mainframe manufacturer to compete successfully in a market where margins were 10 per cent instead of 50 per cent. Speed to market and the competitive spirit would be vital weapons in ICL's battle to win the nationwide British Gas tender.

EIGHT

ICL II

Organisations Sell Products

Whenever John Jones wanted to think he went out on his tractor. It took about four hours to rake the grass and roll the soil on the twenty acres. Piloting the old diesel-powered Fordson methodically up and back one Saturday afternoon, Jones pondered the idea of becoming sole supplier of PCs to British Gas. It was an attractive thought. It was just the sort of high-visibility accomplishment his boss Peter Frank was looking for when he had laid out his master plan at Kenilworth the previous autumn. PCs were a business nobody associated with ICL; if ICL won a contract to supply thousands of them a year to British Gas, everybody there would see the computer supplier had truly changed its spots. Their PCs would sit on virtually every desk in every British Gas office, from Cornwall to the Shetlands, the ICL logo gleaming on the front. What better corporate advertisement could there be?

On Monday morning, Jones began plotting a strategy to win British Gas's PC business. The key would be the 'red tape' factor: how could ICL slice through the mountain of paperwork and bookkeeping required to handle hundreds of PC orders each year? Computers were typically bought by contract. The contract specified the computer, the peripherals that came with it, software, service terms, free trial periods on certain products, and a hundred other conditions, extensions, and provisions. Contracts were thoroughly inappropriate for PCs, which were commodity products. They were bought, off the shelf, like a can of baked beans, with perhaps one item of software (the DOS operating system) pre-loaded. Additional software was loaded either via the office network or also bought, 'shrink-wrapped', off the shelf. If a PC broke, most times the user would simply throw it away and buy another one. What they needed, Jones decided, was a system where any British Gas office in the UK could simply fax an order to a single ICL office, and a PC would arrive at the appropriate place within a guaranteed time, say forty-eight hours. It was the sort of personal customer service ICL often provided, extended to a type of product with which nobody expected to get that kind of service.

A large company like ICL was like a city. Tucked in little alleyways off the main highways and byways were little departments and sub-divisions carrying on obscure, but often vital, tasks, undisturbed for years by the constant hustle, bustle and re-organisation that went on elsewhere. Peter Frank was a master at company networking. With contacts at dozens of these little departments, he knew how to use them to cut through the bureaucracy when he needed to get something done for a customer in a hurry. He hit upon a division based at a warehouse in Stevenage, called ICL Direct. Direct operated a mail-order sales system, mainly devoted to supplying small accessories like printer ribbons to customers. It accepted payment by credit card. It did not take Frank long to convince ICL Direct that it could handle a fax-order and forty-eight hour delivery system to supply British Gas's PC needs. If you win a deal this size, we might need another dozen people to cope, said ICL Direct. Frank went upstairs, to the MD of ICL UK, and secured a guarantee that ICL Direct would get whatever it needed to serve British Gas.

British Gas IT executives immediately saw the advantages of the system Frank and Jones proposed to them. In addition to the no-fuss order and forty-eight-hour delivery system, Frank offered to service their existing and future PC software packages to make sure they ran on every PC on every desk at British Gas. It was a deal combining the service of a mainframe supplier with the speed of a PC retailer. John Allan's IT department decided British Gas would move to a single PC supplier, but they opened the business up to public tender, asking all their PC suppliers to bid. Bidders included computer majors IBM and Olivetti, as well as the PC specialists, Compaq and Dell.

British Gas tested ICL's promise of forty-eight-hour delivery. On a Friday afternoon, at 2 p.m., an IT manager called Frank. Could Frank arrange to have twelve PCs delivered by Tuesday lunchtime to his office at High Holborn?

Frank thought for a moment. 'No,' he replied.

No?

'We'll have them at your office tonight at 6 p.m.'

'But we don't need them tonight. We go home at 5.'

'That's OK. We'll leave them with your security. We're determined to win this. I want you to see that when ICL says we'll do something, we do it.'

While Frank set about clearing the paperwork which would authorise twelve PCs to leave the warehouse, Jones dispatched one of his sales staff to Stevenage to guide the lorry driver to High Holborn and make sure nothing went wrong. When driver and saleswoman arrived at High Holborn, they found the IT manager waiting for them. He had stayed behind to see with his own eyes the four-hour delivery. ICL won the tender. In 1990, they supplied 2000 PCs to British Gas.

The PC competition was a curtain-raiser for the main event, the tender competition for British Gas's national mainframe computer system initiated by John Allan in January 1991. When Frank arrived at Slough that afternoon, straight from his meeting with Allan, he gathered the ten-strong ICL British Gas sales and sales support team into a meeting room. Patiently, he made sure everybody had their coffees, teas, and the little biscuits on white plates served at every ICL meeting. Only then did he solemnly tell them just what they were embarking on and how much was at stake. British Gas was moving from twelve regional computer systems to one national system. If ICL lost the tender competition, then it would have virtually no business with British Gas. If they won, the contract to build a new national computer system and adapt *all twelve* of British Gas's regional systems to the new national system would be worth at least £200 million over the course of the 1990s. It was a massive job, probably the UK's single biggest IT contract of the decade. It would be one of the highest-profile pieces of IT business ever.

ICL had some cards in its favour: only months earlier it had won the exclusive contract to supply PCs to British Gas; Frank's Kenilworth strategy was bearing some fruit as a growing number of the new ICL contacts – the so-called rising stars – rose to more influential positions at British Gas. ICL's reputation was higher than ever before.

But it would be a tough fight. Frank told the team of Martin Goodman's cocky prediction, in the lift at British Gas, that IBM would win the business. IBM was not just any competitor. They were the toughest. Allan had specified that morning that his department was setting up twelve separate sub-committees to consider all aspects of the bids from ICL and IBM. Everything from the design of the computer hardware to the proposals for training British Gas telephonists to use the systems would be considered in detail. The competition broke down into two main areas: first was the 'best of breed' competition. ICL's best of breed was the British Gas West Midlands region computer system. It would be asked to specify a national system based on an expanded version of BGWM, and then explain how it proposed to roll the system out across the country. How long it would take, what were the risks involved, and a hundred other questions would be considered. IBM would be asked to do the same with its best of breed, British Gas South Eastern. Under John Allan, British Gas were pursuing one of the most thorough comparative analyses in the industry's history.

The second half of the competition was a comparison between the two suppliers. Their abilities, reliability and credibility, now and looking forward into the next century, would be compared.

Going head-to-head with IBM on credibility was like fighting an etiquette competition against the Queen. Credibility was IBM's middle name. Moreover, British Gas was being advised by McKinsey. McKinsey was extremely close to IBM. The New York-based consulting firm had advised dozens of clients to use Big Blue (also headquartered in New York) for three decades. McKinsey consultant Ken Ohmae was even a board member at IBM's Far Eastern division.

'This is going to be the fight of our lives, and I want everyone to think of it that way. You're not just fighting for a piece of business. Think of it as you're fighting for your jobs. Because it may be that we are. It may be that if we lose this none of us will have jobs anymore. That's what's at stake.'

ICL's Slough office, housing the GMC (Government and Major Companies) division, was a modern, bright, glass-walled office block. Frank commandeered one of the glass-walled meeting rooms overlooking the central plant-filled atrium for their 'war-room'. The first of many late nights began that evening, as the team sat down to compose answers to the first set of questions from British Gas. The hand of management consultants was evident in the A-level tone of the questions. The first question began: 'Should the Gas business base its IT strategy on a single supplier of mainframe software? Substantiate your hypothesis with reference to areas like market share, cost of software, suppliers' guarantees . . .'

The competition was structured explicitly to test the two companies' responsiveness. They had four days to reply to the first set of questions. Future questions would give them a week or, for the most complex technical and architectural questions, two weeks. The consultants argued that a company that could mobilise to deliver a price quote or a full technical specification quickly was more likely to be efficient when it came to delivering the actual goods and services. The first set of questions given to Frank that morning, asking ICL's views on the 'best of breed' concept, were relatively straightforward. But the salesmen gave them thorough consideration and discussion before they settled upon their replies. It was past 3 a.m. and the table was strewn with cardboard boxes with the congealed remnants of late-night pizzas before the meeting broke up.

Frank reckoned they had one lucky break. Months earlier, he had set up an ICL/British Gas senior executive conference, scheduled for late February 1991. Now it was taking place right as the tender was getting going. The conference had been agreed between Frank and Allan late in the previous year. As deputy chairman of British Gas West Midlands, Allan had been on the list of rising stars drawn up at Kenilworth. Frank's efforts to build a relationship with him paid off in spades when Allan was moved from the region to High Holborn and promoted to director of information technology. ICL ran regular twenty-four-hour conferences at its executive retreat, Hedsor House, a Georgian country house set among trees by the Thames near Taplow. Normally, the senior executive programme involved a day of presentations to senior executives from a customer or potential customer to explain the benefits of investing in computer systems. British Gas knew the benefits of IT. Frank was acutely aware that the issue that preyed most heavily on the minds of Allan and his colleagues was the challenge of transforming British Gas from a former state-owned monopoly to an aggressive competitor. Their new global strategy would work only if the company could remould itself. It was precisely the transition ICL had already achieved. 'British Gas were facing a period of profound and dramatic change, and for an organisation which had such an ingrained culture, which hadn't changed much since the early 1950s, that was going to be traumatic. I realised we had a tremendous asset: we had been through the pain barrier of change. Imparting the knowledge of how you change, how you manage change, would be valuable to them.'

Frank planned a day-long senior executive conference at which top ICL executives would discuss issues of corporate change and ICL's experiences in the 1980s. When he pitched the idea to Allan, the British Gas executive was at first sceptical. 'Peter, you're too good a salesman to get a half dozen Gas executives in a room and *not* try to sell us some piece of IT kit.' But Frank was adamant. Selling would not be mentioned once at the conference, he pledged. Allan agreed to come and enlisted five colleagues from British Gas. None of them were in IT; all were coming to hear about corporate change. Frank arranged for the conference to be hosted by David Teague, director of ICL's government and major companies division. Four senior veterans of ICL's experiences of the 1980s would speak, including Joe Goasdoué on ICL's quality programmes. The final speaker would be Peter Bonfield. Frank himself would not speak at all. He made sure every speaker knew they were not to try to sell ICL products. 'The first thing you have to have is integrity and trust. If you don't have that in large account selling, you don't have anything.'

The British Gas executives were immediately intrigued when David Teague opened the conference. Instead of the banal self-praise and self-promotion to which most companies subject their customers, Teague gave his listeners a crushingly honest assessment of the mistakes and bad management at ICL that brought the company to the brink of bankruptcy in 1981: poor products that were engineering-driven not market-driven, poor financial management, no clear strategy, unresponsive to change, a tradition of designing products and then expecting to sell them with no clear idea of whom to sell them to, and an overmanned, over-unionised, under-motivated workforce. By 1981, those problems made ICL a company with turnover of £800 million but a shareholders' value of just £20 million.

Teague continued: 'Before I hand over to my colleagues who'll tell you more about what's happened since then, I'd just like to sum up where we've got to since our low point in 1981.

'We've been profitable every year since 1982. In fact, we're the *only* major computer company in the world who's been profitable every year since 1982. We have completely shed the old 'shifting iron' mentality. We're customer-led and highly responsive to the market. Nearly half of our business comes from selling software or services now. In hardware, we supply minicomputers and PCs too – as you well know since we won the exclusive contract to supply all of British Gas's PCs. We have partnerships with some of the world's technological leaders, like Sun Microsystems of California. We have an integrated quality programme throughout the company, we invest heavily in our people. We've slimmed down to 22,000 people. We're leaner and fitter. Our people are better paid, and we think they're highly motivated. Our business is growing in the UK, the US and on the Continent. We're pretty proud of what we've achieved.'

The guests were listening attentively when Joe Goasdoué walked to the front of the wood-panelled drawing room to begin his talk. Goasdoué explained ICL's quality programmes, and displayed charts and tables to demonstrate the progress the company had achieved. He stressed the mistakes ICL made in its early attempts to raise quality, the pitfalls of quality programmes, and the costs involved, primarily the enormous amount of senior management time they consumed. He talked about the highest level of quality achievement: when quality became a strategic weapon in the marketplace, when customers chose to buy from you not just because you delivered a quality service but because you had a publicly recognised reputation for quality. Citing Marks and Spencer and Rolls Royce as examples, Goasdoué said that a reputation for quality was a priceless, enduring, strategic asset for any business. A British Gas executive protested, pointing out that British Gas had very high quality ratings in its customer surveys. In areas like the despatch of service engineers within the time frames promised or the reliability of appliances they sold and installed, the company scored high with customers.

In fact, British Gas had a long way to go to gain the sort of public reputation that its private surveys indicated it deserved. (In 1993, it began an advertising campaign aimed specifically at heightening public awareness of the quality of its service.) But Goasdoué didn't want to criticise the utility directly. He finessed the question by returning the discussion to ICL. 'ICL scores very high in surveys too,' he said. 'But we don't believe we've achieved strategic quality yet.' He went on to explain his newest quality programme, entitled 'The Angers and the Delights' a plan to

'Delight the Customer' at every available opportunity. Like all Goasdoué's initiatives, it was far more than cheerleading. Every objective would be quantified, targeted, measured and analysed. In each market segment, ICL would be identifying the two suppliers giving the best customer service, and benchmarking its own performance against them. The aim was to equal or beat the competition within two years.

Bonfield was the last speaker of the day. Unlike the others, he used no graphs or charts, and did not read from notes. He sat in a cosy easy chair at the front of the room. Speaking softly, he recounted how he and his management team had changed ICL. He explained the importance of the technology deals with Fujitsu and others; the people-oriented changes like performance-related pay, and investing in people, ICL's commitment to training and upgrading its people. He discussed how ICL changed from an engineering-led to a market-led company. The process was always continuing, he said. He explained his philosophy of repeatedly employing a 'catalyst for change' to keep the company always moving, always adapting to the ever changing computer market-place. 'We are religious about following the market,' he said.

At the back of the drawing room, Frank sipped a cup of tea and smiled quietly to himself. Customers never failed to be impressed by Bonfield, by the quiet determination and the unmistakeable commitment to make the company successful. He had as clear a grasp on the people issues as he did on the abstruse technical ones. His love and dedication to the company always came through.

When Bonfield finished, the group retired to the bar. There was just time for one cocktail before leaving. 'Did you find it useful?' Frank said to John Allan. 'Very interesting,' Allan replied. They both knew Frank was fishing for a clue about the mainframe tender. Allan was by nature a stickler for the rules. He wasn't about to engage in off-the-record hints or suggestions that might affect the formal tender competition process.

But he was impressed by what he heard at Hedsor. 'You haven't done yourself any harm at all today,' Allan said, shaking Frank's hand on his way out.

The key weapon in ICL's battle to win the tender was the IT system already in use at British Gas West Midlands (BGWM). Under the rules laid down for the 'best of breed' competition, ICL was to show how the BGWM system could be expanded to cover BG's 18 million customers nationwide. The key advantage of the BGWM software packages was that they integrated three distinct databases into one all-purpose, global database, known as Masterbase. Masterbase combined the customer data (names, addresses and gas bill details for West Midland's 1.7 million customers) with the data on consumer gas hardware (for example, details of every British Gas-supplied central heating system filed with the owner's name and account), and details of the stocks at all of West Midland's service depots. That meant that a customer could ring BGWM, query his bill, order a new appliance and book an appointment for an engineer to come to replace a broken radiator valve, which the telephonist could verify was in stock – all in one quick and easy phone call. Every night the system read files from the Post Office and British Telecom to update addresses and telephone numbers on its database. With one *integrated* database, a single update ensured that all files on a customer were updated together. Powered by a four-node ICL Series 39 (ie four of ICL's biggest mainframe processors, working in harmony together), the West Midlands system was fast, always up-to-date, and easy for telephonists to use, guaranteeing a good service for BGWM customers. Or that, at least, was the story as Peter Frank told it.

Not surprisingly, IBM saw it differently. IBM was not entirely happy defending British Gas South Eastern, a computer package they had created with the local Gas board back in the early 1970s. In the late 1980s they set up a joint development project with BG South Eastern at a British Gas site in Dorking to update the existing IT system. It would employ an advanced version of a relational database. Originally invented by IBM in the 1960s, 'relational database' became one of the industry's buzzwords. It was more versatile than the conventional database used in the ICL West Midlands system. It allowed British Gas to access and cross-reference its data in an almost limitless variety of forms. For instance, a marketing executive could specify the characteristics of the typical customer who might buy a central heating system and the relational database could in seconds pull out of a file of a million names every customer who met the specifications. According to IBM's Martin Goodman, the ICL database was obsolete technology.

Thanks to partnerships with Oracle and Ingres, two of the world's leading database programmers, ICL also offered a relational database. But, undoubtedly, IBM had more experience at implementing a relational database than ICL. There was just one catch to IBM's argument: in its two years of existence, the Dorking development project consumed more than £10 million and had yet to produce a tested, proven product.

For three months, the twelve British Gas subcommittees conducting the tender peppered the two competitors with detailed sets of questions. They wanted to know about the proposed structure of the national IT system, the hardware involved, the software packages, the time frames involved to create them, their reliability, security, and of course the prices. Typically, a questionnaire arrived on the fax machine without warning and with an answer requested within seven days. ICL's British Gas team grew steadily to twenty-five people, as Frank drafted in support from all over ICL. The tiny Slough war-room got more and more crowded. Gordon Shortreed, area sales manager for ICL's British Gas accounts in the north of England, was drafted in for one meeting in Leeds and stayed for six weeks. Working eighteen-hour days, he never saw the inside of his Slough hotel room before midnight. 'At Christmas that year, I got a Christmas card from the night shift staff at the hotel,' he recalled later. Shortreed's wife Alison was seven months pregnant, and every night there was a ritual: leaving the office, he would call Alison from the car. She would tell him in detail what he had missed at the day's ante-natal class. He could not help smiling a bit when Alison described these classes, with their boring rituals and their earnest mothers and fathers-to-be. He'd reassure Alison he'd be back in Leeds in time for the birth of their first child in June, hoping to himself that he was right.

The tender competition split British Gas's information technology department into two bitterly opposed factions. The entire IT department employed 3400 people. About 1200 of them worked in the five British Gas regions using IBM mainframe systems and nearly all the rest in ICL regions. It was obvious throughout the company that once the new centralised IT strategy took effect manpower levels would fall dramatically. If ICL won the tender, the years of skills and experience acquired by IBM-region employees would become virtually uselss, while, if IBM won, many of the ICL-trained IT staffers would probably lose their jobs. 'The ICL regions fought like hell for ICL to get it, and on the IBM side we had some quite powerful players who were totally Blue in their thinking,' said IT director Allan. To ensure that all sides saw the competition as fair and unbiased, Allan brought in a London Business School professor, Michael Earl, as another 'nonpartisan' adviser, in addition to the two outside consulting firms he had already employed.

John Jones was on his tractor at the weekend when he hit on the idea later christened the 'hymn sheets'. ICL's greatest advocates, Jones believed, were in the IT department at British Gas West Midlands. They used their IT system daily, and were convinced it was the best in British Gas. They were more than willing to help ICL in any way they could; after all their jobs were on the line. 'Nobody could have been as passionate as we were about winning, but they did feel pretty strongly,' Jones said. The problem was: how to put their goodwill to use. They were IT guys; most of them had never sold anything in their lives. The hymn sheet was Jones's answer. Every Monday morning, he composed a series of half a dozen brief, punchy points to help sell the ICL alternative. Peter Frank called them elevator speeches. Using ICL's internal electronic-mail system, Jones sent the hymn sheet to everybody involved in the campaign inside ICL, and to everybody at BGWM. The BGWM employee could memorise them and mention one to a colleague in a few seconds. It was an ironic situation: ICL trying to turn BGWM employees into salespeople so they could sell their own system to their own company! Hymn sheet comments were always short and to the point: 'West Midlands software package is the best in the gas industry', or 'ICL is committed to change and understands change because of the changes it has had to make' or 'ICL is the only IT company in Europe that enjoyed profitable growth throughout the 1980s'. Some of them were a bit more provocative like: 'British Gas South Eastern software portfolio is seventeen years old'.

While Frank devoted himself primarily to the endless networking involved in securing information or co-operation from other departments in ICL, Jones co-ordinated the editing of the documents that were sent almost weekly to British Gas. In big computer bids, there was no getting away from matrix management and the need for inter-departmental co-operation. Every component of the bid – from data storage to telephone communication systems between the computers, to software, to delivery timetables – had to be specified and priced, requiring input from a myriad of ICL departments. Frank's knowledge of the company and his enthusiasm were invaluable. Gordon Shortreed recalled one evening towards the end of the bid when he and Frank visited Bonfield at his office in Putney. Frank wanted Bonfield to put in a call to Norman Blacker, a British Gas director Bonfield knew personally, and ask him if he needed any further information. When the two men arrived, Bonfield was just getting ready to go home for the day. 'I called him only the other day, and he said everything was fine,' said Bonfield.

'He may have thought of something since then. Just give him a ring,' replied Frank.

Packing his briefcase, Bonfield said he was suffering from the flu and needed to get home and to bed.

'It'll take a minute.' A head taller than Bonfield, Frank was literally hovering over him, blocking his way.

Shortreed stood rooted to his place, watching aghast as Frank nagged and bullied the ICL chairman into finally making the phone call.

'For a while there, I thought you were going to get both of us the sack,' said Shortreed as they left.

Frank smiled. 'When you are up against someone as bloody good as IBM, you've got to use every resource you have. Even the chairman.'

Early in May Frank deployed his chairman again. Over breakfast at the Inn on the Park hotel in London's Mayfair, British Gas managing director Cedric Brown and IT Director John Allan were to discuss the ICL bid with ICL chairman Peter Bonfield. The morning got off to a bad start when Brown spent ten minutes waiting in the hotel lobby. The bellhop assigned to bring him up to the private dining room just off the main dining room failed to spot his prey. The managing director of British Gas sat on a sofa reading a newspaper for ten minutes. Finally, a breathlessly apologetic Frank found him and brought him upstairs. Bonfield gave the salesman a good-natured bollocking and then warned their guests to guard their English breakfasts carefully because one was not normally enough for Frank. The health-conscious Bonfield ate only muesli.

Allan was characteristically blunt in spelling out his worries over ICL's bid for the £200 million computer contract.

'The question we've got to ask ourselves is can we put the strategic future of British Gas on a product that has only 4 per cent of the world market? We're talking about making a commitment into the next century. Even if we felt that in certain ways IBM's offering didn't suit us exactly, or might not suit us in some way a couple of years from now, the fact is that we wouldn't be locked into IBM. Because it's not just IBM you're talking about. We could buy from Amdahl, or any one of a hundred companies – including your friends Fujitsu. They are all Blue. Eighty per cent of the world is Blue.

'Your Achilles' heel is that even if your systems are as good as you say they are, they operate on VME and VME is 4 per cent of the world market. If you buy an ICL box the only thing in the world you can connect it to is another ICL box.'

Frank and Bonfield looked at each other. In a few sentences, Allan had just spelt out the reason for IBM domination of the mainframe computer business for thirty years. For thirty years ICL had fought an uphill battle against this logic. Mainframe computers from different manufacturers could not 'talk' to each other; they could not share the same software. For thirty years, IBM had been saying to potential customers: if you buy from us, we will *guarantee* that when we come out with our next generation of cheaper, faster, better computers, we will move your systems, in other words your valuable accumulation of programs and data, on to the next generation, at a reasonable cost. When a handful of copycat computer producers (led by Amdahl, Fujitsu and Hitachi) began to produce so-called IBM clones, the irony was that that *increased* demand for IBM systems, because customers knew that more companies than just Big Blue would henceforth be investing in improving the IBM family of products, and that the competition would give them choice and a bit of leverage over price.

The other computer companies were a babel. They produced machines that were incompatible with each other. A customer who bought from them was locked into their systems. And the competitive message from IBM was always the same: you may like the current generation of equipment from our competition. Fine. But you don't know you'll like their next generation. You can't even be sure they'll *have* a next generation. ICL's chequered history, its financial crises, made the latter point a wounding one.

Frank launched into a recitation of ICL's standard reply to the arguments about 'lock-in' and incompatibility. A decade before, under Robb Wilmot's leadership, ICL had become a leader in the battle for so-called 'open systems'. ICL fought to convince all the non-IBM-compatible computer companies in the world that if they made all *their* systems mutually compatible, then would they be able to offer customers the same degree of choice and security about the future as IBM. It was not an easy argument, since upgrading a computer's operating system so it could communicate with other computers, read other data, print on other printers, in other words be completely 'open', required a multimillion-pound investment. As usual, European corporate nationalism had impeded progress. But by 1990, the open systems principle was accepted and being (slowly) implemented by most major computer manufacturers. The minicomputer world had seen significant achievements already in 'open-ness'.

'Gentlemen, this information is confidential so I'd ask you to be discreet,' said Frank, lowering his voice to a theatrical hush. He revealed that within a month, ICL would become the world's first computer company to receive an X-OPEN Level 3 accreditation for VME. That meant ICL's Series 39 and its VME language would be the first mainframe operating system recognised as open to the highest international standard.

'We're not afraid of opening the door to allow you to buy from our competitors. We want you to have the choice. We think that it's in your interest to be able to choose the best business solution from the widest field. And we think it's in our interest for VME to inter-connect with the widest range of products. And frankly, we're not afraid of the competition because we believe VME is the best.'

The latter part of Frank's speech was largely for the benefit of Cedric Brown, who was listening attentively. Allan, who had heard most of it before, was studying the table. When Frank finished, Allan took a deep breath before replying.

'Peter, it's all very well you saying that VME opens the door to a whole new world. But the fact is that when you open the door, what's on the other side? Flippin' nothing. Name me one box I can buy that I'd *want* to buy and hook up to one of yours. Siemens, Bull, Unisys? They're all either in trouble or they're still not producing anything that you could honestly call open systems.'

For the first time that morning, Peter Bonfield spoke. 'John, I think you should understand that when you do business with us, it's not just ICL you're talking to. We're in a long-term partnership with Fujitsu, the second-largest IT company in the world. When we say that we will provide you with a system that works, that is state-of-the-art in terms of performance, cost, security, and every other parameter, it's not just us saying that. It's Fujitsu saying that. And when we say we will take you forward into the open world, and into our next generation and the generation after that, it's not just us saying that but Fujitsu as well.'

'What guarantee can you give me of that?'

'We can give you written guarantees. Our legal people will assure you that Fujitsu stands behind us. If you like, you can meet Fujitsu president Tadashi Sekizawa on his next visit to the UK and hear it from him directly.'

Allan and Brown were intrigued. With turnover of $15 billion, Fujitsu was nearly double the size of British Gas. Dear little British ICL suddenly looked very different as a part of the Fujitsu group.

Bonfield was warming to his theme. 'The real guarantee is not on any piece of paper. And it's got nothing to do with the fact that Fujitsu owns 80 per cent of us. We're going to go to the London Stock Exchange some time in the mid-1990s, and Fujitsu's stake will come down considerably.

'The real guarantee of our partnership is the best guarantee there can be in business: mutual self-interest. Fujitsu support us because we are their largest customer for chips. We buy from them because they make some of the best processor chips in the world. They want us as a partner because they believe the world is going towards open systems and we are one of the world's leaders in open systems. That's why they sell our systems in Japan, and why ICL engineers are working on the operating system for the next generation of Fujitsu mainframes.'

For years, computer industry rumours had suggested that one day Fujitsu would pull the plug on ICL's mainframe development, forcing ICL to sell Fujitsu's own IBM-compatible computers. With quiet confidence, Bonfield explained that Fujitsu was relying increasingly on ICL as open systems gained popularity in Europe and the US. Even Japan, stronghold of both IBM and the copycat IBM-compatibles like Fujitsu, was slowly moving towards open systems.

The deadline for submission of the final tender document, which contained details of the entire bid, was Friday 31 May 1991. Empty pizza cartons, Chinese food tins and styrofoam burger boxes piled up every night in the last two weeks of May as the account team worked on writing, rewriting and re-rewriting every section of their document. With Jones as overall editor, the account team divided themselves into 'blue' and 'red' teams. The blue team wrote the document, while the red team read it 'from the customer's point of view', criticising it as vigorously as they could for any lack of clarity, excessive length, or over-technicality. Frank devoted himself to the liaising, conferring and securing agreements to the elements of the bid from all over ICL. The bid included computers, software and details of systems integration, and the retraining ICL would provide to British Gas staff. On some of the newer technologies, ICL was offering free 'try-out' periods on machines, or free training to British Gas staff, or both. Frank needed approval from the relevant ICL departments. 'You sell this kind of big bid twice – once to the customer and once to your own company,' said Gordon Shortreed.

The only time Peter Bonfield had available for a final meeting to approve the bid document was 7 a.m. on a day he was in Bournemouth for a meeting. The night before, Frank and Jones attended a concert with several British Gas executives at Hagley Hall outside Droitwich. There was no question, of course, of cancelling any British Gas entertaining two weeks before submitting the big bid. The two dinner-jacketed salesmen dined, attended the concert, smiled, applauded, said goodnight – and leapt into their cars at midnight to make it to Bournemouth in time for their meeting with Bonfield. Along the way, Jones veered into a motorway service station for a pre-arranged rendezvous with a staffer from Slough who passed through the car window the latest version of the inch-thick bid document. Jones silently thanked god that no policeman was watching. A dutiful constable might not have reacted well if told that the object passed through two car windows in an empty service-station car park at 3 a.m. was a blueprint for a new computer system for British Gas.

The final bid document was a hefty 200-page volume with the words 'British Gas: IT Strategy Review' above a computer-processed image of the globe on the shiny black cover. On the first inside page was a photo of the now thirty-strong account team. With tongue only slightly in cheek, the caption below the photo read: 'The Team that Lives and Breathes Gas'. The team were shattered. It had been weeks since any of them had enjoyed a full night's sleep. As they stared at the pile of freshly printed documents on the desk at Slough, somebody suggested calling a courier to take it into British Gas's London Office. Jones said he would deliver it personally. It would mean he would not reach his farm in Northamptonshire until well into Friday night.

'The last thing you want to be doing on a Bank Holiday Friday is driving into London, but you can't very well talk about personal service and then get a courier to drop off such an important document.' When Jones arrived at High Holborn, he was asked to wait in reception a few minutes. The IT assessment team was in the midst of a meeting. When he was ushered upstairs, the first thing he noticed was that the whiteboard had been scrubbed blank. British Gas was very scrupulous about its confidentiality. The second thing he noticed was a shiny white document on the table with the blue IBM logo on it. His heart sank. 'Blast, I wanted to be first in,' he said. A member of the British Gas IT team told him not to worry: 'IBM phoned up this morning and said do you realise it's a bank holiday weekend, we'll send it down by courier. You've taken the trouble to deliver it personally and we appreciate that.' Jones sat down to a cup of tea. The chat was pleasant but the British Gas men gave nothing away.

Early in June, news came back from British Gas that the assessment team would not reach a decision in time for the original July deadline. The size and significance of the IT tender was such that their decision had to be ratified by the British Gas board of directors, who did not meet in August. The decision, therefore, would not be known until 26 September, the day after the board's September meeting. Few of the members of the account team were able truly to enjoy that summer. As August turned into September, the suspense, and with it the lobbying, reached fever pitch. ICL staffers used every excuse they could to phone up British Gas people, offering minor updates of bid details, asking if they needed any further information, angling for hints or clues as to which way the decision might go. By mid-September, Jones was as exhausted as he was in May, as much from worry this time as from work. 'I rung up Peter Bonfield one day and I said, Peter I have done this, I have called that person, I have done everything I can think of and I have just run out of ideas. Peter had also been talking to British Gas people at the top level and he didn't have a clue either how it would go. He said don't worry, just leave it now. There's nothing we can do except wait for the decision.'

On the morning of 26 September, Peter Frank, John Jones, two colleagues and ICL press relations woman Sara Cole sat around the small table in Frank's cramped, boxlike office in ICL's Birmingham base. Outside the office, a dozen members of the account team sat, stood and idled about within sight of Frank's secretary, Irene. Down at Slough, the rest of the account team milled about, in and around Jones's empty office, waiting for the phone call from Birmingham. Allan had warned Frank he would ring at precisely 10.45 a.m. with news of the decision. Allan had also asked Frank to prepare two press releases: a winning and a losing version. The computer trade press were highly interested in the outcome of the largest IT tender of the decade. As a general rule, Frank and Jones were totally open with their account team. But they prepared the losing press release quietly between themselves. 'We weren't going to introduce the concept of losing into our vocabulary at that stage,' said Jones.

On Frank's wall was a plastic clock, in the shape of a foot-high blue necktie. Made out of bright, translucent plastic, with bright red hands rotating from a central point where a tie pin might be, it was an absurd-looking thing. Frank loved it. It was a gift from his daughter Vanessa. Aged fifteen, Vanessa was exuberantly anti-Establishment. She did not like school uniforms and she thought her father's suits and ties were 'boring'. She enjoyed art, drawing, painting and making things. At thirteen, she had made him the blue necktie clock. It was a precocious creation for a thirteen-year-old and in every office Frank occupied it always held pride of place, high up on the wall. That morning, the blue necktie was the focus of attention in Frank's office. With every passing minute, the five ICL executives glanced up at it more frequently.

At 10.40, conversation dried up. Anticipation overcame their ability to make small talk. The only sound in the room was the ticking of the necktie. In awful silence, they watched the red hands reach 10.45. A minute passed. Silence. They exchanged nervous glances. Frank looked at his hands. They were sweating. At 10.50 the phone rang. From outside they heard Frank's secretary's voice: 'No, there's no news yet and I'm keeping this line clear. Goodbye!' Frank's secretary was as nervous as they were. That morning at 7 a.m. she had rung Frank in his car to tell him that she had not been able to sleep that night worrying about the decision.

At 10.50, Frank said: 'It's not like John to be late.' They all nodded. 'I'm getting a bad feeling about this.' They nodded again, watching the necktie.

Just before 11.00, the phone rang again. 'Of course, Mr Allan. I'll put you right through.'

John Allan thought he would have a little fun. In the most sombre, funereal voice he could muster, he said, 'Peter, I'm awfully sorry to be calling you late, but I called IBM first and the call went on – '

Allan dragged out his apology, until Frank could stand no more. For the first time in his life, he was rude to a customer.

'John, just tell me. Have we won it or haven't we?'

Suddenly, Allan's tone changed. 'Peter, I'm delighted to tell you, you've won. You've done a fabulous job. You couldn't have done anything more to convince British Gas that ICL are the people we want as partners for our new IT strategy.'

Through the phone, Allan heard the room erupt into cheers. Frank thanked him, promised to issue the press release and rung off. His tiny office was now crammed to bursting with the account team, as champagne splashed into plastic cups. The phone began to ring and did not stop. One by one, the account team members rushed off to tell others the news. Jones shook Frank's hand, and departed for Slough to join his people there for a small celebration.

By one o'clock, Frank was sitting across from press relations woman Sara Cole, and the room was again dead silent. They were waiting for the press to call. Restless, Frank asked if he could sneak off to the canteen for a quick lunch. 'Only twenty minutes,' he promised.

As Frank came in, employees sitting in the brightly lit canteen looked up. The room went silent. Suddenly, they broke into spontaneous applause. Frank did not know whether to be proud or embarrassed. He smiled sheepishly, grabbed a tray and went to get his food. His ordeal wasn't over. When he came to the till, the till lady stared at him. 'You're Peter Frank, aren't you?'

'That's right, love,' said Frank, drawing himself up to his full six feet six inches.

She looked at his plate of liver and onions. 'Well, off you go, then. This one's on the catering company. Well done!'

Only the previous day, Frank's wife Irene had come out of hospital where she had had minor surgery. That night, Frank went home to cook dinner for the family. In the evening, ICL UK managing director John Gardner rang Frank to congratulate him. Gardner asked him why he wasn't out celebrating. 'Actually, John, I'm doing the washing up,' Frank admitted. The celebrations would come later. The next day, John Gardner sent a letter to Fujitsu chairman Takuma Yamamoto. It read in part:

> To knock IBM out of six major sites simultaneously is the type of sales success one can only dream about . . .

> Never again will IBM be able to cast doubts on ICL's credibility.

Later, John Allan explained why ICL won the IT bid. He said that ICL's software package for British Gas West Midlands *was* superior, and more easily rolled out to a national scale than the IBM package in use in South Eastern region. But there was also little doubt that, if asked, IBM could produce a first-rate software package for British Gas. Allan stressed the importance of the transformation at ICL. In 1987, as director of marketing in British Gas's North Thames region, Allan had a bird's-eye view of the events surrounding ICL's biggest loss at British Gas. ICL destroyed its credibility at North Thames by failing for years to deliver on promised upgrades to the region's obsolete computer systems. 'It was always coming and it was always tomorrow, tomorrow. We had [Conservative minister] Lord Soames coming to see our chairman saying buy British and it was a very, very hard decision but they lost because of the track record.

'If you look at where they were and where they are, ICL are a transformed business. They have got Fujitsu, they have got a good product, they have diversified well and timely into the solutions market. Some of the other big players are just starting to talk about that, and ICL have essentially done it already and they are throwing in profit at a time when most of the big players, IBM included, are not doing that. They are well positioned and strong and we see them now as a strategic partner. They have a lot to gain from that, and so do we.'

Peter Frank believed ICL picked up points with its customer-friendly attitude. 'Perhaps unintentionally, Big Blue often gave an impression of arrogance.' While ICL made a point of answering every question set by British Gas's IT committees in full, IBM often came back with different options and different ways of achieving what they claimed was the same result. It made comparisons difficult for British Gas. Also, IBM engaged in a lot of behind-the-scenes lobbying with British Gas board members. It was a strategy typical of one of the most influential foreign companies in the UK, but in this case it backfired. ICL also lobbied British Gas hard, but Frank made sure Allan always knew in advance of any meeting between British Gas and ICL directors.

Allan praised Frank's leadership of the ICL campaign, his tenacity and persistence. 'I couldn't get away from him. He was ringing me in my car, at home, and all sorts!' He singled out the role of Bonfield in transforming ICL and in impressing key British Gas executives. 'He is intellectually very sharp and he understands his business through and through, and, perhaps most important in my view, he is a street fighter, he's got that instinct. One got the feeling that if he wasn't an MD or chairman or whatever, he would handle himself well in a stall in the Portobello market.'

In April 1992, ICL recognised the British Gas achievement by inviting the entire account team on the annual 'Atlas Club' incentive trip for the company's most successful salesmen. It was also an opportunity for the team members to repay their wives for the lonely evenings and weekends of 1991. A group of 200 ICL staffers and their spouses spent five days in Barbados. The activities included offshore cruises in 'pirate ships', a frenetic treasure hunt across the island in open-topped jeeps, and, the climax of the trip, dinner *al fresco* on tables set up on the fifth fairway of the Barbados golf course with a fireworks display and live entertainment from 1960s pop star Neil Sedaka. The last night of the trip, in a party in the hotel reception room, Peter Frank was awarded a huge silver cup, as Branch Manager of the Year. He came home with a photo of the account team on a stage before 400 applauding colleagues. Behind them a screen declared, in foot-high letters, 'Peter Frank: Branch Manager of the Year'. As Frank held the silver cup aloft, ICL's senior management team cheered from the side of the stage. Applauding vigorously was Peter Bonfield. Even Vanessa Frank, usually so uninterested in anything to do with ICL or computers, was impressed.

Upon their return to the UK, John Jones was promoted to account manager of ICL's account with the Department of Social Security. The DSS was ICL's largest single account, spending more than £50 million a year on a massive IT system managing the payment of £64 billion of welfare benefits through 1000 DSS offices. Jones had a team of sixty sales and support staff working with him on the account. Under ICL's devolved structure of business units, he would run the team as an autonomous profit centre. He was flattered to get the promotion. 'I'd never seen myself as especially ambitious, but I enjoy my job enormously. I love the challenge of constant change at ICL and I love the success the company has had. It never gets boring.' To commemorate the British Gas victory, Jones named one of his young Irish draft brood mares 'BG'. When he mentioned the name to British Gas managing director Cedric Brown, Brown replied: 'You've got a winner there for sure.' Brown was right. In September, BG cantered off with the award for champion three-year-old from the Irish Draft Society.

1992 was an *annus horribilis* for the computer industry. IBM posted a record-breaking net loss of $4.97 billion. At IBM UK, where sales fell by 6 per cent, the loss was a devastating £616 million, five times greater than IBM UK's 1991 loss, which the company had then termed its worst year ever. Indeed, the 1992 result was one of the largest losses in British corporate history. The UK subsidiary seemed to have adopted all the symptoms of the slow-moving, bureaucratic companies which typified Britain in the 1970s. IBM UK chairman Tony Cleaver even won a knighthood – often a sign of a management devoting more time to corporate image than performance. Cleaver soon resigned as UK chief executive, to be followed months later by his boss, IBM world chairman John Akers. New IBM chairman Lou Gerstner, the first outsider ever to take the helm in that company's history, took office in March 1993. From all sides Gerstner was besieged with free advice, including recommendations that IBM enlarge its software and services business, devolve responsibility down to business units, enter into more partnerships and joint ventures with other IT companies, and make its R&D more commercially oriented. John Sculley, chief executive of Apple, the California-based maker of PCs which survived the recession better than most, sounded similar themes, promising Wall Street that within five years Apple would be big in 'services, software and systems integration'. At ICL the decision to grow in every one of these areas was taken in the *early* 1980s.

Elsewhere in the industry, the news was little better. American minicomputer giant DEC lost $2.8 billion with sales flat at $13 billion. Among the European companies, Olivetti recorded sales down 6 per cent to £3.3 billion and a 1992 loss of £270 million, nearly 50 per cent worse than the 1991 loss. French state-owned computer company Bull saw 1992 revenue drop 10 per cent to £3.8 billion and losses rise to a horrifying £590 million (including a restructuring write-off of £300 million), after an awful 1991 which featured a £412 million loss.

On 7 April 1993, Peter Bonfield announced ICL's results for 1992. The announcement was made in London at the luxurious theatre in the BAFTA conference centre on Piccadilly. Bonfield resented the lack of attention ICL got from the British media. In preparation for the day when ICL would rejoin the London stock market, he made it a point to deliver annual results announcements and analysts' briefings in the City exactly as if ICL was a public company. One hundred journalists, many from Continental trade newspapers, treated themselves to spicy hors d'oeuvres from the kitchens of the Roux Brothers before filing into BAFTA's theatre to hear the ICL chairman speak. With its thick blue pile carpet and plush beige chairs, the cosy theatre telegraphed a clear message: ICL was surviving the worst recession in computer industry history rather well.

In crisp grey suit, a small silver ICL Quality badge twinkling in his lapel, Bonfield mounted the stage. His soft Texan twang – like JR Ewing he swallowed the consonants in the second half of words like profitability and flexibility – made an amusing contrast with the hushed, polite proceedings. His modesty and understatement, however, were completely British. With profits down 38 per cent to £38 million, Bonfield could not be too boastful, and he did not point out that any profit at all in 1992, a 'character-forming' year for the industry, was a major achievement. He talked about 'considerable' achievements like an increase in revenue of 32 per cent to £2.5 billion, including more than £1 billion of revenues from Continental Europe for the first time. He pointed out that with R&D spending of £242 million, ICL was the highest self-funded investor in R&D in the British electronics sector (GEC spent more, but most of GEC's spend was financed by the British government). He talked with quiet confidence about ICL's aim to become Europe's largest IT company.

Only in his closing, did Bonfield allow a trace of emotion to slip through. 'You might think I'm biased, but I think ICL is an excellent company. The results we've announced today demonstrate our resilience and our ability to operate in bad markets.

'I believe we have the right strategy to win in an industry which we understand intimately.'

NINE

Control Techniques

Made in Wales, Exported Worldwide

'There, that's us.'

Trevor Wheatley peered at the newspaper Eddie Kirk held towards him. There was a large photo of two men in suits. Each man was holding up a string of sausages and smiling at the camera. Wheatley did not recognise the men.

'What're you talking about, Eddie?'

'Tha's a company just outside Glasgow. They make sausage casings from collagen. They've got a 94 per cent share of the UK market. And they use our Jaguars to do it.'

Eddie Kirk was the chief UK salesman for the Jaguar, a high-tech drive used for precision control of an electric motor. Jaguars were made by Control Techniques, the company of which Trevor Wheatley was chairman.

Kirk shouted over the roar of the wind and the other two passengers in the small corporate plane listened along with Wheatley as Kirk gave them a thumbnail sketch of the workings of the modern sausage industry. Collagen, a protein taken from the inside of a cow, was the latest development. It had two commercial uses: one was in high-priced cosmetic creams. Collagen's moisture-retention qualities made it a good skin cream, used by women for younger-looking skin. The other use was in sausage casings, where it was steadily replacing traditional cow or sheep gut. The Scottish company profiled in the newspaper manufactured casings in the UK, the US and Australia. Everywhere, manufactured casings were taking a growing share of the £1.9 billion world market away from gut. Kirk kept a keen eye on it.

'Gut's fiddly. Collagen's a lot more economical. You can automate the collagen process. After they scrape the stuff off the cowhide, they make it into a slurry. Then they extrude it into a film, like a half-mile-long balloon. Then they peel it back into six-inch lengths on a machine, like peeling back a giant foreskin.'

'Eddie, for Chrissake.'

Kirk had the Scotsman's predilection for blunt speaking. He was in full flow and carried right on. 'Then another machine rams the sausage meat through, you twist it, seal it and there's your sausage.'

There was a long pause as his three listeners digested Kirk's story. It was not an appetising thought at 6.30 in the morning.

'If you want to taste a really super sausage, wait till we get to Hanover,' said Wheatley. 'A sausage and a beer at one of those stands out in the sunshine, that's one of the treats of the Fair.'

Wheatley opened up a notebook on the table in front of him to a page of figures. 'Eddie, what Mike and I are about to discuss is highly confidential, so whatever you may hear, can you make sure to forget it when we get off the plane?' Kirk nodded his assent. He was already explaining further nuances of the sausage industry to Control Techniques' sales director David Reece.

The plane was scheduled to arrive at Hanover at 9 a.m., in time for the start of the 1993 Fair. The annual Hanover Fair was Europe's premier trade show for industrial and electrical machinery. Control Techniques always had a big stand at the Fair. Wheatley always looked forward to the frenetic seven days of socialising and gossiping with customers and exploring what competitors were up to. This year he was more excited than usual. He had a meeting planned that afternoon with senior executives from VEE, Austria's premier manufacturer of drives. VEE was in financial difficulties. In 1992 its owners contacted Wheatley with a proposal to sell the company to Control Techniques. It was a golden opportunity for the British firm. At its ultra-modern factory at Newtown in mid-Wales, Control Techniques made the best drives in the world. A drive controlled the speed of an electric motor. Drives were one of the fastest-growing segments of the large industrial controls industry. With sales of £11 million, VEE was number one in the drives business in Austria. If the deal was successfully completed, it would boost Control Techniques' 1993 sales over £100 million. More importantly, they could double profits at VEE by shutting down the Austrian company's manufacturing and replacing their product line with the superior Control Techniques products made in Wales. With the VEE sales network producing CT products, CT market share would grow further. Control Techniques had followed the same strategy with previous acquisitions in Germany, Italy and the US.

The biggest potential obstacle to the deal was VEE's Vienna factory where 300 employees produced drives. Wheatley had been there. It was a classic low-quantity, high-cost production site. VEE was a 50/50 joint venture between Germany's largest maker of papermaking machinery, JM Voith, and Elin, a state-owned Austrian machinery conglomerate. During the past year of discussions, Voith was always keener on the deal than Elin. Wheatley suspected Elin's management dreaded the prospect of redundancies in Vienna. Wheatley was more than willing to confront the problem – provided Voith and Elin sold 51 per cent of VEE so Control Techniques would have a free hand. Wheatley would not get involved in any structure which required tri-national approvals for decisive action. Their best hope, Wheatley explained to Control Techniques finance director Mike Robins, lay in Voith chairman Michael Rogowski's eagerness to shed the loss-making VEE albatross. Rogowski recognised that VEE was an uncompetitively high-cost producer. With drive technology advancing all the time, the race was best ceded to efficient, state-of-the-art manufacturers. Like Control Techniques. The question was whether Rogowski had persuaded Elin chairman Heinrich Trescher.

'He's good, Rogowski. You'll like him,' Wheatley told Robins.

They studied VEE's numbers. From 1990 to 1992 the company enjoyed an unblemished record of operating losses. In 1993, VEE was projecting a sudden return to profit of £700,000. Robins' finger alighted on the 1993 sales figure, projecting an increase of 50 per cent over 1992. It was a big jump, especially since Germany and Austria were still mired in recession. 'I shall want to know the background to this figure,' said Robins.

'Talk to Hirsch. Or Agis. They'll both be there. VEE has two joint managing directors, one German, the other Austrian. Honestly, I don't know how they ever make a decision.'

'Victor Romeo Bravo Lima Kilo requesting clearance to land.' They were at Hanover. The radio voices boomed out from the cockpit at the front of the plane. The control tower asked the pilot to squeeze in quickly ahead of a 747 just beginning its descent. The tiny Gulfstream Commander turboprop dropped suddenly and banked sharply to the right. The four men watched the ground rush up to them and bounce hard against the three-point landing gear. The airport gleamed brilliantly in the early spring sun. They taxied into the private plane area and parked alongside a corporate jet. The jet was twice the size of CT's Gulfstream, and painted midnight blue. Across the fuselage was scrawled in giant letters 'BON JOVI', and on the nose a smaller inscription read 'Keep the Faith'. It belonged to an American heavy metal band. The jet's windows were bordered with swathed curtains inside. Empty bottles of wine were visible on a table inside. Robins eyed the jet. 'It'd be nice to have a personal jet, wouldn't it?' Robins asked nobody in particular.

Wheatley eyed him curiously. It was an unusual remark coming from their abstemious finance director. What flamboyance there was at Control Techniques came from Wheatley, who looked the part of the dynamic, successful company chairman. A full head of immaculately trim silver-grey hair lent an air of distinction to his squat, bulldog-like frame. An ex-salesman, he was usually talking or joking in his North Country accent, playful blue eyes sizing up everyone and everything, the bright red silk tie from Hermès and the gold watch hinting at the success he enjoyed as founder and chairman of Control Techniques. Having mastered the art of flying a small plane, he had recently acquired a helicopter licence.

'It's probably got a sauna in the back,' Robins added. He was still studying the Bon Jovi jet.

'Why don't you set up a team to look into buying us one?' Wheatley teased. Earlier that year, they'd decided the Gulfstream was adequate for the company's needs. It did 300 mph. It had leather upholstery in the company colour, pale green. The Control Techniques logo, a green circle with a white lightning streak across it, adorned both walls.

Robins was still contemplating the parties Bon Jovi must have enjoyed in the back of their jet. 'Why does everyone always think accountants are boring?' he said.

Wheatley stood before the Control Techniques stand inside the bright sunlit Hanover exhibition hall. He nodded his approval. The stand was eighty feet long, wrapped around one corner of the hall. At the corner a tall structure in white steel tubing rose towards the atrium roof, like a mini-Eiffel Tower. At the top was the green CT logo. In the wall display below was CT's latest product, the Dinverter. It was the smallest mass-produced drive in the world, a compact plastic cube about five inches across packed with electronics. The Dinverter handled up to 0.37 kilowatts of power, enough to drive small pumps and industrial motors. It was, of course, pale green. A hundred of them were arranged against the white wall to form an eight-foot-high circular CT logo. On either side CT's larger drives were displayed, some accompanied by demonstration motors spinning merrily.

Jerry Hooper was handing out abstract, almost psychedelic, pale green ties to all the CT employees at the stand, explaining that customers would prefer a gift of an abstract tie to one with a logo. Hooper was the MD of Control Techniques Germany. He was also the company's 'hit man', despatched to every new acquisition to teach them the Control Techniques way. For eight months he had been living in Hennef, outside Cologne, setting up CT's German operation. They had bought two family-owned German drives companies, substituted the British products, and almost overnight outgrown their premises. Despite the German recession, sales were running 30 per cent over the levels a year earlier.

'C'mon Mike,' said Wheatley to the finance director. 'Let's have a look at Hall 11.' Wheatley headed purposefully towards the glass doors, pocketing the abstract green tie. He would stick with Hermès.

Hall 11 was the central hall, the most coveted location at the Fair. Here were all the giants of German industry, accompanied by a handful of famous overseas names. There was just one British presence, a shared stand squeezing in half a dozen British companies. Most were industrial has-beens, dependent on British military contracts for much of their business. When the electronics trade association asked Control Techniques to join the exhibit, Wheatley offered instead to take the whole stand. He hated the concept of one British stand. 'That's no advertisement for Britain, crowding all these companies, good, bad and indifferent, in together,' he said. They declined his offer, and Control Techniques took its own stand in Hall 13, twice the size of the entire British stand.

As they walked, Wheatley and Robins passed several stands displaying Control Techniques products. French motor manufacturer Leroy Somer had a Control Techniques Commander on show, rebadged, of course, with the French company's name. Made in Newtown, it was identical to the one sold in Britain except the plastic box was grey instead of the CT green. French electronics firm Cegelec also sold a rebadged Commander, but in yellow. German electronics giant AEG sold the Commander in their company colours, red and white. AEG was Wheatley's destination. The billion-pound German electronics giant sold several million pounds worth of Commanders to German customers. They were one of Control Techniques' top distributors worldwide and Wheatley always tried to visit them on the first morning of the Fair. Wheatley stopped briefly at the Siemens stand. Stretching for 100 metres in every direction, it was the biggest at the Fair. Everything electrical – from microchips depicted with moving multicoloured photographic enlargements, to giant power systems – was on show. Siemens was the largest maker of drives in the western world. That was the position Wheatley was aiming for. He stopped and studied the stand and the latest Siemens products. He saw no features that could not be found on a CT drive. Satisfied, he turned and headed for AEG.

'Herr Rensch! Frau Hoch!'

'Herr Wheatley! Good to see you!'

The AEG stand was busy. Wheatley and Robins shook hands with the two AEG drives executives and the foursome retired to AEG's free restaurant upstairs.

'*Ein Apfelsaft, bitte.*' The two Germans smiled at Wheatley's Derbyshire-accented German. Both of AEG's sales managers for drives were women. With swept-back blonde hair streaked with grey, and well-lined steely grey eyes, Frau Hoch was a tough cookie. She wore a pink skirt suit with chrome buttons the size of small hubcaps. On the weekends, she drove a Harley-Davidson. Herr Rensch was an older, highly cultured man, a native Berliner recently retired as MD of AEG's drives division. The two had led a fight at AEG in 1986 to convince their bosses to allow them to stop making their own AC drives under 75 kilowatts and sell Control Techniques' instead. It was no easy decision for a proud company like AEG.

They told the Englishmen that sales in 1993 were running well ahead of 1992. The worst of the German recession was, they hoped, over. But the former East Germany was still mired in recession, with new layoffs announced almost daily. Rensch described a recent visit he had made to Turkey to see a large company building a new factory. They needed drives to power their conveyor lines and Rensch suggested buying Commanders from AEG. The Turk replied that he had already ordered some Commanders, direct from Control Techniques' new office in Istanbul. 'Do you know the story about the hedgehog who challenged a rabbit to a race?' asked Rensch. 'He had his twin brother wait at the finish line and when the rabbit arrived, exhausted, he saw the hedgehog's brother waiting with a big smile.

That's how it is with Control Techniques, Herr Wheatley. Every time I go somewhere, you are there already!'

Wheatley smiled at the compliment and asked the older man how he was enjoying his retirement.

'Oh, I still do some consulting. There are some eastern companies who think my knowledge can be of some use to them.' Massive construction was turning Berlin once again into a great capital city. 'I told my daughter to become a lawyer,' Rensch said. 'It is the career of the future. Berlin will be a city of public administration. Under German laws they will soon have to employ 50 per cent women. Lawyers and public administrators, they make everything function.'

'No they don't, Herr Rensch,' replied Wheatley. 'It's people like us, who make things, who manufacture. People like us make the world go round.'

Rensch smiled at the Englishman's pugnacious self-confidence and shook his head. 'Lawyers, they are the obstacle-removers. And today in Germany, we have many obstacles.'

Wheatley had just enough time for a sausage on a stick and a glass of lager at an outdoor stand in the noonday sun, before it was time for the meeting with Voith-Elin Elektronik. The Voith stand was at the front of the now bustling hall. It seemed to be trying for a disco effect. Purple neon strip lighting blazed above a rabbit warren of glass cases displaying Voith products, shiny painted steel boxes full of gears, shafts and electronics. One glass case held three Control Techniques Commanders, this time in purple. The label omitted to explain that the product was made not by VEE but by Control Techniques. Rebadging was wide-spread in industry, but nobody liked to admit to it unless asked. Wheatley and Robins idled about, studying a four-foot-high mechanical gearbox. 'Whenever a mechanical company gets into drives, it goes wrong,' Wheatley whispered to Robins. 'They just don't understand the electronics business.' An electronic drive did the same job as the traditional mechanical gearbox more precisely, reliably and economically. When electronic drives first appeared, mechanically-based companies like Voith quickly moved into producing them for their customers. But designing and developing electronic products required six-figure upfront investments in designing circuitry and software. The headlong technological progress in microchip power meant that every two years a whole new generation of drives came on the market. In the days of mechanical drives, progress was measured in decades, not years. Most mechanical companies soon realised that they had neither the volume nor the technological skills to compete in their new industrial niche. Voith and its Austrian joint venture VEE was just coming to that realisation.

Michael Rogowski came over, beaming. 'Good to see you,' he said, pumping Wheatley's hand exuberantly. 'How is Wales?' He escorted the Englishmen to Voith's private bar/restaurant, hidden behind the stand. It was a dimly lit room, with thick, dark blue carpeting, more blue neon strip lights, Monet prints on the walls, and boxes of shrubbery atop the partitions, ensuring privacy for each group of comfy black leather chairs. A young waiter came up and suggested an alcohol-free cocktail. Five men sat on one side of the low cocktail table, and Wheatley and Robins on the other. Wheatley took in the size of the Austro-German contingent. It suggested they were ready to do a deal.

Jovially, Rogowski introduced his colleagues, another Voith board member, the president of the state-owned Elin, and both managing directors of VEE. 'This is my finance director, Mike Robins,' Wheatley said. 'I always bring him along whenever there's any danger of me spending money.' Rogowski and Elin president Heinrich Trescher lit cigars and leaned back in their chairs to listen to Wheatley explain his proposal. Quickly and succinctly, Wheatley went through his plan to take over VEE, and sell the British products to VEE's Austrian and German customers. All drives up to power levels of 150 kilowatts would be manufactured at the Newtown plant, the low-cost production site. The entire explanation took less than a minute. 'It's a simple, straightforward plan. I'm a simple straightforward guy,' Wheatley said, smiling.

'We agree that there should be only one place of production up to a certain level of kilowatts,' said Rogowski. 'But above that level, we have some of our own technology in Vienna. We have established something there and we think we should try for a while longer to get that thing going.'

Rogowski looked to be in his early forties, surprisingly young for the president of a large German company. Relaxed, in a green blazer and blue trousers, he was frank and to the point. He gave the impression of having already decided exactly how far he would go to solve the problem of his loss-making VEE subsidiary. Trescher, the older, grey-haired, grey-suited Austrian sitting next to him, was a different kettle of schnitzel, cautious, vigilant, almost suspicious. With his head tilted back, staring down his nose at Wheatley as the Englishman spoke, he looked like the front end of a new Honda, eyes squinting like halogen headlights beneath a balding dome. If Wheatley didn't charm the Austrian, he'd get run over.

Cheerfully, Wheatley explained Control Techniques' manufacturing strategy. They produced smaller drives at the Newtown factory. Producing 10,000 drives a month, Wheatley believed it was the highest-quality, lowest-cost drive plant in the world. He wanted to build a similar production line for larger drives, but had not yet decided where. 'We have no preconceived ideas,' he said. 'We manufacture wherever it's best to manufacture. We need to do a very careful analysis. I think for two or three years we will probably not change very much, until our analysis is concluded.' It was a signal that there would be no immediate closures or redundancies at VEE.

It was the compromise Trescher was looking for. He leaned forward and the tension in his face seemed to evaporate. 'That's good,' he said. 'Sudden changes at VEE could cause problems with some of our other contracts with the Austrian government.'

They discussed how they would assess the value of VEE's assets and the course of events after the deal was signed. Rogowski suggested they agree on the sale price within twelve weeks. The hurry that Voith and Elin were in to wash their hands of their subsidiary was almost unseemingly, thought Wheatley. Trescher and Rogowski said they would like payment for VEE in the form of CT shares. It was a vote of confidence in Control Techniques.

'How much of Control Techniques could we own?' Rogowski asked.

'You can buy up to 29.9% per cent in the market. But it would be expensive.'

'How would your other partner feel about that?' Control Techniques already had a 29 per cent shareholder, American firm Emerson Electric, Inc.

'No problem,' said Wheatley. Rogowski was enjoying himself. Wheatley answered in a single sentence questions for which other chairmen might have set up a study group and investigated for months. The two men recognised kindred spirits in each other. Rogowski asked Wheatley about his long-term strategic aims.

'It'll all be in the business plan. But it's simple. To be number one in drives.'

Rogowski smiled. 'Ah! Perhaps we will buy Hitachi.'

For the first time, Wheatley was shocked. He did not like the Japanese competition. He did not even like joking about them. They were very quick to sell in Europe, but made it almost impossible for a European manfacturer to sell over there. 'Why buy Hitachi?'

'Are they not number one in drives?'

'No. Siemens are number one in the west. In the Far East, they're all about equal, Hitachi, Fuji, Yaskawa, and Mitsubishi. At the start of this year, we took £5 million of business off Hitachi in France. Our products are much better than theirs. We wouldn't take Hitachi's drives business if you offered it to us on a platter.'

Rogowski eyed Wheatley carefully. 'To be number one in the world, is this a serious vision?'

Wheatley eyed him right back. 'It's not in my nature to be number two,' he said.

Rogowski's face creased into a big smile. 'It is an exciting idea, Mr Wheatley . . . Trevor. I look forward to our co-operation.' He rose and extended his hand.

On the way back to the Control Techniques stand, Wheatley

and Robins passed the Siemens display again. Once again, Wheatley paused and studied the world leader's display of drives. He turned to Robins. 'You don't have to be number one in too many countries, and number two in a few more, before you're number one in the world,' he said.

The Hanover Fair meant a lot to Trevor Wheatley. It was there, twenty years earlier, that Control Techniques was born.

Like many industrialists, Wheatley's roots were in the coal industry. He grew up in the mining village of Poolsbrook, Derbyshire. His father drove an ambulance for the National Coal Board. All three Wheatley boys went into the coal industry after school. Young Trevor qualified as a mining electrical engineer. After a short time working down the mine, he decided there had to be more pleasant ways to earn a living. 'I'd seen some salesmen and they seemed to have a pretty good life, not too much work to do, fancy cars, and expense accounts,' Wheatley recalled. 'I thought: that looks like the kind of life I could enjoy.' After eight years with the Coal Board, he took a job as a drives salesman with Mawdsley, a long-established motor and electricals manufacturer. Electronic drives were then a new industry. Most of Mawdsley's salesmen did not know them well enough to sell them well. Before long, Wheatley was Mawdsley's top-performing drives salesman. He went back to school at night to earn a DMS (Diploma of Management Studies), to back up his engineering skills with some business knowledge.

By the time he received his DMS, Wheatley accounted for half of Mawdsley's drives sales in the UK. His boss suggested he put his new education to use by drawing up a business plan sketching out how Mawdsley could become number one in the UK drives market. He gave Wheatley a month off to work on his plan. 'It was a typical case study, like the ones I did on the DMS course,' Wheatley recalled. He devised a detailed plan to take Mawdsley to number one in the business. Wheatley figured in the starring role, of course. His boss liked the report tremendously. But it was far too ambitious for Mawdsley's, he said. They preferred steady, not spectacular, growth. What happens next, Wheatley asked. His boss suggested he seek employment elsewhere, at a firm more suited to his talents and ambitions. Wheatley had written himself out of a job.

His next stop was a small electronics company in the Manchester area. The managing director ran the company with an iron hand. He offered Wheatley an attractive-sounding opportunity. 'He made vague promises about equity stakes and directorships,' Wheatley recalled. He soon discovered the company was in a serious plight. The order book was about one third of the level required for the company to break even. It was a little company in grave danger of going bust. Wheatley threw himself into his job with determination. He worked harder then, he said later, than at any other time in his life. It paid off. At the end of three months, the company's order book had trebled.

'I took a weekend off, dusted down my old report, and rewrote it to suit the needs of this small company,' he recalled. On Monday morning, he brought it in and gave it to the managing director. For two hours, Wheatley explained how the little company could transform itself into a market leader in the young, fast-growing drives business. Wheatley's boss listened in silence. At the end, he told Wheatley it was a fantastic plan. 'Just hang on a moment,' he said, slipping out the door. The next office was shared by two women, one the MD's wife and his secretary. They had shared the office for ten years. For two minutes, Wheatley heard whispered discussion through the door. Finally, the MD re-emerged. He shook his head. 'Sorry, Wheatley. The girls don't like it.'

It was one of the few times in his life that Trevor Wheatley was at a complete loss for words. 'What I should have said was here's your car keys,' he commented later. 'But I couldn't afford to resign. I had a wife, two children and a mortgage on a big house in Manchester.' Instead, he just walked out and drove home. But he knew he could not continue to work for a company that made its decisions in such a way.

That was in March of 1973. A few days later, Wheatley turned thirty. He was at Hanover the next month for the Fair. He sought out Ken Briggs, head of drives design at Mawdsley's, and suggested they meet for drinks that night at the Munchener Hall, the Fair's giant beer hall where bosomy *fräuleins* in fancy dress served armfuls of beer steins to thirsty businessmen from around the world. That evening, the two men bemoaned the lack of ambition among the electronics companies in Britain. They decided the only answer was to start their own company. As the empty steins crowded the table, they pledged to begin work on the idea immediately upon returning to England.

Drives were then, as now, a little-known industry. But it was growing fast. Electric motors provide the power for a vast multitude of moving parts in the home, office and factory. A household vacuum cleaner, the fan inside a desktop computer, the escalators in the London underground, the conveyor lines at a food manufacturer, and the mile-long rolling mills at a steel-maker are all driven by motors. Electronic drives enable the user to control the speed, power, acceleration and electricity consumption of a motor. The growing power of microelectronics and their tumbling cost made it economic to attach a drive to more and more motors. More than half of all the electricity produced in the world is consumed by electric motors. In 1973, the potential for the electronic drives industry looked great. (Today it is a $6 billion a year industry and still growing at double-digit rates.) Wheatley's boundless optimism was as much a factor in their decision as the industry's long-term potential. With the country encumbered by strikes, three-day weeks, and government spending cutbacks, it took optimism and some courage to start a new manufacturing venture.

Ken Briggs was as quiet and diffident as Wheatley was flamboyant. Wheatley regarded him as the best design engineer he knew. Briggs had an uncanny knack for coming up with unexpected, cost-efficient solutions to design problems. But the basis on which they formed their new company was simpler. 'In those days in Britain, everybody delivered late, usually months late,' Wheatley recalled. 'I believed all we had to do to be successful was give people a delivery date and stick to it.' They invited in a third partner, Kevin Curran, also from Mawdsley's, to run their manufacturing. For an entrepreneurial start-up operation, it was an extremely well-balanced team: Wheatley on sales and marketing, Briggs on product design, and Curran responsible for manufacturing. They named the company KTK (for Ken, Trevor, and Kevin).

As new prospective employers, KTK received an offer from the Welsh Development Agency of low-cost factory space and housing for the three partners. The Agency had a factory space just the right size in the small Severn-valley town of Newtown. Located in mid-Wales, in the shadow of Powis Castle, Newtown was one of the most inaccessible sites in Britain, equally removed from south Wales, Birmingham, and north Wales by an hour's drive over small, windy country roads. Even after improvement of the roads around Shrewsbury in the 1990s, the town still remained a daunting drive from most centres of civilisation. Clothing designer Laura Ashley sited her factory in Newtown specifically because it was so cut off, believing the views of the Welsh hills would nourish the workforce's appreciation of the pastoral culture inherent in the Laura Ashley style. In June 1973, Wheatley, his wife Patricia and their children had a picnic on the banks of the Severn. The sun shone, the birds chirped and the decision was made in favour of Newtown. Wheatley and Briggs sold their houses and put in £4000 start-up capital. Curran, then just twenty-four, did not own a house and could afford to put in only £2000. He worked for nothing for the first year to balance up his contribution, supported by his wife. In October 1973, with the three wives helping out with screwdrivers, KTK Newtown Ltd produced its first drive.

Right from the start, Wheatley's penchant for unconventional marketing singled out the young company. In one of their first advertisements, Wheatley bought space on the front page of *Industrial Equipment News*. In those days, a KTK drive was a waist-high steel box. The KTK ad contained a photo of a drive – with a smiling nude girl sitting on top. 'In terms of class, it was probably the worst ad I've ever seen,' Wheatley admitted. 'But the impact was massive!' They received many orders directly from the ad. Protests from women's groups gave the tiny company some much needed publicity.

The week the ad appeared, an engineer from Rolls Royce's Shrewsbury office rang, in urgent need of a motor and drive. KTK had in stock the products he needed, and Wheatley was asked to come in that afternoon to take the order. He sat around a table with three Rolls engineers working out the specifications. 'We enjoyed your ad,' commented one of the Rolls engineers. 'What ad?' asked another. 'Oh, you've got to see this,' said the first, rushing out to find a copy of the magazine. He returned and spread the magazine out on the table. The other engineer froze. 'But – that's Jillie!' Wheatley did not stick around long enough to find out how he had come to put a customer's model girlfriend in the altogether on the cover of a national trade magazine.

There were two keys to the 1980s success of Control Techniques (as the company was renamed when it joined the stock market in 1985). The first was their early fixation on volume production. 'Right from day one, Trevor was determined to sell our products worldwide,' commented Jerry Hooper, who joined the company in 1974, also from Mawdsley's. The British electronics industry had a tradition of personal, customised service. Electronics engineers spent months, sometimes years, designing a unique control system for a factory, a mill, or a conveyor line. In the spirit of the Victorian craftsman, personal service was supposed to be synonymous with quality. But it was not anymore. The unrelenting forward march of technology fundamentally changed the equation. Large volume production became the only way to generate the profits that paid for the investment in new technology that brought the quality. In London, if you walk down Savile Row or visit any of the old luggage-makers in Mayfair, you still find craftsmen talking about the wonder of the handmade British suit or the weekender or suitcase. The wonder may be there. But the quality of the fabric in a Giorgio Armani suit or the construction in a Louis Vuitton bag is far higher. The state-of-the-art textile mills and luggagemakers that weave Armani's wools and stitch Vuitton's leathers produce to a quality level craftsmen can only dream about.

Eddie Kirk saw the same phenomenon in drives. He worked for Thorn in the 1960s and GEC in the 1970s. Each company was a major force in the UK drives market in its day. Both have since reduced their presence in the business dramatically. 'It was a combination of lack of investment and over-ego,' said Kirk. The ego took the form of an obsession with large custom-designed systems for prestige customers. Such projects would occupy dozens of engineers, make for glossy pictures in magazines, and deliver large sales figures, but often very little profit. 'They would rather do one deal at £100,000 than sell 100 drives at £1000 each,' Kirk said. Small profit, low investment and insufficient focus on product development spelt decline for the old giants. Their personal service culture meant that design engineers were often too busy working on individual customer applications to develop new products. From the start, KTK had a separate R&D department, led by Briggs. Its task was to develop new products which would be saleable round the world. Right from 1973, KTK had its eye on the global market. As early as the late 1970s when their turnover was still under £1 million, Wheatley went looking for overseas sales. He found his first overseas distributor by putting a KTK drive in the back of his Ford Escort and tootling around industrial sales companies in Rotterdam demonstrating it.

The second key development for Control Techniques was technological. The company's major breakthrough came with the opening up of the market for AC drives. Until the mid-1980s, most industries used motors powered by DC electricity. DC motors were more complex, required more maintenance, operated only in a dry, well-ventilated environment, and were typically made to specification, requiring waits of ten weeks or more for delivery. But DC motors had one great advantage: their speed was inherently variable. Vary the voltage through the motor and the speed changed. An AC motor was a more robust, standardised, cheaper product. You could buy an AC motor off the shelf. But its drawback was that it was inherently fixed speed. If the AC current alternated at fifty cycles per second (the European standard) then an AC motor rotated at fifty cycles per second.

When they set up KTK in 1973, the founders knew that the continuing rapid pace of development in electronics would soon make it possible to produce a drive which would manipulate AC electricity to give an AC motor the flexibility of DC. From the very beginning Briggs worked on developing AC drives. In 1983, Control Techniques brought out the Commander, its first volume-produced AC drive. It was a small, green plastic box, ten inches high, six inches wide and eight inches deep. Inside the plastic box was a densely packed club sandwich of electronics. The latest transistors gave it the capacity to handle high voltages and microchips gave it unprecedented speed and flexibility.

At that point, Wheatley made an unusual move: he appointed independent equipment distributors IMO to distribute the Commander in the UK. Many bosses in Wheatley's position, especially a former salesman, would have expanded their in-house sales force to sell the new product. But Wheatley's eye was firmly fixed on his goal of volume production. He did not want the company to be distracted running a sales operation. It was exactly the same strategy followed by Nissan when they first led the Japanese car industry into exports. They appointed sales agents in the UK and elsewhere in Europe who knew the local markets, while they concentrated on designing and manufacturing a quality product. 'We took a leaf out of the Japanese's book,' admitted Kevin Curran. Control Techniques *did* have a UK salesforce. But Wheatley told them to stick to selling DC drives. The potentially higher-volume AC product went outside to the IMO salesforce.

'It was a far-sighted, courageous decision, to recognise that AC and DC were sibling rivals and set up two salesforces in direct competition,' said Eddie Kirk. Kirk was the drives manager for IMO who, in 1984, undertook the marketing of CT's Commander, which he renamed the IMO Jaguar. The UK market leader in the smaller AC drives segment was then Danish company Danfoss. Their standard AC drive was three feet tall and just as wide. Kirk produced an advertisement featuring a little boy sitting on a Danfoss drive holding an IMO Jaguar in his hand. Small size was significant not only because it meant convenience and a better price; to electronics engineers, compactness on the outside suggested state-of-the-art electronics inside. Within three years, IMO/Control Techniques was number one in the UK market. The entire market grew as customers embraced the newer technology. By 1992, AC drives accounted for 60 per cent of the UK market, up from 35 per cent in 1986.

Kirk gave the examples of a chocolate bar manufacturer looking at replacing the motor and drive running a conveyor line carrying chocolate bars and cooling them in a giant tumble dryer. Their DC motor and drive gave them the accurate speeds they needed – if it tumbled too slowly, a single one-ton sweet would emerge from the dryer. But DC motors produced dust and played up if something spilled on them. The IMO Jaguar was small enough to fit into the existing cabinet, drove an AC motor to the required tolerances and cost less. And since both motor and the Jaguar were standard, off-the-shelf products, if either went wrong they could be replaced in a matter of hours. The Jaguar was tremendously attractive to food and drink manufacturers: its AC motor would not produce dust to contaminate their products, and spillage of their products could not damage the motor. Or as Kirk put it in his inimitable Scotsman's language: 'You can stand there and piss on an AC motor all day long and it won't get wet inside.'

Soon, hundreds of factories who had never heard the name Control Techniques used IMO Jaguars. Overseas, Wheatley pursued a similar low-profile strategy. Soon after he signed up IMO, he was showing a Commander at a Brighton trade show. A group from German electronics giant AEG passed by and were drawn by the drive's small size and clean good looks. 'How much?' they asked. '7.5 kilowatts', replied Wheatley. 'So. *Point seven five* kilovatts,' replied the German. 'No, *seven point five* kilowatts,' Wheatley said. A pencil was produced to ensure they had the decimal point in the right place. The Germans were astonished to see so much power in such a small drive. Days later, Wheatley was bound for Berlin at AEG's invitation. They signed a distribution deal for Germany, rechristening the product the AEG Microverter.

Control Techniques had a five-year headstart on most of their competitors in AC drives. By the time competitors got around to designing comparable products, CT was into its third or fourth generation of AC drives. How did CT take such a lead on world-class electronics firms twenty times its size? Part of the answer was old-fashioned entrepreneurial flair. CT saw a new product opportunity and a need before the competition. They were so sure it would pay off that they bet their company's future on the AC drive. The old electronics giants never took such risks. Eddie Kirk described how at one of the large drives companies he worked for years ago no new development project could get underway until the development engineers *proved* to the finance people there was a market for it. 'It was a chicken and egg situation,' Kirk recalled. 'You couldn't prove there was a market until you had a product out there and you couldn't put a product out there unless you could prove there was a market.'

'Drives have been a poor relation in many companies,' said Ken Briggs. With unkempt white hair protruding over his ears and a soft-spoken, almost mumbling, manner of speaking, Briggs seemed like an absent-minded professor. Boasting was completely out of character for him. He was uncomfortable explaining why CT's drives sold so well around the world. 'Look at this,' he said seizing a screwdriver. In the R&D lab at their Newtown headquarters was a new model of an AC drive from Hitachi. It was about twenty-four inches tall. He unscrewed the front cover and a spaghetti-load of jumbled wires tumbled out. The drive was stuffed with circuit boards mounted in all directions. Between the boards components stood, lay and swayed in the breeze. By contrast, a Control Techniques Commander was half the size. Inside, it was neat and tidy. There were very few wires, most of the connexions were made on the circuit boards. Everything plugged or slotted in. With scarcely any screws, there were few components that could shake loose.

The simplicity of the inside of a CT drive was due in large part to the extensive use of microchips. They were the first company in the world to use application-specific integrated circuits or ASIC chips in an AC drive. ASICs were customised chips, designed and produced for a specific use. They were widely used in consumer products like cameras or video-recorders, but less common in industry. CT's development team designed ASICs to do many of the major functions of the drive. It cost £80,000 to design a single ASIC, but with volume targets in tens of thousands, ASICs were worth investing in. They made the drive less costly to produce and more reliable, as well as smaller and neater. CT was also the first company to use custom-moulded plastic casing for their drives instead of flat panels screwed together. The initial investment to create a plastic moulding could be as much as £50,000, but, once again, volumes made it worthwhile.

In 1983, CT's sales were £3.7 million. In 1992, its sales were £88 million. Its pre-tax profits were £6.2 million. CT succeeded by maintaining a small company mentality in an industry dominated by big companies. While it grew at an incredible pace, its three founders never lost touch with the business and the customers. In 1992, CT's factory moved across Newtown to larger premises at the town's new industrial estate. But the executive offices remained at the older St Giles estate, one flight up from the R&D department. When the St Giles offices were once again bursting at the seams, the finance department was shifted to the new site. The three founder-directors insisted on being close to R&D. New products were the company's lifeblood. They were frequently to be found wandering around the R&D area, looking at the progress of new projects, or talking to the design engineers about new ideas or suggestions from customers.

Wheatley's irrepressible drive and action-orientation infected the whole company. By the end of 1993, Control Techniques would be a £100 million company. Yet it did not *look* like a £100 million company. The St Giles head office was a modest two-storey building just off Newtown's high street, surrounded on both sides by the green Welsh hills. On the ground floor was a reception area where two secretaries worked. Upstairs, in a large open-plan office were the three founders' desks. None of them had a private office. None of them had a private secretary. They were all hands-on in the fullest sense. Every Monday morning, group managing director Kevin Curran received the five key numbers they used to monitor the business from the company's offices in the Far East, the US and Europe. He entered them personally into the computer, printed out the totals, and gave copies of the print-outs to Wheatley and Robins. Wheatley often typed his own letters into his desktop computer. He operated a one-page report system – 'if it's got to be done in writing'. He preferred face-to-face discussion and on-the-spot decisions whenever possible.

Everyone at Control Techniques shared Wheatley's action-orientation. It was like a company religion. Electronics engineer Mike Cade joined CT's R&D department in 1991. Prior to that he was at NEI (now part of Rolls Royce). He spoke despairingly of the time wasted in meetings at NEI. Young and keen, Cade tried to initiate a project to design a new drive controller for NEI. He spent hours in meetings trying to justify it to the sales department and the senior management. A year later, a sales executive came to tell him they were close to approving his proposal. He replied he had just accepted a job offer from Control Techniques. At CT, he loved the 'do it now' ethic. 'I actually want to come to work here each morning,' Cade said. 'There's not masses of paperwork and documentation. You work on stuff that's been decided. You get it done and out the door as quickly as possible.'

Factory manager Bob Millard was hired to run CT's printed circuit board factory after he toured the factory and told Wheatley there were far too many trolleys. The one-metre-square steel-wheeled trolleys were used for holding work-in-progress and Millard wanted to move the company to a more demanding just-in-time system, with minimal amounts of work-in-progress. 'What would you do with the trolleys?' said Wheatley. 'I'd throw 'em away,' said Millard.

293

'On his first day, he just threw away sixty-five trolleys,' Wheatley recalled. 'Fantastic!'

Wheatley's action-orientation sometimes got him in trouble with larger, slower-moving companies. In 1989, Control Techniques formed a joint venture with the American Warner Electric (subsidiary of the $4 billion industrial conglomerate Dana Corporation). The venture aimed to sell Control Techniques drives to US industrial customers, a market Warner Electric knew well. Control Techniques typically supported its business with Drive Centres, local operations who combined many drives into systems for customers and offered service and support. Under the terms of the joint venture, Warner Electric people ran the joint venture's Drive Centres. Wheatley quickly grew unhappy with the joint venture's sales figures and the financial performance of the Drive Centres which lost money. In response, Warner set up a special 'hit squad' to cut costs in the joint venture. After a year, the hit squad had saved $100,000. At a meeting with Warner executives and the heads of the joint venture, Wheatley asked how much further the hit squad aimed to reduce costs in the coming year. Another $100,000, they hoped. How much is the hit squad costing us, he asked. $160,000 was the response. 'Well then, let's get rid of the hit squad!' replied the Englishman impatiently. They don't do things that way at Warner Electric, he was told.

A year later, Control Techniques terminated the Warner joint venture when a new, more promising way to attack the American market emerged. In late 1990, Jean-Paul Montupet, the French-born head of the industrial controls division of American electrical group Emerson Electric, invited Wheatley to visit Emerson's American drives subsidiary, ICD Drives, Inc. during his next trip to the States. Wheatley immediately accepted the offer. He never turned down an opportunity to see what the competition was doing. Wheatley knew Montupet and Emerson. With $7 billion sales, Missouri-based Emerson was one of America's most successful electronics companies. Montupet had previously explored the possibility of buying Control Techniques but the three founders were not interested in selling.

The ICD plant was at Grand Island in upstate New York, midway between the city of Buffalo and Niagara Falls. Wheatley knew ICD's AC drives. Their technology was outdated. ICD's AC drive took up ten times as much space as CT's Commander. Wheatley was not impressed with the factory he saw at Grand Island. They used old-fashioned assembly processes with little automation and too much unskilled labour. Inside the Emerson company jet after the tour, Montupet asked Wheatley what he thought of what he had seen.

'May I speak frankly?' asked Wheatley.

Montupet nodded.

'It's crap.'

'What would you do with it if it belonged to Control Techniques?'

'We'd shut down production of drives and use their sales force to sell our standard product which is made in Wales at far lower cost and higher quality levels than that place could ever dream of.'

'OK. How would you like to buy ICD?'

Wheatley was momentarily stunned. With sales of $56 million, ICD would more than double Control Techniques' business in the US. It would greatly increase the volumes and profitability of the Newtown plant.

In June 1991, a deal was announced. Control Techniques bought ICD for £24 million. It paid in the form of Control Techniques shares: Emerson took a 29.9 per cent stake in CT and Montupet joined the CT board. It was standard procedure for the American giant, which maintained many autonomous fast-growing subsidiaries within the group.

In the autumn of 1991, Jerry Hooper arrived from Newtown to take over as president of ICD. Hooper's critique of the company he found in New York gave an insight into what made Control Techniques so successful. His first observation was that ICD lacked strategic direction. ICD's previous president was an accountant. Drive companies, said Hooper, needed an engineer at the helm. 'With the best will in the world, an accountant could not have any real understanding of the product or drive markets,

295

so the best he could do is hold his own in market share, but more likely he would lose market share as other more aggressive players pushed forward and came out with newer, better products,' said Hooper.

ICD's main product, a DC motor drive, proved the point. By 1991, it was technologically outdated. 'It was broadly similar to the DC drive we replaced in 1987,' said Hooper. ICD had recently completed the development of a new product, a fully digital DC drive, comparable to the Mentor drive Control Techniques brought out in 1988. The product was grossly over-engineered, a common problem when marketing and development departments did not work in close harness. 'The drive had everybody's whims incorporated,' Hooper said. With too many features, the drive would have to be priced far higher than the Mentor and the Japanese competition. It showed little sign of the *manufacturability* which was the hallmark of all Control Techniques products. The ICD drive contained three microprocessors compared to one in the Mentor. Each of ICD's complicated microprocessors cost more than Mentor's single processor, yet the drives were similar in performance. ICD's manufacturing process was shortsighted, with wages screwed down to the limit. The mostly unskilled workforce could not have operated the automated machinery which would have delivered economies of scale. 'With one skilled person and a machine, you can often replace five people and manufacture more efficiently and effectively,' said Hooper.

Manufacturing quality was the most damning indictment of the New York factory. Hooper cited the first-time-pass rate at the printed circuit board (PCB) factory. The first-time-pass rate for PCBs at Newtown was 98 per cent. At Grand Island, the rate was around 50 per cent. One ICD product never passed its first test in all the months Hooper was there. Quality manufacture was a powerful long-term competitive advantage in the global market-place. 'It took us years to build up to the quality levels we have in Newtown,' said Hooper. 'You can't recreate that overnight.'

In 1992, Control Techniques opened its new, expanded drive

assembly plant. In a very real sense, the new factory was the heart of the company. Management and employees were as proud of the state-of-the-art factory as they were of any of their most successful products. It was unique in the worldwide drives industry. The company had formerly made some drives at a plant in Singapore. But after the ICD acquisition, all volume production was concentrated at a new factory at Mochdre, Newtown's new industrial estate half a mile off the high street, where the verdant countryside began. A visit to the new factory in 1992 was an exercise in collective democracy. The visitor found himself surrounded by two, three or more guides, including Wheatley or one of the divisional managers or a shopfloor worker. All spoke at once in their enthusiasm to explain the workings of the most automated, sophisticated drive assembly plant in the world.

Drives division chief Bob Brayshaw, who led the creation of new plant, explained his philosophy: 'The UK has always been very good at innovative, entrepreneurial engineering and manufacturing ideas. We have always been let down by the other side of it, actually making the product. We've put such a lot of effort into manufacturing because we know that if we are very good at making it cost-efficiently and cost-effectively as well as thinking up new ideas and new products, and provided we continue down the path of continual improvement and the total quality ethic inherent in that, then we will remain the best.'

Twenty years ago, factories made an impression by the amount of automated gadgetry that went into them; today's truly impressive factories are the ones where you can see the thought that's gone into them. The Mochdre factory was a vast steel shed brightly lit from wrap-around windows high up the wall. The floor was a shiny white with a giant CT logo in green. Hanging from the ceiling, a sign read 'CONTROL TECHNIQUES WORLD MODULE ASSEMBLY'. Two production lines ran the 100-foot length of the building. Even while operating at capacity, Mochdre seemed eerily quiet and half-empty. It took only 135 people (half of them working directly on the production lines) to build 120,000 drives a year, two thirds of them for export. Production was organised on a pallet system: each drive was strapped to a nylon pallet which moved along a conveyor. The drive was also plugged into the pallet electronically. The pallet made contact with the conveyor which was attached to the mains. The drive was powered up and tested as it ran along the conveyor.

Every morning Brayshaw and his team looked at the orders and decided what drives would be built that day. Kits containing all the components including the plastic cover for the drive and the relevant badge (blue for IMO-distributed product, red for AEG, orange for VEE, etc.) were collected by a worker and put on a pallet at the start of the conveyor. The conveyor belt delivered the kit to the assembler when she – most were women – signalled for one. She assembled the drive, plugged it into the pallet and sent it down for its first test. If it failed it was sent to an inspector to diagnose the fault. If it passed, it travelled upstairs on a dumb-waiter-style lift which delivered it to the mezzanine level for the 'soak' test. Running the full eighty-foot length of the line, the upper level consisted of 128 stations. Each looked a bit like a domestic washing machine. For four hours, the newly built drive passed from one washing machine to the next. It rested at each station for eight minutes where it was alternately 'soaked' at full power, powered down for eight minutes, soaked again, and so on. 'Our task is to break the product before it leaves the plant,' explained Kevin Curran. 'We literally beat the shit out of it. Then when it goes in a box and out that door we are reasonably sure that it will be OK in the field.'

At the PCB factory, Control Techniques used cellular manufacture and statistical process control (spc) to monitor and continuously improve quality levels. The factory produced 30,000 circuit boards a month, to quality levels that held their own against any competition in the world. A £600,000 'placement' machine placed up to 10,000 components per hour on to circuit boards. But the responsibility for organising and supervising the production rested with the 100 workers, most of them women. The first cell formed at the factory named themselves Cell Block H, in honour of their favourite Australian television soap opera. Most had no previous experience in electronics. The company trained them to use the high-tech equipment and sophisticated manufacturing systems. Amanda Sharrock, twenty-five, used a powerful microscope, a stereo dynascope, to examine the boards for defects. She said she enjoyed her job, despite the fact that she worked harder than at any of her previous jobs. She took pride in meeting, or beating, the week's quality targets. 'I care about what I do,' she said. 'When I find a problem, I'm eager to sort it out. We're all really chuffed when we get 100 per cent for the week.'

Ironically, many of the women at Control Techniques worked previously at mid-Wales's textile and fashion manufacturing companies. In the past, the poor quality of British-made garments was criticised. The bosses of those companies told the press and the politicians that British labour was too high-paid and too shoddy in its work to compete with the Far East. The truth was the local labour force was always capable of world-class production. It was the poor systems and the poor management – often swilling champagne at the fashion shows of London and Paris when they should have been managing their businesses – that was the real cause of those companies' decline. At Control Techniques, every employee from top to bottom had his heart and soul in Newtown. Factory manager Bob Millard was always to be found in one of the factories, wandering around talking to people or holding informal meetings, often over a cup of tea at the makeshift snack bar in one corner. 'It's getting everybody to think logically about it whenever something goes wrong, it's getting them to be proud of zero defects, and it's communication,' said Millard. 'Lots and lots of communication.'

The automated assembly and testing process for drives was light-years ahead of the traditional 'bench' assembly still used by many of Control Techniques' competitors. Testing a drive by hand was a boring, monotonous job. An engineer could not help but occasionally make a mistake. He might misread a meter, or cut short a soak period. CT's custom-designed automatic soak machines did not suffer from wandering concentration or sick leave. Product quality, not cost-cutting, was the driving-force behind automation.

'We brought the American salesmen here from ICD and they were stunned,' said Brayshaw. 'They'd never seen anything like it.' Even the Japanese were behind in automated production of drives. 'We deliver within four weeks of an order,' said Brayshaw. The typical Japanese delivery was twelve to sixteen weeks. He added: 'If it breaks and you call the Japanese manufacturer, he tells you to find someone to fix it. If you call Control Techniques, somebody will be on his way to you with a replacement product in the boot of his car probably that same day.' In April 1992, the Duke of Kent presided over the opening of the Mochdre factory. As vice-chairman of the British Overseas Trade Board, the Duke visited many factories around the world. At Mochdre, he was sufficiently impressed that he stayed well past the allotted time in his schedule, producing severe jitters among the police waiting outside. 'We couldn't get him off the shopfloor,' Brayshaw recalled. 'He was in and out of everything, asking what does this do and why have you linked this up to that, what does this computer do?'

Mochdre was also a marketing tool. Customers were frequently invited to visit. Control Techniques was confident that customers, most of them in manufacturing themselves, seeing the quality inherent in the production process, would want to buy the Control Techniques product.

That was exactly what Jerry Hooper found when he moved from New York to set up Control Techniques' new German drive centre in the summer of 1992. In October 1990, CT bought a small German drives company called Reta Electronic in the old town of Siegburg, not far from Cologne in the heart of the German industrial belt. At first, CT left Reta in the hands of its German boss. When that did not work out, Wheatley asked Hooper to take over. Hooper explained: 'You can't really use a local [as MD] because what we're trying to do is implement the CT strategy worldwide and you've got to have someone who understands what the hell we're trying to do and believes in it.' In short, a manager needed to have done time in Newtown and imbibed the company's culture. 'It's a culture of quality and customer support,' said Hooper. 'It's about getting things done. It's a culture which says it doesn't take a year to make a decision.'

In 1992, Control Techniques opened an all-new Drive Centre to house its German operations, in Hennef, a new town near the ancient Siegburg, equipped with large, modern factory buildings and good autobahn connexions. CT's fifteen Drive Centres offered personal customer service to complement its off-the-shelf standard products. A conveyor line might use ten, twenty, or more drives. At a Drive Centre, Control Techniques would assemble the drives and the other electrical components into a system, typically housed in a row of six-foot-high cabinets. The Drive Centre was the face of CT that the larger customers saw. It had to embody CT's high-tech, customer-oriented image. Hooper supervised the design and decoration of the Hennef Drive Centre closely. 'It's like McDonald's. Every Drive Centre is a clone of the original in Newtown,' said Hooper. The modern, two-storey glass and steel structure at Hennef was decorated in the company colours, green and grey. Every glass door was adorned with the green CT logo.

Hennef's first floor was a large open-plan office with sales staff on one side and the software engineers who wrote the programmes that went into the drives on cards. At first, the German engineers resisted the open-plan layout. They preferred the traditional German honeycomb of offices where size of office related to status. Hooper overruled them: 'It's all about communications. Open offices, open doors, lack of hierarchy. We want to bring together sales, purchasing, engineering support, to support each other and the customer.'

The staff put aside their doubts when they saw the new business brought in by the CT products. In no time, the Hennef Drive Centre was operating close to the capacity of its workshop. Hooper made frequent use of the CT turboprop, taking prospective customers on day trips to Newtown to see the new factory. They always came back impressed. 'Every single customer who has been to the factory switches on to our product,' Hooper crowed. 'It's like having a fifth ace in your pack.'

Reifenhauser GmbH, one of the world's largest makers of plastic extrusion machines, watched Control Techniques' takeover of Reta carefully. Reifenhauser sold its plastic-making machines to companies all over the world, and serviced them for years after. It needed to feel confidence in all the components in the machine. Reifenhauser's engineers examined Control Techniques' products, visited Newtown, and discussed in detail the implications of the change of ownership at Reta. They were impressed by the superior technological capabilities of the microchip-driven Control Techniques drives. 'For us it is very important to be able to tell our customers we have the newest technology,' explained Reifenhauser engineer Bernd Hübner. 'The new products from Control Techniques were leading-edge products. Perhaps there are a few companies in Germany also with digital products and perhaps they are no worse than Control Techniques' products. But we are only half an hour away from the Reta factory and we knew the Reta people well. We knew they worked hard. Whenever we had a problem they were there for us. So it was no question to stay with Reta.'

Control Techniques engineer Frank Borchardt, formerly with Reta, said he was very happy with the Control Techniques takeover. The former management recognised the move to digital too late. They lacked the financial resources to catch up. Also, he pointed out, CT's worldwide network of Drive Centres allowed the company to offer a level of service support Reta never could. Borchardt said that the image of British industry in Germany had changed dramatically between his father's generation and his own. 'Older people know the production problems, the strikes and the negative attitude of the government. But today, British industry has become more flexible.'

Today, Borchardt thought, German industry had many problems. Hübner agreed. Many of Germany's small and middle-sized private companies, backbone of the nation's industrial success, the famous *Mittelstand*, suffered from a succession problem as the founders who led them in the *Wirtschaftswunder* years of the 1950s and 1960s grew too old or passed on the company to less dynamic heirs. 'If you have a very old big boss, it can be difficult to create new machines,' said Hübner. 'We are fortunate that Mr Reifen-hauser has two very modern-thinking sons and that Reifenhauser is a little bigger than average so we have the finance and manpower to change.'

Control Techniques' managers shared a great admiration for Germany's machinery industry. Wheatley always told people with pride that he owned three cars, all German: a Mercedes, a Porsche and a Trabant. In 1992, the state of German industry worried them. Before buying Reta, Wheatley spent five years looking at German companies, trying to find a suitable drives company. Many he saw had fallen behind in the technological race, often because the wife or children who had taken over the business lacked the understanding, or the will, to invest in new technology. 'Germany today is in a similar position to that we were in twenty years ago,' said Wheatley. 'They build good quality, but a lot of their equipment is overpriced and their export order books are collapsing because of it.' Hooper caused a storm at the German electronics trade association when he insisted on offering a five-year warranty on CT's drives. It was CT's standard policy worldwide. The German trade association's standard was six months. The flexibility, productivity and quality of Britain's new wave of manufacturers was winning growing recognition in Germany. 'Our German customers are very aware that there is a strong lobby in Germany to reduce the working week, ask for big increases in wages, and a bigger threat of strikes than ever before,' Hooper said. 'We are virtually immune to that. We can't be held to ransom by the test department, the most important technical department in the factory, because our testing is automatic. If we want to double our production overnight we can do it. You couldn't find 100 test engineers overnight.'

While international growth gathered pace, Control Techniques continued to introduce new products. In 1988, it announced the Vector, an innovative AC drive employing sophisticated microelec-

303

tronics to offer virtually the same precision performance as a DC drive. It was aimed squarely at the mainstream DC market, customers such as plastic extruders, where extremely precise control of the motors was essential. New products did not take off instantly; it took years to convince conservative industrialists to try a new technology.

An unconventional customer who was converted to the Vector was Jim Douglas's theatrical lighting company, Unusual Automation. Douglas was hired to build a light show for Yumi Matsutoya's Japanese tour. Yumi looked like a Japanese Madonna but sang songs more like a Whitney Houston. Her annual tour of Japan, stage-designed by her husband, was always fitted out with the latest high-tech special effects. The Matsutoyas wanted spotlights that started out shining upwards from under a clear plexiglass stage, and moved on giant square rails around the sides and up over the stage, all the while swivelling to light Yumi and her band. They contacted Douglas after Japanese rigging companies told them the synchronisation was impossible. 'We were the only ones in the world who could do it,' said Douglas. 'Or *said* they could do it.' Douglas was a London-based electronics engineer with a decade's experience in the theatre. In December 1992, he flew to Tokyo to design and build a set with eight light pods, each on its own rail, all individually controlled from a computer keyboard. Each light pod was driven by a Vector. 'It was the only drive I knew that offered the precision and was controlled by a microprocessor,' he said. The effect of the finished show, with the multicoloured lights racing around the stage, in perfect sync with each other, and in time to the music, was spectacular. 'The audience loved it,' said Douglas. 'It was like they were watching fireworks.' Douglas did not have much time to stay around and enjoy the shows; in January 1993, he was back in London to design the system that would move the stage sets for the London production of *Crazy For You*. The rig used thirty Vectors.

Other products Control Techniques introduced in the early 1990s included a range of servo-drives, higher precision drives used for positioning equipment like tools to tolerances of thousandths of an inch, and a computer controller for machine tools, based on a product originally developed at Cranfield Institute of Technology. This last was a very high-tech product in a sector dominated by the Japanese Fanuc and the German Siemens. Once again, the world's electronics companies were intrigued by Control Techniques' audacity in challenging the established giants. Like many of the great Japanese successes of the last thirty years, Control Techniques' strategy was to expand from lower-priced, high-volume products (the ordinary DC and AC drives) into related, higher-priced products.

Wheatley saw the world's electronics and machinery industries as a colossal three-cornered race between Europe, North America and Japan. The emergence of a single European market would strengthen Europe's electronics industry, he believed, enabling Europe to pool its technological resources and sell to the unified market. Control Techniques' successful move into servo-drives illustrated the potential. Servo-drives controlled the *positioning* of motors rather than speed. Offering great precision, they were used on precise equipment like machine tools. Control Techniques acquired its servo-drive technology when it bought Italian servo-drive manufacturer Soprel in 1988. They boosted sales of the Soprel-designed servo-drives throughout Europe, while Soprel's Italian sales network made Control Techniques market leader in AC drives in Italy. Wheatley was especially thrilled to be number one in the large Italian industrial market because they knocked out Japanese firm Hitachi from the top spot. 'Anybody who's tried to sell in Japan knows we don't fight on a level playing field,' said Wheatley. 'This is no lover's tiff, this is an economic war.'

Wheatley had the bull-headed determination and patriotism (or pan-European patriotism) of an earlier Englishman, Winston Churchill. He combined audacity, persistence and optimism in equal measures. Yet he was realistic in assessing the difficulties in Control Techniques' achieving the target he'd set – number one worldwide in the drives business. There were five western companies ahead of CT and five companies in Japan. Their greatest advantage, he said, was Control Techniques' focus. 'We are the only one that is just a drives company,' he said. 'It won't be easy becoming number one, but that is the target. It has to be. Nobody is going to be satisfied being number two, are they?'

By 1992, Wheatley's shares in Control Techniques were worth over £5 million. Had he retired immediately, he probably would not have lived long enough to spend all his money. Yet his enthusiasm for building Control Techniques was as great as it was twenty years earlier when he founded the company. Love of manufacturing, and enthusiasm for building a global business kept him going. Drives, he said, were a fascinating industry, with new products and new applications emerging all the time. They were at the heart of many vital industrial processes. 'Without manufacturing we are nothing,' he said. 'Absolutely nothing.'

In 1986, Wheatley was too sophisticated to use a nude model to promote a product. But when Control Techniques introduced its innovative all-digital DC drive, Mentor II, Wheatley wanted a theatrical launch. Brainstorming with his team, they hit upon a dramatic way to demonstrate the precision timing made possible by digital communication between a main computer and any number of drives. For four weeks, staff at Newtown laboured night and day to prepare the complex launch demonstration. 'Trevor's favourite saying was: "There's twenty-four hours between now and this time tomorrow. Let's use every one of 'em,"' recalled one of the team. On the appointed day, fifty members of the industry and trade press filed into the Queen Elizabeth Hall in London to find two Mentor II drives and two motors on the stage. Attached to each motor was a two-foot wide wooden disk with a white stripe painted on it. Wheatley explained that the drives were hooked up, via telephone, to a computer at Control Techniques' Drive Centre at Rhode Island, USA. The hall was also on live telephone link with an engineer at the Rhode Island facility. Wheatley asked the audience to call out instructions to the engineer, who would send an instruction, via the computer, to the drives on stage. For an hour, the audience told the operator to move the disks: half a revolution clockwise, now a full revolution, now backwards by ten degrees. The parallel white stripes showed the motors stayed in precise sync throughout. The next demonstration was a bit more lighthearted. Motors make whirring noises at recognisable musical pitches, with the pitch dependent on the speed of the motor. Mentor II controlled a motor so precisely that it could 'sing'. Wheatley asked the audience to call out musical notes. 'C', 'F sharp', 'A flat', called out the audience. The engineer in Rhode Island pushed buttons, and the notes sounded. The audience laughed and applauded.

'There's just one more thing before you go, ladies and gentlemen,' said Wheatley, and he shouted at the microphone. As Trevor Wheatley strolled towards his seat, the two motors played a recognisable, if electronic, version of the Welsh National Anthem.

Appendix

Renaissance Principles

UNIPART

1. 'If you combine the natural flair and ingenuity of the British people with the systems for quality manufacture invented by the Japanese, you would create a company with an unbeatable formula for world-class success.' – John Neill, Unipart chairman
2. 'Understand the real and perceived needs of your customer better than anyone else and then serve those needs better than anyone else.' – John Neill
3. 'Our aim is total commitment to customer service and outstanding personal service to create an environment where everybody's contribution counts, and ultimately to make us a world-class company.' – Sue Topham, head of people development
4. 'Every team leader is like a mini-managing director.' – Frank Burns, Premier Exhausts MD
5. 'Nobody understands a machine better than the man who operates it all day.' – Melvin Thornton, team member, Oxford Automotive Components

GUINNESS

1. 'The business we're in is for people who appreciate good quality, and who want other people to be able to recognise that they appreciate quality.' – Tony Greener, Guinness chairman
2. 'I'm a great believer in sticking to our knitting. This business [beer and spirits] is something we think we know something about, and we also believe we can run it a hell of a lot better in the future

than we are doing today. Our best odds for being successful are to continue what we're doing, but do it better.' – Tony Greener on focus

3. 'As people become more affluent, they don't buy more holidays, motorcars, or clothes, but *better* holidays, motorcars and clothes.' – Sir Anthony Tennant, Guinness chairman 1988–1992, on the market for luxury products

4. 'An international business especially is totally dependent upon the people on the ground, and unless you give them the room and the space to operate and expect them to operate, you'll never get good results.' – Tony Greener

5. 'We would never have produced Canned Draught Guinness if there wasn't a direct client inside the company.' – Dr Alan Forage, head of R&D, Guinness Brewing Worldwide, on the product champion

VIRGIN

1. 'Western companies do not concentrate enough on their staff, looking after them and making sure they're happy and satisfied. If you put your staff first, then your customers also come first because the staff are the public face of your company.' – Richard Branson, Virgin chairman

2. 'If you promote somebody above what they'd expect, they will be determined to give their all and prove you've made the right decision.' – Richard Branson

3. 'It's more important that everybody from the managing director to the receptionist knows how we're doing each day than that we keep the figures secret from the competition. Knowledge breeds confidence and ignorance breeds fear.' – Robert Devereux, Virgin Communications chairman

4. 'Companies grow old quicker than their managers.' – Patrick Zelnik, Virgin Records France chairman

5. 'I look for someone I can get on with. If I like them and they're nice as individuals, I think they'll be good at motivating other people.' – Richard Branson on how to spot a good entrepreneur

TI

1. 'The Japanese have taught the world that quality sells a product. If you add quality to knowledge and service, you have a product with which you can compete on a global basis.' – Sir Christopher Lewinton, TI chairman
2. 'If you want to change the culture of a company, close the headquarters.' – Sir Christopher Lewinton
3. 'We're in the business of applying technology, not originating it.' – Sir Christopher Lewinton
4. 'Any guy in a factory, on a machine or sweeping the floor or wherever, has the potential to be incredibly creative in improving his job or improving other people's jobs. The only limitations are in people's minds.' – Bob Gibbon, UK managing director, John Crane
5. 'This is a forward-thinking company. They are not frightened to invest, they are not frightened to try new ideas, and they involve everybody from the top down to the bottom.' – Steve Adkins, cell supervisor, John Crane
6. 'Loners achieve nothing. Team players achieve everything.' – Sir Christopher Lewinton

ICL

1. 'Products don't sell products. Organisations sell products.' – Robb Wilmot, ICL managing director 1981–1984
2. 'We are religious about following the market.' – Peter Bonfield, ICL chairman
3. 'In this industry which is constantly changing, if you aren't changing so fast that it feels painful and on the edge of being do-able, then you aren't changing fast enough.' – Peter Bonfield
4. 'I try to go out and bring a catalyst for change into the company on a very regular basis and use it to say to people: which way are we going? is it right? do we need to change?' – Peter Bonfield
5. 'In the next five years our manufacturing will concentrate totally on flexibility, not high volume. The key will be very, very fast response to the marketplace.' – Peter Bonfield

CONTROL TECHNIQUES

1. 'You address the global market. You design the product cost-effectively. You create volume, you concentrate your manufacturing in one place. You don't get sidetracked by niches. Leave them to the opposition. It keeps them busy while you take what you want from the marketplace.' – Kevin Curran, Control Techniques MD

2. 'Europe is not exporting. It's our home market.' – Ken Briggs, Control Techniques technical director

3. 'This is no lover's tiff. This is global economic war.' – Trevor Wheatley, Control Techniques chairman

4. 'The new breed of UK manager is more aggressive, more shirt-sleeves, less insular, more prepared to get out and find out what the world is doing, and really address the global market in a head-on fashion.' – Kevin Curran

5. 'It's not in my nature to be number two.' – Trevor Wheatley

Index

Abbott, Trevor 177, 191, 197, 198–9, 200, 208
Abdullah Brothers 128
Adkins, Steve 119–20, 122–4, 310
AEG 277–8, 290–1
Agis, Herr 275
Air Florida 168
Airbus 141
Akers, John 218, 269
Alexander, Nick 167, 171, 174
Allan, John (British Gas) 210–14, 247, 248, 250–1, 253–4, 256, 258–61, 265–6, 267–8
Allegheny International 132–3
Allen, W.H., publishers 193–4
Anderson, Lisa 158, 192
Anheuser-Busch 67–8
Apple computers 269–70
Argyll, bid for DCL 81
Arnault, Bernard 96, 97, 98, 106–7
ASIC chips 292
Assembly lines criticised 12–13
Ayeroff, Jeff, 197–8

Bain, management consultants 50–3, 79–81, 82, 88, 92, 101
Baker, Kenneth 229
Baldock, Brian 75–6, 92
Ball, Roger 11–12, 13–14, 17, 21, 28; and OAC 30–1, 33–4, 35, 37, 38, 41, 42
Baric company 230
BBC, and Superchannel 183
Beans Engineering 11
Beecham's 77
Beer market 54, 55–8, 66–7
Benetton xv
Benn, Tony 226
Berry, Ken (Virgin) 158, 161–2, 200, 202, 203, 204, 205, 207
Beta Television 185–6, 187

Betteridge, David 190
Biggam, Robin (ICL) 231, 235–6, 237, 239
Blacker, Norman 257
Bland, Christopher 185
Blank, Victor 7
Body Shop xv
Boeing 141–2
Bonfield, Peter (ICL) xii, 222, 236, 237, 238, 239–40, 270–1; reform of ICL 240–2, 243, 244; and British Gas 251, 253, 257, 258, 259, 260–1, 262, 264, 268; quoted 310
Borchardt, Frank 302–3
Boutari Brothers 104
Bowler, Ian 25
Branson, Joan 148
Branson, Richard 149–50; partnership with Simon Draper 156, 158–9; and John Brown 144; and Storm Model Agency 146–7; and music 158; sale of Virgin Records 162, 195, 201–2, 204; purchase of Rushes 163; style 163–4, 170, 174, 175–6, 189–90, 196; working conditions 147–9; and Virgin Atlantic 166–74; and Music Box/Superchannel 180–1, 187–8; staff first policy 175, 188; and South African Airways/BA monopoly 189; takes Virgin Group public 191; Virgin Group divided 199–200; gains from sale of Virgin Music 201; criticism of 207; present position 208–9; quoted 309
Brayshaw, Bob 297, 298, 300
Briggs, Ken (CT) 285, 288, 289, 291, 311
British Airways 178, 189
British Atlantic Airways 165–6
British Gas 220, 225; and IBM 210–14, 254–5, 256, 263, 267; and ICL 210–14, 218–22, 245–6, 247–55, 256–68
British Leyland (BL) 3–4, 5, 6, 7; see also Rover Group

313

Index

Index

Index

Index